T0355708

Harold Pinter

MICHIGAN MODERN DRAMATISTS
Enoch Brater, Series Editor

Michigan Modern Dramatists offers the theatergoer concise, accessible, and indispensable guides to the works of individual playwrights, as interpreted by today's leading drama critics. Forthcoming books in the series will consider the works of Sam Shepard, Samuel Beckett, and Wendy Wasserstein.

Harold Pinter

THE THEATRE OF POWER

Robert Gordon

THE UNIVERSITY OF MICHIGAN PRESS
ANN ARBOR

First paperback edition 2013
Copyright © by the University of Michigan 2012
All rights reserved

Published in the United States of America by
The University of Michigan Press
Printed and bound by CPI Group (UK) Ltd, Croydon, CR0 4YY

2016   2015   2014   2013   5   4   3   2

A CIP catalog record for this book is available from the British Library.

Library of Congress Cataloging-in-Publication Data

Gordon, Robert, 1951 Nov. 28–
    Harold Pinter : the theatre of power / Robert Gordon.
        p.   cm. – (Michigan modern dramatists)
    Includes bibliographical references and index.

    1. Pinter, Harold, 1930–2008–Criticism and interpretation.   I. Title.
    PR6066.I53Z653   2013
    822'.914–dc23   2012005026

ISBN 978-0-472-05124-3 (pbk. : alk. paper)

For Olaf

Acknowledgments

I wish to thank Sam Aaron for his judicious advice on the first chapters of the book and Brian Pearce for his encouragement and advice. My thanks go to colleagues in the Pinter Centre for Performance and Creative Writing at Goldsmiths for their enthusiastic support of this project. To Enoch Brater I owe a debt of gratitude for encouraging me to contribute a volume in this series, and to LeAnn Fields and Marcia LaBrenz at the University of Michigan Press much thanks for their kind help and encouragement.

Contents

Introduction:
Understanding Pinter's Drama

The award of the Nobel Prize for Literature to Harold Pinter in 2005 was a fitting acknowledgment of his international standing as the preeminent living dramatist in the English language. Although physically weakened by esophageal cancer, he used his televised acceptance speech to communicate to a global audience his passionate opposition to the imperialism that he believed had come to characterize Western democracies. While those who have come into personal contact with him have attested to his personal kindness and generosity, Pinter's determined pursuit of truthful expression in life as in art gained him a formidable reputation for appearing as difficult as his drama has seemed to be obscure. His death in December 2008 prompted obituaries that were predictable in their celebration of his originality and significance as the greatest and most influential postwar British dramatist but which tended to treat his later plays, by contrast with his early masterpieces, as disappointingly didactic political propaganda.

Major Themes

Focusing on Pinter's work in the theater, I aim to challenge this oversimplified view by exploring his continuously innovative experiments in theatrical form, while tracing the recurrence of a consistent set of ethical and epistemological concerns throughout his career.[1] The ceaseless desire for power is the prime motor for the action in almost all of Pinter's drama. Represented in his work as a compulsive drive to achieve or maintain dominance—whether it be the struggle to defend one's own territory from intruders, the father's battle with his sons to assert his patriarchal position in the family, the manipulation of erotic feelings in the gender warfare that motivates sexual relationships, the abuse of brute force by dictatorships and democracies, or simply the masculine obsession to dominate.

Pinter's earliest plays, *The Room* (1957), *The Birthday Party* (1958), *The Hothouse* (written 1958, produced 1980), *The Dumb Waiter* (written 1958, produced 1959), and *A Slight Ache* (1959), introduce a cluster of themes arising from the play of power relations that are repeatedly recapitulated, rethought, and elaborated in new ways in later plays. Throughout his career, he experimented with new variations of core structural and thematic motifs, whose origin can usually be traced to an initial idea from an earlier play. These thematic concerns may conveniently be comprehended in terms of four primary notions:

1. *The territorial imperative:* the struggle to defend one's territory and protect one's identity. Exploiting the clichéd settings of the well-made West End thriller, the scenic structure of a number of the plays marks the boundaries of a territorial battle to defend private space from potentially hostile strangers.

2. *The exercise of power through the language of authority:* how language functions both to disguise and to authorize the operations of power. Echoing the preoccupations of Hollywood film noir as much as those of Kafka's fiction, Pinter's works elaborate a drama of interrogation, evasion, and silence that exposes a crisis of subjectivity at the core of human identity. The questionable motives of both criminals and detectives in stage and film thrillers find parallels in the failure of Pinter's authority figures to valorize their often brutal exploitation of power.

3. *Sex, gender, and the construction of identity:* focuses on how the performance of gender is formative in the construction of identity, and how sexuality manifests itself through, between, and across gendered identities, manifesting its force in language and behavior. Exploiting the sophisticated wordplay of English comedy of manners in a postmodern context, the plays challenge realist assumptions about behavior, revealing character as a performance,

whose "truth" is relative to the context and form of its enact-
ment.

4. *Questions of time and memory:* addresses the radical subjectivity
of memory, exposing the attempt to retrieve the past as a struggle
for power and control. Apparent in Pinter's drama after 1968, the
interest in the constitutive function of memory and the experience of temporality appears to have been stimulated by his work
in adapting fiction such as L. P. Hartley's novel *The Go-Between*
to the screen (1968) and, more profoundly, by writing a screenplay
for a film by Joseph Losey of Proust's *A la Recherche du Temps
Perdu (The Proust Screenplay, 1972)*, which was never made.[2]

Social and Political Context: Resistance to Authority

Whether, as more recently, concerned with state abuses of power, or
with the micropolitics of human relations that constitute the key
motif in his work until 1981, much of Pinter's drama examines both
the brute reality and the language of power, so that a paradoxical continuity can be traced from his early—apparently apolitical—attitude
and his later, explicitly political plays. Pinter has attested to the fact
that as a Jew growing up in the East End of London during the Second
World War his imagination was haunted by the crimes committed by
the Nazis, but his own personal attitude as a citizen was also formed
in response to the violence of British fascist gangs he personally encountered at the end of the war. Although he asserted that, had he
been old enough, he would have been prepared to fight in the war
against the Nazis, it is ironic that at the age of eighteen he felt compelled to risk two years' imprisonment as a conscientious objector to
conscription into the army because he believed Britain, the United
States, and the Soviet Union to be pursuing a Cold War that was precisely what the allied forces had recently been fighting to prevent.
The young Pinter's first public act as a citizen was thus characterized
by a stance that persisted through the whole of his life: while he did
not consciously espouse any particular ideology, his life and work
were politically engaged in resistance to any social order or political
structure that threatens the freedom of the individual. In his words,
"I've always had a deeply embedded suspicion of political structures,
of governments and the way people are used by them" (Smith, 70).

The Aesthetics of Pinter's Theater: Political Agitprop versus Poetic Drama

Notwithstanding his own extreme sensitivity to the political environment in which he existed, Pinter never in his plays deliberately manipulated characters and situations to express a preexisting point of view. In an interview for a magazine in 1961, he claimed to "object to the stage being used as a substitute for the soapbox, where the author desires to make a direct statement at all costs, and forces his characters into fixed and artificial postures in order to achieve this" (Smith, 45). This assertion is surely not contradicted by Pinter's retrospective opinion in 1988 that his "earlier plays are much more political than they seem on the face of it" (Smith, 85). In the same television interview with Anna Ford for *Omnibus* he explained,

> I've been writing plays for thirty years and many of them have to do with that mode of operation—of terrorizing through words of power—verbal power, verbal facility. In *The Birthday Party*, I think it's most evident. I was a boy in the last war, you know, and the sense of the Gestapo was very strong in England. They weren't here, but we as children knew about them. (Smith, 83)

Although he was clear that the didactic approach to writing ran counter to the unconscious process of his own creativity, Pinter acknowledged his own careful attention to linguistic and dramaturgical form in shaping the material generated by the spontaneous work of the imagination that produces "specific and concrete images [. . .] you've got to have an impulse, and the impulse must come from a specific image [. . .] I have the impulse, and then I have to organize that impulse and make it coherent" (Smith, 90–91).

While acknowledging his increasing concern with political issues as both writer and citizen since the eighties he continued to insist, "My plays are not political discussions. They are living things. They are certainly not debates . . . I do not have an ideology in my plays. I just write; I'm a very instinctive writer. I don't have a calculated aim" (Smith, 93).

The earliest critical responses to Pinter's work linked him either with the playwrights categorized by Martin Esslin under the rubric of theater of the absurd, or with the working-class naturalism of the Royal Court,[3] such as Arnold Wesker's *Chicken Soup with Barley*

(1957) and *The Kitchen* (1959), which are paradigmatic of the genre, or John Arden's only naturalistic drama, *Live Like Pigs* (1959).[4] In his *Theatre of the Absurd* Martin Esslin placed Pinter's early plays in the category of European existentialist drama, pointing out that their minimalistic deployment of stage action echoes the theater of Samuel Beckett in its revelation of the void beyond the sphere of social interaction, while their exaggeration of the banality of everyday conversation resembles Ionesco's grotesque depiction of the phatic nature of human communication, its lack of meaningful content paradoxically disclosing a substratum of anguish and aggression. Finding *The Room, The Dumb Waiter*, and *The Birthday Party* baffling, early critics latched on to labels like Irving Wardle's "comedies of menace" to indicate the peculiar—and unresolved—mystery that characterizes each of these fragmented thrillers of working-class life. In the early sixties Esslin's label of absurdist theater provided a useful if eventually misleading way to comprehend plays that seemed both too fragmentary and too artfully unresolved to be properly naturalistic.

While his early plays came to be identified, on one hand, with so-called kitchen-sink British naturalism[5] and, on the other, with Continental European dramatists of "the absurd" such as Sartre, Beckett,[6] Ionesco, and Genet, it soon became apparent that Pinter's work was more complex and original than either such identification would imply. Ruby Cohn was the first critic to demonstrate that Pinter marries the minimalism of Beckettian theater with the anti-establishment "anger" of the post-1956 Royal Court writers.[7] A useful strategy for avoiding the false and simplistic dichotomy of naturalism versus absurdism was elaborated by Katherine Burkman, whose focus on the uncannily ceremonial quality of each play's stage action applied notions of narrative and performative structure drawn from the "myth and ritual" school of criticism[8] to illustrate that the action of Pinter's dramas functions realistically while at the same time forming patterns of archetypal significance. While never wholly abstract or deliberately obscure in the manner of Ionesco, Pinter's plays are almost always set in an ordinary social environment, with people represented quite literally as part of a material world that remains in place, even when the motivations of the characters and the strategic power games they play may produce disturbing, mysterious, and at times illogical outcomes.[9] According to Pinter himself,

I start off with people, who come into a particular situation. I certainly don't write from any kind of abstract idea. [. . .] I'm convinced that what happens in my plays could happen anywhere, at any time, in any place, although the events may seem unfamiliar at first glance. [. . .] what goes on in my plays is realistic, but what I'm doing is not realism. (*Harold Pinter: Plays Two*, viii, ix)

Language on Stage and the Language of Theater

The tension between realist and abstract styles of stage representation that underpins Pinter's theatrical forms can be attributed directly to the opposition between his own personal taste in modernist literature (particularly Kafka and Beckett) and the typically pragmatic attitude to drama of the professional British stage actor of the fifties. Working under the stage name of David Baron, he learned about the craft of dramaturgy by exploring histrionic strategies for realizing a playwright's effects in performance before an audience. His early plays in particular are both funny and suspenseful, demonstrating a mastery of the nuts and bolts of the dramatist's craft. The actor's theatrical know-how manifests itself in the way the relationship between stage action and language is conceived:

> [W]hen I write the last draft, I carefully work out the movements as I visualize them, and the pauses too. The thing must be capable of realization, and it must work visually for me [. . .] I always write in direct relation to the visual image of people walking about and standing on the stage. (Smith, 47)

In *The Peopled Wound* (1970), Martin Esslin drew attention to the complex and varied dramaturgical functions of Pinter's language as stage speech. By 1970 certain features of Pinter's linguistic style had become so recognizable that the word "Pinteresque" had entered the language as a way of indicating the phatic communication[10] constituted by his characters' peculiar mannerisms of verbal repetition and circumlocution. Esslin pointed out that, far from demonstrating the failure of people to communicate, Pinter's dramatic technique revealed in a subtle and complex manner the many strategies through which they actually *do* communicate: the equivocation, evasion, and euphemism that characterizes their linguistic expression are "strategies for covering nakedness," allowing these characters to mask those aspects of themselves they wish to hide while projecting themselves as they wish to be seen by others. In so doing, Esslin pointed out the affinity between Pinter's sophisticated deployment of the oblique relationship between what people literally say and the situational context of their speech and Anton Chekhov's complex use of a "subtext" of thought and feeling which underscores (and may in fact contradict) what is directly spoken by the characters.[11] This approach to the dramatic function of speech anticipated Austin Quigley's reconceptualization of Pinter criticism in *The Pinter Problem* (1975).[12]

As an actor, Pinter was always extremely sensitive to the rhythm and sound of his drama in performance, composing the shape of speech and action with the precision of a musician. This feature of his writing has resulted in the ubiquitous "Pinter pause," probably the most widely circulated cliché concerning his writing style. Three kinds of breaks are indicated in the scripts of his plays as directions for actors: an ellipsis (. . .) represents a momentary cessation in the flow of speech, "pause" represents a longer break, and "silence" a complete interruption of thought and action. Pinter later regretted the way these directions were endowed with exaggerated portentousness by critics and actors, claiming that he preferred his plays to be performed swiftly and without overemphasizing the pauses and silences.[13]

Early on in his career, an uncanny ability to pinpoint a mental attitude in a particular mode of demotic speech was identified by critics as a source of Pinter's effectiveness as a playwright; missing the subtle stylization of his dialogue, some critics even suggested that his precision in rendering the humor of the London working-class vernacular was achieved with the aid of a tape recorder. But Pinter's ear for the rhythm of speech and the idiosyncrasies of vocabulary and syntax surely demonstrates an unerring histrionic sensitivity. His performances as Goldberg in the television production of *The Birthday Party* (1987), Nicolas in *One for the Road* (2001)[14] and Ben in a reading of *The Dumb Waiter*[15] are brilliant demonstrations by an actor of the comic effects produced by exploiting the detailed musicality of sound and syntactical structure as these are written. These comic effects are never arbitrary, however, but arise from a vision of the manifold complexity of human experience. In Pinter's own words, "The old categories of comedy and tragedy and farce are irrelevant" (*Harold Pinter. Plays Two*, xi).[16] John Lahr[17] compared Pinter to Chekhov in order to explicate Pinter's more radical strategy of inviting the audience to seek subtextual information that is ultimately denied them, the obvious implications receding to a vanishing point where commonsense historical explanations for the action on stage become self-contradictory or remain hauntingly equivocal.

One of the most remarkable features of Pinter's career is the commercial success achieved by a number of his plays that have been regularly revived in London's West End, playing for six months or more to audiences who enjoy the plays as dark and sophisticated comedies.[18] Katharine Worth's *Revolutions in Modern English Drama* (1972) anticipated later Pinter critics[19] who concentrate on the impact of his actor's knowledge of the convention-bound English theater of the early fifties, by focusing on his highly original integration of the seemingly opposite linguistic and theatrical vocabularies of his predecessors, the experimental poet-dramatist T. S. Eliot, and the comic realism of the commercially driven Noël Coward. The positioning of avant-garde plays within a commercial theater system might retrospectively be seen as a postmodern aesthetic strategy that challenges boundaries traditionally separating "high art" from popular entertainment. Scenographically, most of Pinter's plays employ the staging conventions of the well-made plays of the British theater in which he developed his craft as an actor. While subtly exploiting the theatrical possibilities of scenic action, his plays never mimic the vivid and at times surreal theatricality of Beckett's abstract stage landscapes. The aesthetic of his theater is founded on a minimalist redaction of naturalistic conventions; its animation of complex games of scenic and histrionic deconstruction renders every stage object, every tic of behavior and every word spoken, strange or problematic. No utterance can be taken at face value, just as no detail of an actor's gesture or movement and no item of scenography can be seen to represent reality unequivocally—and the status of the reality being represented is itself uncertain. The verbal and the visual are startlingly counterpointed or intertwined, the theatrical effect of each speech act being generated by the subtle and at times surprising contrast with its material and spatial context of utterance. In Pinter's words, "It is a matter of tying the words to the image of the character standing on the stage. The two things go very close together" (Smith, 46).

Some critics have interpreted the lack of coherent exposition ("backstory") and the linguistic stylization of Pinter's plays as a reason to search for allegorical or wholly symbolic meanings.[20] While the action of the plays is occasionally metaphorical, the clinically accurate representation of observed behavior in particular social environments is interwoven with a direct expression of the subjectivity of consciousness to render the complete experience of a recognizable world. Pinter has himself criticized the tendency to allegorize the meaning of his drama: "When a character cannot be comfortably defined or understood in terms of the familiar, the tendency is to perch him on a symbolic shelf, out of harm's way" (Dukore, 7). By contrast, Pinter claims to be "objective in my selection and arrangement, but, as far as I'm concerned, my characters and I inhabit the same world" (Smith, 45). Most of the strange, puzzling, and apparently irrational aspects of speech and action in a Pinter play derive from the playwright's blurring of conventional distinctions between representation of the subjectivity of perception and the "objective" reality of behavior. The seeming illogicality of motive and action in Pinter's plays involves an innovative dramaturgical means of portraying the irrationality of human behavior itself rather than a technique for producing purely aesthetic effects. Lucinda Pacquet Gabbard's *The Dream Structure of Pinter's Plays* adopts a psychoanalytic approach to character and action as archetypes, an approach that in general terms received guarded assent from Pinter himself.

A Note on My Critical Approach

In order to respect Pinter's insistence that his plays are visions of the world he inhabits that are not conceived abstractly as didactic parables, I have attempted as far as possible within the limits of chapters 1 to 5 to trace how the meaning of key plays might unfold in a putative performance.[21] This is a phenomenological approach[22] that aims to capture the way that each drama is conceived as a pattern of lived experience to be grasped by the audience in its moment-to-moment presentation in space and time.[23] Beginning with the dramatist's exploitation of scene, I proceed to show how speech and behavior enhance the stage image by complementing or contradicting the visual image to enable the construction of character (most often puzzlingly indeterminate in Pinter) and the further elaboration and patterning of action. This is in some respects a straightforward approach to the analysis of a play, but it has the advantage of grounding the reader's interpretation in how action—and therefore meaning—might unfold in performance, preventing her/him from privileging abstract or conceptual language over the "language" of stage action in tracing the genesis of each play's felt significance in time.[24]

From chapter 6, I assume that the reader is familiar with this approach to apprehending each play as a unique shaping of experience in space and time, so I do not follow the order of events of individual plays, condensing the analysis in order to convey a sense of how motifs recur from one play to the next, or how Pinter begins to elaborate certain themes that dominate much of his later work. My own grasp of the "felt significance" of every play has been generated by a phenomenological interpretation of it as a happening in space and time, but in order to direct the reader toward salient points of analysis or conclusions that indicate key arguments in the field of Pinter criticism, I have attempted to avoid the repetitiousness that would result from such detailed analysis of the genesis of theatrical meaning and assumed that the reader will be able to use the method of analysis followed in earlier chapters to test my interpretations against their own. Clearly, the interpretation of the plays analyzed in the book is mine, and every reader will construct a somewhat different interpretation, depending on how she construes the dialogue and stage directions of each play, how she feels each mood, how she responds to the tone of every speech, how she reacts to the characters' behavior, and so on. The dialogue between one reader and another—in the theater, one spectator and another—about the meaning of the play in itself constitutes a significant part of its experience. I intend my analysis of each play to serve as a guide to *how* the play means rather than a prescription of *what* it means.

In an effort to avoid the inevitable oversimplification and distortion that arise when plays are categorized strictly according to ideas or themes, I have surveyed the plays written before *Betrayal* (1978) chronologically, in order to show how dramaturgical forms and thematic motifs were introduced, explored, and reconceived from one play to the next, gradually coming to constitute webs of thematic interest and recognizable approaches to dramaturgical structure that subsequently sparked off new notions of the relationship between content and form. As many of Pinter's two- or three-act dramas are anticipated by one or more one-act plays in which he seems to have experimented with the interrelated nature of his formal innovations and the new insights into human experience that are more fully elaborated in the later plays, I usually preface the analysis of a full-length play with a discussion of the short play/s that gesture toward it. After *Betrayal*, Pinter's plays become shorter (the longest lasts seventy minutes) and, although he wrote numerous screenplays, his output of original stage plays was far smaller than in the preceding two decades. In chapters 8 and 9, I have therefore elected to group the plays in such a way as to identify the consistency in his approach to the two pervasive motifs of (*a*) time, absence, and death, and (*b*) political repression and torture; while in chapter 10, I group together his three last plays in order to examine his reflections on the individual's contamination by the globalized culture of consumer capitalism.

The book will concentrate on Pinter's work in the theater, excluding analysis of his writing for film and television in order to limit the text to a manageable length without risking oversimplification of individual works. Occasional references will be made to radio or television plays where this illuminates discussion of the theater plays. All three-act plays will be explicated in detail in order to offer an in-depth comprehension of Pinter's dramaturgical strategies, while others will be briefly analyzed in more general terms with the aim of comprehending Pinter's entire theatrical oeuvre in synoptic terms. In doing so, I aim to demonstrate the adventurousness of Pinter's experimentation with form while at the same time exposing the ethical, epistemological, and aesthetic preoccupations that have persisted with remarkable consistency throughout his career.

All phases and aspects of Pinter's writing are characterized by an ethical commitment to expressing himself honestly and precisely. His politics can ultimately be seen as an artist's critique of the debased forms of representation that promote double standards in public and private life. By insisting on the proper use of language throughout his career as a writer and public figure he conducted a courageous battle against the deception (and corresponding self-deception) that is caused by imprecise or dishonest speech. His mastery of a unique theatrical language exemplifies the possibility of truth-telling in the face of the "habit of lying" people come to accept as ordinary conversation.

CHAPTER I

Territorial Imperatives:
The Room

On its initial production at Bristol University in May 1957, *The Room* seemed bafflingly avant-garde,[1] its strangeness and originality inhering not only in its deliberate refusal to resolve the contradictory assertions by different characters to produce a coherent exposition that integrates all its strands of narrative information, but also in the strategy of delaying the play's only striking stage action until the last two minutes. Despite the play's apparent obscurity, it is less subtle and complex than the plays that followed it, therefore making it useful as an introductory illustration of how the meaning of Pinter's drama emerges *in* and *through* performance.

Bernard Dukore aptly explicates Pinter's aesthetic by quoting Beckett's reflection on James Joyce's *Finnegans Wake:* "Here form *is* content, content *is* form. [. . .] His writing is not *about* something; *it is that something itself*" (Dukore, 7). The title of *The Room* itself proposes as the core of its drama the struggle to inhabit and possess a room of one's own. Not merely a motive that determines the behavior of its characters, the territorial imperative—the necessity of demarcating and defending the boundaries of one's own territory—also provides a structural principle for the play's scenic action. Nothing in the directions for the stage scenery prepares an audience for the avant-garde nature of *The Room.* These directions are written in the typical style of the Samuel French acting editions used by both professional repertory and amateur theater companies in the fifties, precisely specifying minimal stage settings and actors' blocking (positioning/movement). The detail of the furnishings is clearly indicated, as is the position of every object onstage, the "door down right" allowing for the five entrances and four exits to and from the room that serve to divide the action into six segments, while the gas stove and sink, window, table and chairs, and rocking chair are all working props that function as elements of the unfolding action. The foot of the double bed that protrudes from an alcove in the right-hand back corner of the stage implies that the flat occupied by Rose and Bert Hudd is a bed-sitting room within the large house specified in the directions.

The layout of the scene and the plotting of action within the space embody the human imperative to protect one's own territory from invasion or destruction by outsiders. Virtually every aspect of the drama either comically or menacingly represents the threat of the other—the intruder, the stranger, the foreigner, or possibly, even the insider, who is feared because he refuses to participate in the normative rituals of everyday domestic communication. The window positioned upstage in the center and the door on the audience's left downstage create a double focus for Rose's foreboding. Although her response initially appears as no more than curiosity about what is happening outside the flat, her persistent questioning establishes a cyclical rhythm of nervous anticipation and disappointment that anticipates the shocking event at the climax of the play:

> *She rises, goes to the window, and looks out.*
> It's quiet. Be coming on for dark. There's no one about.
> *She stands, looking.*
> Wait a minute.
> *Pause.*
> I wonder who that is.
> *Pause.*
> No. I thought I saw someone.
> *Pause.*
> No.
> *She drops the curtain.* (104)[2]

The questions concerning whom—or indeed what—may be seen from the window give way to Rose's repetitious musings on the room as a safe and cozy haven from the hazards of bad weather and the unexplained danger of outsiders. ("This is a good room. You've got a chance in a place like this.") This thought leads to further reflections on the architectural configuration of the house and on its occupants: "[W]hen they offered us the basement I said no straight off. I knew that'd be no good . . . I wonder who has got it now. I've never seen them, or heard of them. But I think someone's down there" (105).

The initially unsettling feature of the drama is that, although first Rose and later the landlord, Mr Kidd, talk to him without letting up for over a third of the play's duration, Bert remains entirely silent, not uttering a word, even on his exit. The obvious effect of this unconventional dramaturgical device is to provoke the audience to question why he says nothing, thereby drawing attention to the subtext of his unexpressed thoughts and feelings and emphasizing the peculiarity of Rose's relentless stream of small talk. The surprising contrast between Rose's garrulity and Bert's uncanny lack of communicativeness heightens the audience's awareness of the way in which spoken language functions as a form of action. Already in his first play, Pinter demonstrates a mastery of the naturalistic technique of subtext perfected by Ibsen and Chekhov and brilliantly exploited in English for the purpose of comedy by Noel Coward. This emphasis on the peculiar nature of such a one-sided conversation, however, transforms the traditional function of subtext, problematizing the relationship between speech and silence in order to expose the gulf between the surface conversation and the underlying matrix of motives and feelings that are both concealed and revealed by the contrast of excessive talk with unexplained reticence.

Since she has very little of import to communicate, Rose's unceasing chatter begins after a few minutes to register as a series of utterly banal domestic clichés, voiced while she bustles around the still and silent figure of Bert seated at the table in the center of the stage with his tea. Rose's rambling attempts at conversation return over and again to a topic that is repeated so insistently it appears as an obsession that progressively acquires significance as the symptom of an apparently all-consuming anxiety. Rose seems excessively concerned with the need to protect herself from the unspoken dangers that might be imagined to lurk outdoors or even immediately beyond the small confines of her bed-sitting room. Why is she preoccupied by the fact that it is cold, wet, and becoming dark outside? This would surely be normal on a winter afternoon. Why does she seem so concerned that Bert is going out for a while? Why is Bert's reason for going never explained? Why does Rose constantly reiterate the fact that it is safe, warm, and cozy in the room? (This is somewhat ironic as the stage directions indicate that it is sparsely furnished with rather basic, purely functional items.) And why does she seem so anxious to know the precise layout of the house and to determine the identity of its occupants? The fact that, no matter how she rationalizes it, her anxiety over her immediate circumstances is never clearly explained or logically motivated, prompts the audience to search for a hidden motivation for her insecurity. As none is revealed in the course of the action, the audience may well assume that the anxiety is endemic to her condition, the symptom of an existential anguish Rose is unable either to confront or repress.

Seconds later, there is a knock on the door. Rose's concern about what is outdoors and who inhabits the rest of the house contributes to the tension created by the knock, which is prolonged by two further knocks and the corresponding silences that greet Rose's enquiries as to who it is. Tension is diffused by the comic sequence that follows:

> *Pause. The door opens and* MR KIDD *comes in.*
> MR KIDD: I knocked.
> ROSE: I heard you.
> MR KIDD: Eh?
> ROSE: We heard you.
> MR KIDD: Hallo, Mr Hudd, how are you, all right? I've been looking at the pipes.
> ROSE: Are they all right?
> MR KIDD: Eh?
> ROSE: Sit down, Mr Kidd.
> MR KIDD: No, that's all right. (105–6)

The entrance of Mr Kidd so early in the action introduces a structural pattern of entrances and exits that constitutes the major source of dramatic tension in *The Room*. Every time a new character enters, the audience will expect to discover who they are and how they relate to Rose and Bert Hudd—but such knowledge is precisely what the dramaturgical scheme of the play is designed to render obscure or ambiguous. The pattern of repeated entrances and exits is exploited as a symbolic device that gives concrete theatrical shape to the terror of having to defend one's territory from intrusion by unidentified forces.

During *The Room*'s fifty minutes of playing time, four sets of entrances and exits occur, as well as one entrance shortly before the play ends. Mr Kidd's first entrance appears to be a theatrical non sequitur. Over approximately ten minutes of stage time, the conversation between Rose and Kidd meanders through a series of comic mis-apprehensions and lapses of memory and hearing. Pinter's skill in the construction of stage dialogue can be seen to encompass not only Rose's fifteen-minute stream-of-consciousness chatter but also a wonderfully confused and confusing exchange of false assumptions and misunderstandings during which the characters cannot manage to communicate any specific information about their respective lives in the house as landlord and tenant. What seems at first to be a brilliantly mannered portrayal of the comedy of linguistic obfuscation that typifies so much everyday conversation[3] is intensified through repetition so that in the next segment of the drama the confusion experienced as a consequence of the inability of language to map one's own environment accurately, becomes a symptom of the individual's alienation from his or her own world.

Rose's unexpected discovery of Mr and Mrs Sands when she opens the door to put out the garbage bin seconds after Bert has exited, ushers in an episode of complicated and silly cross-talk redolent of traditional humorous sketches from the British music hall or fifties radio comedy, so that now the linguistic stylization draws attention to itself and points up even more obviously the failure of the characters to establish the facts that would normally comprise the basic "backstory" of any well-made play.

> MRS SANDS: Why don't you sit down, Mrs—
> ROSE: Hudd. No thanks.
> MR SANDS: What did you say?
> ROSE: When?
> MR SANDS: What did you say the name was?
> ROSE: Hudd.
> MR SANDS: That's it. You're the wife of the bloke you mentioned then.
> MRS SANDS: No she isn't. That was Mr Kidd.
> MR SANDS: Was it? I thought it was Hudd.
> MRS SANDS: No it was Kidd. Wasn't it, Mrs Hudd?
> ROSE: That's right. The landlord.
> MRS SANDS: No, not the landlord. The other man.
> ROSE: Well that's his name. He's the landlord.
> MR SANDS: Who?
> ROSE: Mr Kidd.
>
> *Pause.*

MRS SANDS: Is he?
MR SANDS: Maybe there are two landlords.

Pause. (112–13)

By ridiculing the characters' repeated attempts to establish a straightforward context of exposition within which to comprehend the events they are experiencing and the information they are given, the episode not only draws attention to the conventional nature of the Sandses' stereotypical marital relationship but at the same time comically exposes the unexpressed insecurities of characters who, like Rose, appear unable to ascertain the correct spatiotemporal co-ordinates of their world:

ROSE: How long have you been here?
MRS SANDS: I don't know. How long have we been here, Toddy?
MR SANDS: About half an hour.
MRS SANDS: About thirty-five minutes.
. . . .
. . . .
MR SANDS: Well. If I wanted to get hold of . . . [the landlord], where would I find him?
ROSE: Well—I'm not sure.
MR SANDS: He lives here, does he?
ROSE: Yes, but I don't know—
MR SANDS: You don't know exactly where he hangs out?
ROSE: No, not exactly.
MR SANDS: But he does live here, doesn't he?

Pause.

MRS SANDS: This is a very big house, Toddy. (114–15)

Rose's inability to answer with absolute certainty Mr Sands's questions concerning her landlord may well lead the audience to wonder whether Mr Kidd is indeed the landlord and to question Rose's reasons for regarding him as such. In this way the possibility that Mr Kidd may have been lying to her is introduced, causing the audience to review what appeared as a rather pointless episode with him and retrospectively call into question Mr Kidd's motives. As Mr and Mrs Sands claim to need a place to rent, their alleged reason for visiting the house is to find the landlord in order to make arrangements for their tenancy. Mrs Sands recounts an episode in which they stumbled upon a man in the dark basement while searching for the landlord. Mrs Sands tells the story in a long speech that interrupts the easy to-and-fro of the previous conversation, its Kafkaesque atmosphere of dislocation and disorientation evoking a vivid experience of the uncanny:

> MRS SANDS: . . . [I]t was very dark in the hall and there wasn't anyone about. So we went down to the basement . . . I didn't like the look of it much, I mean the feel, we couldn't make much out, it smelt damp to me. Anyway, we went through a kind of partition, then there was another partition, and we couldn't see where we were going, well, it seemed to me it got darker the more we went, the further we went in, I thought we must have come to the wrong house . . . And then this voice said, this voice came—it said— well, it gave me a bit of a fright . . . but someone asked if he could do anything for us . . . And this man, this voice really, I think he was behind the partition, said yes there was a room vacant. (117)

Rose is unsettled to learn about the man in the basement, and even more shaken to discover that the room said to be vacant is hers.

> ROSE: You won't find any rooms vacant in this house.
> MR SANDS: Why not?
> ROSE: Mr Kidd told me. He told me.
> MR SANDS: Mr Kidd?
> ROSE: He told me he was full up.
> MR SANDS: The man in the basement said there was one. One room. Number seven, he said.
>
> *Pause.*
>
> ROSE: That's this room.
> . . . .
> . . . .
> ROSE: This room is occupied.
> MR SANDS: Come on.
> MRS SANDS: Good night, Mrs Hudd. (118)

The individual accounts given by Rose, Mr Kidd, and the Sandses contradict one another, so neither Rose nor the audience can be certain that Mr and Mrs Sands are telling the truth. If the landlord is *not* deceiving Rose, there is no one in the basement and Kidd has no intention of asking her to leave, which exposes the married couple as cunning intruders who have been planning to maneuver Rose and Bert out of their own bed-sitting room.

This Pirandellian conflict of one subjective version of reality with another is set within an atmosphere reminiscent of a forties film thriller in which the viewer is compelled to explain the facts of a crime by examining a complex web of obscure motives that appear to lead further and further from a solution until the startling reversal at the film's conclusion reveals the truth as having actually been visibly present from the start. *The Room* transposes its central conflict from a material to a mental level as the battle for the possession of territory is transformed into a noir mystery in which no one is who he says he is and the question of "Whodunit" is ultimately replaced by "Who am I?"

Mr Kidd's second entrance no more than thirty seconds after the Sandses' exit, confirms the suspicion that he was not telling the whole truth in his previous encounter with Rose. After a few minutes of talk at cross-purposes in which both Rose and Mr Kidd manage to communicate nothing more than their feelings of panic, Kidd confirms one aspect of the Sandses' story that he could not do in Bert's presence:

> MR KIDD: . . . I've got to tell you, that's all. I've got to tell you. I've had a terrible week-end. You'll have to see him. I can't take it any more. You've got to see him.
>
> *Pause.*
>
> ROSE: Who?
>
> MR KIDD: The man. He's been waiting to see you. He wants to see you [. . .
> . . . .]
> He's downstairs now . . . He said that when Mr Hudd went out I was to tell him. That's why I came up before. But he hadn't gone yet . . . I said, well when he goes, I said, you can go up, go up, have done with it. No, he says, you must ask her if she'll see me . . .
> . . . .
> ROSE: Who is he?
>
> MR KIDD: How do I know who he is? . . . .
> . . . .
> MR KIDD: He hasn't given me any rest. Just lying there. In the black dark. Hour after hour . . . Mrs Hudd, have a bit of pity. Please see him. Why don't you see him?

ROSE: I don't know him.
MR KIDD: You can never tell. You might know him.
ROSE: I don't know him. (119–21)

Mrs Sands's image of the man whom she heard but could not see in the dark of the basement is progressively amplified by Kidd to form the picture of a man waiting a whole weekend in the dark until Bert's departure gives him a chance to meet Rose on her own. The new information conveyed somewhat hysterically by Mr Kidd confirms aspects of Mrs Sands's story but does not explain why the man has said Rose's room was vacant. Mr Kidd's fear and Rose's illogical insistence—without even seeing him—that she does not know the man introduce a new dimension to the detective mystery aspect of the plot. Who is this man, and what motive does Rose have for not wanting to see him? Pinter's powerful manipulation of the audience's dramatic expectations is very economical, utilizing the minimal disposition of conventional stage business derived from entrances, exits, and domestic conversations to generate intense feelings of apprehension and curiosity. As in the best stage and screen thrillers, the less the audience actually witnesses, the more vividly it will imagine the concealed reality.

The entrance of the blind black man Riley, and the odd exchange that follows, create the grotesque effect of a grim fairy tale. Before Riley can tell Rose what he has come for, he is subjected by her to a stream of unmotivated abuse. When the play was first performed in 1957, racial difference may have prompted extremely emotional and occasionally prejudiced responses among members of a British audience. Their first real experience of black people living in Britain was a result of the initial wave of immigration from British colonies in Africa and the West Indies beginning with the arrival on the "Windrush" of 400 Jamaican immigrants in 1948. At this time, black people were exotic and alien to most inhabitants of Britain, so in this context Pinter's characterization of Riley as a black man with a stereotypically Irish name was not only unsettling but challenged the incipient prejudice of the audience by revealing Rose's apparent overreaction to Riley as itself potentially racist. Riley's message from her father to Rose whom he calls "Sal," is delivered in an incantatory rhythm and its startling content evokes the bizarre fascination of a cautionary tale:

RILEY: Your father wants you to come home.

Pause.

ROSE: Home?
RILEY: Yes.
ROSE: Home? Go now. Come on. It's late. It's late.
RILEY: To come home.
ROSE: Stop it. I can't take it. What do you want?
RILEY: Come home, Sal.

Pause.

ROSE: What did you call me?
RILEY: Come home, Sal.
ROSE: Don't call me that.
RILEY: Come, now.
ROSE: Don't call me that.
RILEY: So now you're here.
ROSE: Not Sal. (124)

The putative outline of a detective thriller that the spectator has thus far been witnessing is transformed into a Sophoclean drama of identity. How does Riley know Rose and why does he call her Sal? If he knows who she is, why does she not recognize him? If she has moved away from home to stay "here," what was her reason for doing so? Why does she reject the name Sal? Riley later says, "*I* want you to come home" (emphasis added), so is it possible that he is her father? Or is he lying? And if so, why does she so forcefully reject the appellation "Sal"? Having been aggressive in her first response to Riley, she finally becomes philosophical in acknowledging that Riley knows her from somewhere else ("I've been here") and begins to treat him compassionately before Bert arrives home, "*She touches his eyes, the back of his head and his temples with her hands.*" On his return Bert gives a stereotypical and repetitiously sexualized description of driving the car "down there" on icy roads before tipping up Riley's chair, throwing him to the ground, and kicking his head a few times against the gas stove. When the curtain falls the audience does not know whether Riley is alive or dead, while at the closing line Rose appears suddenly to have gone blind ("Can't see. I can't see. I can't see" [126]).

The audience is left wondering why Bert has hit and kicked Riley so viciously (he has no apparent reason for wanting to do this) and why Rose has gone blind after touching the blind Riley on the eyes and temples. Is Bert jealously afraid that Riley has come to take Rose away from him and back to the bosom of the family from which Bert may have rescued her? Is Rose's blindness a symbol of her kinship with Riley? The play has certainly moved beyond the confines of naturalism toward a more abstract form of symbolic drama. Despite her desperate efforts to retreat from the world into the room, Rose—or is she Sal?—cannot ultimately prevent the truth of her past life from breaking through the defenses by means of which she attempts to maintain her present position. The play's surprise reversal consists in the discovery that what Rose has been trying to escape is not any external danger but an interior crisis or secret that she has attempted to hide. Although it is never explained, the spectator experiences a sense of the mystery of Rose's identity and the concealed trauma of her past by witnessing the inexplicably sudden attack of blindness that uncannily links her with the blind Riley.

Pinter's view that "people fall back on anything they can lay their hands on verbally to keep away from the dangers of knowing, and of being known" (Smith, 58) does help to explain the degree to which Rose and the other characters remain unknowable to one another and the audience; nevertheless the play's refusal to explicate in more detail the psychosocial identity of these individuals cannot be accounted for in naturalistic terms but constitutes an entirely original dramaturgical strategy. By deliberately withholding plot resolutions or character motivations, Pinter places responsibility on each member of the audience to explicate the fictional situation in a process that involves a confrontation with her or his own personal fears, needs, prejudices, insecurities, guilt, secrets. All that can be said with any degree of certainty is that Rose is hiding in this room in an attempt to avoid the demands of a past life from which she believes she has escaped. In the archetypal psychological pattern of an Oedipal narrative, she discovers that it is impossible to escape from her past—that in some sense it exists within her.[4]

The Room unflinchingly shows us the world as it is. People are irrational, jealous, and violent and their behavior may not be entirely explicable with reference to logical cause-effect relationships. Pinter himself defends the representation of apparently arbitrary violence in some of his plays with reference to a psychological analysis of human behavior:

The world *is* a pretty violent place, it's as simple as that, so any violence in the plays comes out quite naturally. It seems to me an essential and inevitable factor . . . The violence is really only an expression of the question of dominance and subservience, which is possibly a repeated theme of my plays . . . I wouldn't call this violence so much as a battle for positions, it's a very common, everyday thing. (Smith, 60–61)

The foregoing analysis of the dramaturgy of *The Room* illustrates Pinter's first elaboration of the technique he deploys in the plays written from 1957 until *The Homecoming* in 1965. The play does not so much reject as deconstruct the model of the well-made thriller or "drawing room" drama that occupied most of Pinter's early career as the actor David Baron. *The Room's* structural scheme is akin to Terence Rattigan's well-made one-act masterpiece, *The Browning Version* (1947), one of the best-known and most highly regarded plays produced after the war.[5] In this play, the web of bourgeois hypocrisy, euphemism, and petty duplicity that represents the milieu of an English public school is gradually exposed through a series of conversations in a living room, constructed as duologues and trios of characters who come and go in much the same way as those in *The Room*. The difference is that through his concise and careful plotting Rattigan unambiguously evokes an image of the environment contiguous to the living room and unequivocally reveals the true identity of each character, so that by the end of the play, the hero recovers the nobility of his vocation in an act of self-assertion that demonstrates the truth of who he is, whereas in *The Room* what information is gained by means of the series of conversational encounters merely complicates the mystery, raising more and more questions about the identity of the protagonist and undermining the possibility of ever establishing or verifying a true state of affairs.

The play establishes the aesthetic terms of Pinter's early theater, which does not aim to communicate an overarching "meaning" in an allegorical or symbolic manner, but which invites the spectator to "live through" the experiences of a group of people in a virtual universe that operates in parallel to her or his everyday world. By removing the conventionally logical exposition of a "well-made" naturalistic play that functions to reassure the spectator that it is possible to piece together all the parts of the dramaturgical puzzle in order to supply a coherently historical rationale for the action, the revelation that there may not ever be a logical explanation for the events of a human life comes as a genuine shock. The contradiction of one character's "back-story" with another's is never satisfactorily explained; neither is the opacity of the mental processes motivating the characters' seemingly arbitrary actions ever penetrated. Consequently, every character's version of "reality" conflicts with that of every other, producing the unsettling experience for the spectator of the human inability to provide a satisfactory account of what she sees, hears, and feels. By removing the frames of belief or rationalization through which we habitually attempt to organize and explain our experience, Pinter's drama undermines our commonsense assumptions about the world, insisting that we confront the bare facticity of an existence that the preexisting categories by means of which we order our lives fail to accommodate.

The Room does not therefore simply exploit the histrionic capability of actors to present pretense. It locates acting as key to an epistemology of everyday life in which everyone is an actor instinctively manipulating surface behavior to conceal truths they need to hide in order to protect themselves from being manipulated by others in turn. Human interaction is thereby conceived as a series of games of impersonation, in which each individual creates a personality that he acts for the benefit of positioning himself in relation to others. In this radical epistemological context, the commonsense view of the human situation disintegrates to disclose a world fraught with ambiguity and equivocation. The room one lives in is contingent on a mysterious geography, a fragment of an unknown house in an alien neighborhood. The people one knows and meets are strangers: familiar bodies, faces, and voices whose conventional gesticulations, grimaces, and babble are merely clichés, empty of human significance. In Heidegger's existential philosophy, truth is not contained within the logic of a linguistic or symbolic proposition, but is experienced as an historical moment of "unconcealment": truth is a "coming into being."[6] This is precisely the "meaning" of The Room. It cannot be translated into analytic language in order to abstract from it a kernel of wisdom or knowledge. Its truth is experienced as a progressive "unconcealment" of truth from the accretions of falsehood consequent on the social habit of equivocation. Without offering the convenient historical rationalization of traditional realist dramaturgy the play's anagnorisis asserts the archetypal social and psychological truth of the Oedipal myth as a happening in time: the ending leads back to the beginning.

CHAPTER 2

Questions of Authority:
The Dumb Waiter,
The Birthday Party

Although Pinter was engaged in writing *The Dumb Waiter* at the same time as he was working on *The Birthday Party* (1957), it was only in 1959 that it received its premiere in Germany before being given together with *The Room* at the Hampstead Theatre Club in London in 1960. The influence of the crime thriller is obvious in both *The Dumb Waiter* and *The Birthday Party*. Written in one act, *The Dumb Waiter* lasts only fifty minutes and its plotting is extremely concise, producing a great build-up of tension with minimal means. While containing a number of surreal elements, the action is tightly structured and leads with the inexorable force of a Greek tragedy to the shocking reversal that is its climax. The focus of the play is on the agents rather than on the victim, who is not identified as Gus until the last moment of the action. In waiting for their assignment to begin, Ben seems to share Gus's anxiety but, in contrast with the obsessive need Gus has to question the details of their methods and instructions, Ben maintains a blind faith in the system, and demonstrates a mechanical obedience to the letter of his instructions right up to the moment when it becomes apparent that his accomplice is in fact his designated victim.

The Dumb Waiter is one of Pinter's most frequently performed plays, totally convincing in its depiction of the banal routine of the hired killers and the anxiety generated by their being obliged to wait in unfamiliar surroundings for the signal to execute their task, yet achieving surreal flights of verbal and visual comedy at particular moments. As they engage in seemingly nonsensical quarrels over the wording of trite local newspaper stories and the correct language for petty activities like *lighting* as opposed to *putting on* the kettle, the audience observes the terms of their relationship: Ben is the senior partner and more dominant personality, while the more sensitive Gus is the junior partner who defers to Ben's authority as leader. The power play that characterizes this partnership is located in the context of the absolute power of the organization that employs them and chooses their victims, effectively assuming the power of life and death over people whom Ben and Gus never know. In some respects, Ben and Gus represent Pinter's wry take on Vladimir and Estragon, perpetually in waiting for Godot to reveal the meaning of their existence. In Pinter's more naturalistically plotted drama, however, the two who wait are located in an environment that can be located as somewhere in or near Birmingham, in a real room that appears to be the basement of a defunct restaurant. What is reminiscent of both Beckett (and Kafka) is the fact that the institution that authorizes and controls their actions—and therefore invests what they do with meaning—is invisible, somewhere offstage, manifesting the power to determine their fate without ever identifying the source of its authority to do so. As in *The Birthday Party* the reality of power is revealed as arbitrary force, authority as an illusion, always hidden or absent.

The image of *The Dumb Waiter* possesses multiple layers of significance. As ignorant victim, Gus is a dumb waiter—fearfully curious about the minute details of the job such as how the corpses are disposed of and queasy about having to kill women, without recognizing his own blind complicity in a system that has doomed him to death. Ben's unthinking acceptance of authority, manifest in his failure to question his instructions, also makes him a dumb waiter, trapped by the mechanism of a malign system into assassinating his own partner. The dumb waiter is also literally present as part of the scenery—a contraption used by small restaurants for transporting meals from the kitchen to the dining room on another floor. Ben's conversations on the attached speaking tube are a startling visual and aural metaphor for his blind service of a faceless authority, while the increasingly absurd orders for meals that descend as written notes on the dumb waiter are a surreal evocation of the irrational demands of modern life, in which the power structures that control repressive sociopolitical systems are concealed and their agents both anonymous and blind.

The Birthday Party

Although the milieu of *The Birthday Party* is represented in more complex detail and the action is far less schematic, many of the thematic motifs of the one-act play are elaborated and explored in a different context in the full-length play. There are obvious similarities between the pairs of agents in *The Dumb Waiter* and *The Birthday Party*. In some ways Goldberg and McCann in the latter play can be seen as variants of the hired killers Ben and Gus. Apparently under instructions to insinuate themselves into the Boleses' house in order to extract some kind of confession from Stanley, instead of killing him at the conclusion of the play they forcibly remove him from the house to be treated for his unspecified condition by someone called Monty, who it can only be assumed by the audience is the head of their organization. *The Birthday Party* was Pinter's first three-act play. Its London premiere was his first and only flop, the production closing after five performances at the Lyric Theatre, Hammersmith. Although it had elicited enthusiastic and perceptive responses from audiences and critics during its short pre-London tryout in Cambridge, Wolverhampton, and Oxford, it proved incomprehensible to all of the reviewers in the London daily newspapers.[1] These London reviewers were not alone in their demand that *The Birthday Party* be explicable in neatly discursive terms. In a letter to the *New York Times* after its New York premiere in 1967 a woman asked Pinter for clarification on three points:

> Dear Sir, I would be grateful if you would kindly explain to me the meaning of your play. These are the points which I do not understand: 1. Who are the two men? 2. Where did Stanley come from? 3. Were they supposed to be normal? You will appreciate that without the answers to my questions I cannot fully understand your play. (Quoted in Esslin, 37–38)

Pinter's answer is a witty parody of such literal-minded attempts at pinning down meaning as though it were merely the solution to a puzzle:

> Dear Madam, I would be obliged if you would kindly explain to me the meaning of your letter. These are the points which I do not un-

derstand: 1. Who are you? 2. Where do you come from? 3. Are you supposed to be normal? You will appreciate that without the answers to my questions I cannot fully understand your letter. (Quoted in Esslin, 37–38)

In the light of this exchange it is ironic that *The Birthday Party* comes closest to the form of the well-made play that Pinter is continually intent on deconstructing: it is set in the familiar living room of a run-down English seaside boarding house, and it has elements of the kind of comedy-thriller in which Pinter himself, as David Baron, had often performed. Just as *The Room* does, however, the play deliberately frustrates the expectations of an audience for unequivocal exposition, failing to confirm or deny the truth of its characters' ambiguous and occasionally contradictory assertions about their histories or motives, and refusing to satisfy the conventional demand for a neat conclusion. By rejecting the conventions of the thriller in its refusal of any logical explanation as to why the protagonist Stanley is at last escorted out of the boarding house to see Monty—or exactly who Monty is—*The Birthday Party* parodies the pat resolution of such drama, and undermines its "commonsense" moral assumption that a policeman's authority derives from a system of justice designed to protect the citizens of a democratic society.

As with *The Room*, the idea for *The Birthday Party* came from a real experience that Pinter's imagination wholly transformed. In the summer of 1954, while on tour with a play in Eastbourne he was obliged to share an attic room in a seaside boarding house with a man he had met in a pub:

There was a terrible landlady, and it was all quite incredibly dirty. And at the end of the week I said to this fellow, who turned out to have been a concert pianist on the pier: "Why do you stay here?" And he said: "There's nowhere else to go." I left with that ringing in my ears. (Bakewell, 630)

The situation in Eastbourne seems to have resonated with Pinter's heightened sensitivity to the horrors of the Second World War:

He was a totally lonely man. That's all I knew about him, but his image remained with me for some years. I thought, what would happen if two people knocked on his door? [. . .] The idea of the knock came from my knowledge of the Gestapo. I'll never forget. [. . .] The war had only been over less than ten years. It was very much on my mind. (Gussow, 71)

The Birthday Party begins in a style of trite conversational naturalism that evokes the reassuring normality of the well-made play of the fifties, albeit in a linguistic register that indicates the less educated class that had begun to be regularly represented in English drama after *Look Back in Anger* (1956) and *A Taste of Honey* (1957). As in the opening episode of *The Room*, a man (in this case, Petey Boles) sits at a table trying to read the newspaper while his wife interrupts him with her repetitious chatter. This time, however, the woman (Meg) is initially merely an offstage voice and the man does reply. As in the earlier play, the woman is serving the man a meal (in this case, breakfast) and commenting, merely to keep up a conversation:

> MEG: I've got your cornflakes ready. (*She disappears and re-appears.*)
>   Here's your cornflakes [. . . . .
> . . . .] MEG *enters by the kitchen door.*
> Are they nice?
> PETEY: Very nice.
> MEG: I thought they'd be nice. (*She sits at the table.*) You got your paper?
> PETEY: Yes.
> MEG: Is it good?
> PETEY: Not bad.
> MEG: What does it say?
> PETEY: Nothing much. (19–20)[2]

But in contrast to the parallel opening of *The Room*, neither Meg nor Petey seems to be concealing any repressed anxiety, and no mystery appears to be concealed by the conventionally naturalistic social interaction. The action represents the typical attempt of a bored and lonely housewife to engage her husband in talk. The obvious lack of genuine informational content in Meg's conversation foregrounds as a comic ritual the stereotypical nature of most everyday social discourse.[3] Even in this first phase of his career, such comic virtuosity in the exposure of the emptiness of much social conversation became a hallmark of Pinter's technique as a playwright.

The absurd pointlessness of the exchange is emphasized when Petey obliges Meg by reading out extracts from his newspaper, so that the casual introduction of the "crime thriller" motif a few minutes later goes almost unnoticed in the flow of conversational chitchat:

> PETEY: (*turning to her*) Oh, Meg, two men came up to me on the beach last night.
> MEG: Two men?
> PETEY: Yes. They wanted to know if we could put them up for a couple of nights.
> [. . . . .]
> MEG: What did you say?
> PETEY: Well, I said I didn't know. So they said they'd come round to find out.
> [. . . . .]
> MEG: They must have heard this was a very good boarding house. It is. This house is on the list. (22)

This conversation surreptitiously introduces a crime mystery motif as a motor of the plot. Although the audience does not feel it yet, the anticipated arrival of the two men will become a source of tension when Stanley later appears apprehensive about the two men whom the naive Meg welcomes into her house without suspicion.

After Stanley has come downstairs for breakfast and Petey has left for work, the inappropriateness of Meg's regressively girlish flirtation with Stanley suggests the Oedipal ambivalence of a relationship in which Meg is simultaneously the protective mother and predatory lover:

> MEG: Was it nice?
> STANLEY: What?
> MEG: The fried bread.
> STANLEY: Succulent.
> [. . . . .]
> MEG: You shouldn't say that word to a married woman.
> [. . . . .
> . . . .]
> MEG: Stan?
> STANLEY: What?
> MEG: (*shyly*) Am I really succulent?
> STANLEY: Oh you are. I'd rather have you than a cold in the nose any day.
> MEG: You're just saying that. (27–29)

The conversation conveys Meg's infatuation with Stanley as well as his teasing complicity that alternates with revulsion when her flirting becomes too physical:

> STANLEY: (*violently*) Look why don't you get this place cleared up?
> . . . I need a new room!
> MEG: (*sensual, stroking his arm*) Oh, Stan, that's a lovely room. I've had some lovely afternoons in that room.
>
> *He recoils from her hand in disgust* [. . . . . . .
> . . . .]
>
> MEG: I like cigarettes. (*He stands at the window, smoking. She crosses behind him and tickles the back of his neck.*) Tickle, tickle.
> STANLEY: Get away from me.

Every bit of stage business is visually imagined in relation to speech, Pinter's dramaturgical economy being manifest in the way the apparent randomness of the characters' chatter is carefully designed to build rhythmically toward the moment of shock when Stanley hears of the anticipated arrival of the two men. The stillness indicated in the direction to speak "without turning" marks this moment as potentially fraught with significance, posing the question for the audience as to the nature of Stanley's relationship with these men.

> MEG: [. . . . .] I've got to get things in for the two gentlemen.
>
> *A pause.* STANLEY *slowly raises his head. He speaks without turning.*
>
> STANLEY: What two gentlemen?
> MEG: I'm expecting visitors. (29–30)

Meg takes advantage of his apparent nervousness to taunt him about the visitors' anticipated arrival but her naive belief that they are merely businessmen arriving to stay overnight is putatively overlaid with irony as the audience begins to infer that Stanley may suspect them of some sinister purpose:

> STANLEY: They won't come. Someone's taking the Michael. Forget all about it. It's a false alarm. A false alarm. (*He sits at the table*) Where's my tea?
> MEG: I took it away. You didn't want it.

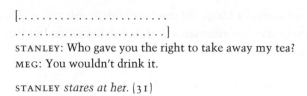

[. . . . .
. . . .]

STANLEY: Who gave you the right to take away my tea?
MEG: You wouldn't drink it.

STANLEY *stares at her.* (31)

Stanley's aggressive tantrums are emotionally disproportionate to Meg's provocations, masking an anxiety that seems excessive in the given situation. His bluster about his status and his rights constitutes an unsuccessful attempt to overcome his growing panic, the insistent self-assertion betraying a deeper insecurity and introducing questions of authority and identity that will ultimately manifest themselves as dominant tropes:

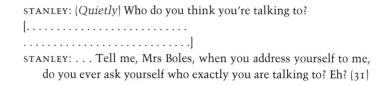

STANLEY: (*Quietly*) Who do you think you're talking to?
[. . . . .
. . . .]
STANLEY: . . . Tell me, Mrs Boles, when you address yourself to me,
do you ever ask yourself who exactly you are talking to? Eh? (31)

The spectator may well wonder if Stanley has indeed been concealing a secret about himself, thereby perceiving this overreaction as a further clue in a stage thriller focusing on Stanley's identity as either criminal or victim. Is Stanley on the run? And if so why? What is his relationship with the two men? The tension subtly builds to the entrance of Goldberg and McCann, the audience's curiosity being skillfully manipulated by the deliberate withholding of expository information.

Pinter's skill in writing for actors is beautifully illustrated here in his economical contrivance of stage action. Stanley betrays the intense nature of his panic by the surprising contradiction in movement of his previously supercilious speech to Meg:

Silence. He groans, his trunk falls forward, his head falls into his hands.

MEG: (*in a small voice*) Didn't you enjoy your breakfast, Stan? (31)

The complexity of this brief interaction reveals a mastery of histrionic effect. Within the rhetorical terms established by the play, the lapse from speech into silence, followed by the actor's groans as he falls forward on to the table, signify a huge emotional crisis that has been repressed beneath the surface playfulness of Stanley's teasing conversation with Meg, but at the same time her rueful attempt to comfort him, comically exposes the great gulf of incomprehension that separates her perception of things from his.

Further plot tension is generated by the succeeding discussion of Stanley's earlier career as a pianist, which acts as a conversational red herring. Blithely unaware of Stanley's real reason for reacting so emotionally to the news of the two visitors, Meg does not question him about this but resorts to chatting about his career as a way of rousing him from his anxious state. In so doing, she only helps to intensify his feelings of self-disgust:

> MEG: (*She approaches the table.*) Stan? When are you going to play the piano again? (STANLEY *grunts.*) Like you used to. (STANLEY *grunts.*) (31)

Meg's encouragement prompts Stanley into an escapist fantasy in which he appears to be pretending to Meg that he has been offered a world tour as a concert pianist. He then somewhat fancifully recalls a triumphant solo concert at Lower Edmonton that gives way to a maudlin account of a humiliating subsequent engagement that nobody attended:

> STANLEY: . . . My next concert. Somewhere else it was. In winter. I went down there to play. Then, when I got there, the hall was closed, the place was shuttered up, not even a caretaker. They'd locked it up. (*Takes off his glasses and wipes them on his pyjama jacket.*) A fast one. They pulled a fast one. I'd like to know who was responsible for that. (*Bitterly.*) All right, Jack, I can take a tip. They want me to crawl down on my bended knees. (33)

The long speech from which the above is quoted constructs Stanley's past career as a musician in the self-pitying way he has chosen to see it—as a classic narrative of betrayal in which he is the sensitive and talented artist-hero, deserted by friends, critics, and public ("they"), whose rejection has reduced him to servility and creative impotence. The comic oddity of certain images and particular details serves to alert the audience to the possibility that Stanley's account may not be entirely reliable—a defamiliarization technique[4] typically deployed by Pinter to emphasize the ways in which idiosyncrasies of speech express the equivocal or subjective nature of a character's self-dramatization. The succession of reflections forms a stream of consciousness that might be projecting memory, fantasy, dream, or a combination of all three, establishing an uncommon approach to the representation of mental states that anticipates one of the chief preoccupations of Pinter's later plays. Significantly, there is no way for an audience to ascertain which part of Stanley's narrative is true and which false. Speech in a Pinter play can never guarantee an objective representation of the facts of any human experience, because a person's self-consciousness is always subjective; memories are, *ab origo*, contaminated by the subjectivity of desire, imagination, dream, fantasy, and self-idealization, produced in a process of creative self-fashioning that renders them as unverifiable as purely imagined states of being.

Classic thriller techniques continue to be deployed in order to sustain and heighten tension. After a threatening exchange in which Stanley projects on to Meg his fears that the two men are coming to take him away in a van, there is a knock on the door but instead of the anticipated entrance of Goldberg and McCann, it is Lulu, who has come at Meg's behest. Furthermore the spectator's curiosity is aroused by the effect of having Lulu speak to Meg offstage for a few moments prior to her entrance, with Stanley present onstage listening, although unable to comprehend their conversation. The subsequent exchange between Stanley and Lulu putatively evokes the notion of a stereotypical sexual liaison between the two young people that contrasts with the improperly Oedipal relationship of Stanley and Meg that has previously been entertained. Stanley's mock-flirtation with Lulu and the almost parodic nature of his invitation to elope ("How would you like to go away with me?" [20]), together with Lulu's final put-down ("You're a bit of a wash-out, aren't you?" [20]), reinforces the sense of Stanley's neurotic impotence, while further delaying the anticipated arrival of the "two gentlemen."

A further exploitation of the classic formula by which a stage thriller enhances dramatic tension through a deferral of anticipated conflict is engineered when after Lulu's exit Goldberg and McCann arrive but enter the living room without knocking so that the expected confrontation with Stanley is delayed yet again because he is in the kitchen and exits through the back door without their noticing him. This bit of stage business not only ensures a plot twist as comically complicated as classic farce, but significantly creates a change in perspective so that the audience now has an opportunity to watch the unfolding of action from the intruders' viewpoint. Here Pinter's originality can be recognized in his inversion of the stage cliché in which the well-practiced and cunning criminals plan their campaign. Like Gus in *The Dumb Waiter*, McCann is feeling insecure and Goldberg is obliged to bolster his confidence:

> MCCANN: What now?
> GOLDBERG: Don't worry yourself, McCann. Take a seat.
> MCCANN: What about you?
> GOLDBERG: What about me?
> MCCANN: Are you going to take a seat?
> GOLDBERG: We'll both take a seat? [. . .
> . . . .]
>> Sit back, McCann. Relax. What's the matter with you? I bring you down for a few days to the seaside. Take a holiday. Do yourself a favour. Learn to relax, McCann, or you'll never get anywhere. (37)

The uncertainty of the two figures about how to position themselves on the stage implies that the intruders are unsure of how to play the roles in which they have been cast. It is funny because it not only establishes Goldberg and McCann as the stereotypical stage Jew and stage Irishman in a time-honored comic variety turn but it suggests that beneath the intimidating masks they assume as invaders of Stanley's territory are two insecure actors who are not entirely in control of their script. The construction of social identity is thus problematized in the contrast between the initial difficulty they have in adopting authentic roles with which to engage Stanley and their subsequent ruthlessness in terrorizing him. Goldberg's attempts to calm McCann's nerves echo the exchanges between the two contract killers in *The Dumb Waiter*, where, while they wait in a basement room to receive their orders, Gus's fretful questioning of small details of procedure prompts Ben to try unsuccessfully to calm him down by emphasizing the routine nature of their job. Like Goldberg, Ben as the senior partner seems to have internalized the rationale of the organization that employs them, while Gus remains anxious and unmotivated. In *The Birthday Party*, Goldberg possesses an ability to valorize the authority structure in whose name he acts in more sophisticated terms than Ben. While Ben mechanically parrots his instructions without having the sensitivity or intelligence to interrogate either their efficacy or moral implications, Goldberg expansively elaborates a bravura rhetorical display of the well-worn clichés of family, community, and country in an apparently endless series of variations on the benefits of social conformity. .

The real irony derives from the fact that the authority of the English Establishment is here represented by the two oldest outsider figures in the history of English drama—the Irishman and the Jew. Pinter's comic improvisation around these two stage stereotypes is not only brilliantly observed, but it represents an early instance of a postcolonial attitude that had only recently begun to be reflected on the British stage in the mid-fifties. The gradual disintegration of the British Empire that began after the war gave rise to a new—and often anxious—awareness that English culture might not forever dominate the English-speaking world; the various waves of immigration to England by Irish people, Jews, Indians, Pakistanis, Chinese, Africans, and Afro-Caribbeans precipitated a newly multicultural society whose authority might be assumed by individuals other than those who had formerly inherited the ideology of upper-middle-class Englishness.[5] The Jewish Goldberg is an uncannily prescient representation of the phenomenon of the arriviste who ironically makes a more effective representative of the authority of English values than an upper-middle-class graduate of a public school. As Goldberg's speeches comically suggest the demotic patois that invokes London Jewish culture, so is his ventriloquizing of the platitudes of democratic authority wonderfully parodic, the alien quality of the dialect grotesquely rendering the values of traditional Englishness as the paternalistic jingoistic clichés to which the current context of post-imperial history has reduced them.

On their arrival, Goldberg's attempts at calming McCann seem equally intended to reassure himself of his own status, as if blowing his own trumpet was an effective way to advertise his authority. The language hilariously mimics the jargon of the door-to-door salesman expounding the supposed benefits of relaxation as the key to a healthy life:

> GOLDBERG: (*sitting at the table, right*). The secret is breathing. Take
> my tip. It's a well-known fact: Breathe in, breathe out, take a

chance, let yourself go, what can you lose? Look at me. When I was an apprentice yet, McCann, every second Friday of the month my Uncle Barney used to take me to the seaside, regular as clockwork . . . After lunch on Shabbus we'd go and sit in a couple of deck chairs—you know, the ones with canopies—we'd have a little paddle, we'd watch the tide coming in, going out, the sun coming down—golden days, believe me, McCann. (*Reminiscent*) Uncle Barney. Of course he was an impeccable dresser. One of the old school. He had a house just outside Basingstoke at the time. Respected by the whole community. Culture? Don't talk to me about culture. He was an all-round man, what do you mean? He was a cosmopolitan. (37)

Goldberg's philistinism is exposed in the relish of his precise itemization of the deck chairs "with canopies," his view of his Uncle Barney as an "impeccable dresser," and his reference to "culture" as a commodity. The sentimental lower-middle-class English cultural idyll invoked in Goldberg's nostalgic recollections of a faux Edwardian milieu of such seaside beach resorts as the one serviced by Petey and Meg is comically traduced in Goldberg's catalog of clichés. Beneath the bluff overassertiveness of his salesman's patter, however, lies the insecurity of the outsider whose garrulous assumption of friendship with potential customers barely conceals the fear that his outsider status will never allow him to be accepted as a member of the club.

> MCCANN: What about this, Nat? Isn't it about time someone came in?
> GOLDBERG: McCann, what are you so nervous about? Pull yourself together. Everywhere you go these days, it's like a funeral.
> MCCANN: That's true.
> GOLDBERG: True? Of course it's true. It's more than true. It's a fact.
> (38)

The joke of course is that McCann is almost certainly a hired gun, so that wherever he goes he does leave a corpse to be buried! The stylized rhetoric of the assimilated English Jew with his conservative appeal to family ties and the sentimental Irish Londoner with his traditional IRA loyalties provides grotesquely comic music hall–style cross talk,[6] the lugubrious yet occasionally sinister speech of McCann contrasting with the ingratiating bonhomie of the loquacious

Goldberg. The effect of such unexpected racial stereotyping on stage is in its own way as disquieting as that produced by the appearance of the blind, black figure of Riley at the end of *The Room*. Since *The Birthday Party* deals in comic types, there can be no question of racism here; Meg and Petey are as stereotypical in their representation of the intellectual poverty of lower-middle-class English culture as Goldberg and McCann are of their respective cultures. McCann's naive trust in Goldberg's authority together with Goldberg's unquestioning belief in the fatuous jargon of authority are comically undercut by McCann's unthinking ascription of Christian values to a Jew.

> GOLDBERG: I would never deny that I had a position.
> MCCANN: And what a position.
> GOLDBERG: It's not a thing I would deny.
> [. . . . .]
> MCCANN: You've always been a true Christian.
> GOLDBERG: In a way. (40)

The language of officialdom that Goldberg invokes is devoid of content:

> GOLDBERG *sighs . . . then speaks in a quiet, fluent, official tone.*
>
> GOLDBERG: The main issue is a singular issue and quite distinct from your previous work. Certain elements, however, might well approximate in points of procedure to some of your other activities. All is dependent on the attitude of our subject. At all events, McCann, I can assure you that the assignment will be carried out and the mission accomplished with no excessive aggravation to you or myself. (40)

Goldberg's language is empty of concrete detail, its bureaucratic generality exposing the arbitrary nature of authority (the law, the church, science, the family, the community) in whose name he claims to speak. Meg's subsequent entrance causes the men to adopt their typical social pose. Goldberg's insinuating gallantry is a way of manipulating the gullible Meg to tell him as much as he needs to know about Stanley, while his idea of a party to celebrate Stanley's birthday introduces a new set of plot expectations that establishes further tension when after their exit Stanley returns and pressures Meg to recall Goldberg's name. Meg's enthusiastic and unthinking collusion with Goldberg in throwing Stanley a birthday party reveals the emptiness of her social life while at the same time it provokes in Stanley an inexplicable dread that she blithely misinterprets. When Meg insists that Stanley unwrap her grotesquely inappropriate gift of a boy's drum a concrete image of Stanley's infantilization is manifested and his assumption of the role of naughty child in which she has cast him marks his own hesitant participation in a game from which he is gradually exposed and ejected as social outsider:

> STANLEY: *(flatly)* It's a drum. A boy's drum.
> MEG: *(tenderly)* It's because you haven't got a piano [. . .
> . . . .
> . . . .]
>
> (STANLEY *looks into the parcel. He takes out two drumsticks. He taps them together. He looks at her.)*
>
> STANLEY: Shall I put it round my neck? (46)

Act 1 ends with an eerily evocative pantomime sequence in which Stanley slowly starts to march around the table beating the drum, at first in a regular rhythm, but after finally losing control, banging it erratically until, as the curtain falls, he stands in front of Meg, "his face and the drumbeat now savage and possessed" (46). This disturbingly antisocial action expresses the violence of Stanley's repressed feelings in the form of an impotent and childlike rebelliousness, ritualizing the undercurrents of terror and defiant aggression hinted at in his odd behavior throughout the act and foreshadowing the way the celebratory ritual of a birthday party spirals into an nightmarishly atavistic experience in act 2. The idiosyncratic manipulation of stage action is a further illustration of Pinter's mastery of theatrical form. The sound of the drum, the unexpectedly savage demeanor of Stanley, and Meg's blind incomprehension of the true state of affairs intimate a state of hysteria and violence that signals the disorientation and existential alienation repressed beneath the humdrum routine of this lower-middle-class English milieu. The reassuringly cosy milieu of the seaside boarding house has been revealed as an illusion, masking a terrifying battle for dominance and control by mysterious agents who assert the right to freely infiltrate the private sphere of any citizen's existence. In parallel with this unmasking, the sedate naturalistic habit of interpretation is exposed as a response whose banal conventions of signification screen the audience from the Nietzschean battle taking place among the inhabitants of this room.

Once the banal surface of this shabby environment has been punctured by the mysterious entrance of Goldberg and McCann, the action of *The Birthday Party* gradually becomes less comprehensible on a naturalistic level. In act 2 the metaphorical significance of the surrealistic succession of images and events is indicated by the increasingly exaggerated stylization of speech and action. On the surface, the action of the play is conventionally plotted as a comic thriller, with Meg's motherly desire to celebrate Stanley's birthday being exploited by Goldberg as reason to hold a party. A number of putative reasons for their arrival and subsequent intimidation of Stanley are proffered by Goldberg and McCann, yet there is never an unequivocal explanation of why they have been hunting him down and where they intend to take him. In withholding definitive evidence of their true identity Pinter alerts the audience to the possibility of a more sinister explanation of the men's appearance and of why their behavior is enough to reduce Stanley to a state of helpless subservience. While it heightens the sense of the uncanny, the inexplicable menace created by Goldberg and McCann in the second and third acts further complicates the deliberate strategy of refusing to provide conventional exposition. The events represented in the first part of act 1 are the kind of everyday occurrences that one might expect to occupy people's time in such a domestic milieu but, as so often with Pinter, its pattern of arbitrary repetitions and non sequiturs drains the banal routine of the Boleses' domestic life of any meaningful content, its grotesquely comic effect exposing the characters as empty vessels who perform pointless daily rituals that offer little or no personal satisfaction.

When Goldberg and McCann at first try to assert their dominant status over Stanley by tricking him and then forcing him to sit down, he attempts childishly to resist them until Goldberg's unspoken threat of force obliges him to comply. There follows an extended game of questions that exhibits the linguistic virtuosity for which Pinter is justly famous. Its darkly comic representation of the Orwellian process by which agents of authority isolate and neutralize social rebels or nonconformists through verbal mystification promotes a horrifying vision of a totalitarian state that uses interrogation as a form of mental torture aimed at coercing recalcitrant individuals to become well-drilled automatons, passively conforming to behavioral norms appropriate to childhood:

> GOLDBERG: Why do you pick your nose?
> MCCANN: I demand justice.
> GOLDBERG: What's your trade?
> MCCANN: What about Ireland?
> GOLDBERG: What's your trade?
> STANLEY: I play the piano.
> GOLDBERG: How many fingers do you use?
> STANLEY: No hands! (61)

Goldberg's domineeringly insistent litany of trivial questions concerning Stanley's personal habits and his job is nonsensically interrupted by the stock "stage Irish" gesture that demands proof of loyalty to the Irish Republican cause, the through-the-looking-glass absurdity of the actual questions emphasizing the absolute power of state authority to render Stanley a non-person:

> GOLDBERG: No society would touch you. Not even a building society.
> MCCANN: You're a traitor to the cloth.
> GOLDBERG: What do you use for pyjamas.
> STANLEY: Nothing.
> GOLDBERG: You verminate the sheet of your birth. (61)

In a bizarre sequence of apparent linguistic non sequiturs, the interrogation switches without warning from the simplistic rhetoric of domestic hygiene, family allegiance, and patriotism to the more subtle theological register of a religious inquisition, only to descend immediately to the rapid-fire questioning of a radio quiz show:

> MCCANN: What about the Albigensenist heresy?[7]
> GOLDBERG: Who watered the wicket in Melbourne? (61)

These surreal shifts from one topic to another have the effect of conflating all the primal fears an individual might have of being found out, the interrogation thereby evoking archetypal antisocial fantasies as in a nightmare of guilt and punishment. Stanley's retreat to Meg's boarding house involves a disregard for social norms that

Goldberg and McCann must "correct" before he can be rehabilitated as a "healthy" member of society.

> GOLDBERG: But we've got the answer to you. We can sterilize you.
> MCCANN: What about Drogheda?
> GOLDBERG: Your bite is dead. Only your pong is left.
> MCCANN: You betrayed our land.
> GOLDBERG: You betray our breed.
> MCCANN: Who are you, Webber?
> GOLDBERG: What makes you think you exist?
> MCCANN: You're dead.
> GOLDBERG: You're dead . . . You're a plague gone bad. There's no juice in you. You're nothing but an odour. (62)

In this context, the flouting of social norms is presented not only as a betrayal of one's country but as the symptom of a kind of disease that must be cured,[8] so the pair acts to reduce Stanley to a state of complete subservience before taking him for "special treatment" to Monty—according to Goldberg "the best there is" (95). The repetition of Monty's name implies that he is a psychiatrist, but this is never confirmed by Goldberg; however, the contexts in which he is mentioned conjure up an impression of Monty's institution as a state mental sanitarium of the kind used by totalitarian governments to carry out behavior modification treatment on dissidents. These two representatives of authority may just as easily be criminals as agents of social cohesion. Although they pose as beneficent, paternal figures who have the interests of the community at heart, the arbitrary threats of force with which they intimidate Stanley are not backed up by any proven authority, while their drunken and bullying behavior at the party in act 2 ultimately evokes an image of the pair as brutal intruders whose motives are to kidnap Stanley and seduce Lulu, rather than to help and protect either character.

Pinter hereby implies that the behavior of officers of state authority is indistinguishable from that of agents of organized crime. The only means of distinguishing one from another may by an examination of the ethical values of the authority in whose name they act, but a private individual never has any guarantee that agents of authority will act according to their professed principles. Force is force, for whatever reason it is deployed. As early critics of the play have pointed out, the Jewish Goldberg and the Catholic McCann can be interpreted as emblematic of the institutionalized—and increasingly archaic—authority of the Judeo-Christian value system underpinning Western societies.[9] Pinter's brilliant comic rendering of their typically facile and mechanistic invocation of this ideology as a means of justifying their irrational behavior and arbitrary use of force is reminiscent of the hollow rhetoric of those who would justify the exploitation of military force and police brutality in the name of justice and democracy.

The purely associative logic that underpins the display of the author's astonishing linguistic virtuosity in the scene of Stanley's interrogation highlights the absurd nature of Goldberg and McCann's allegations against Stanley, the musicality of the dialogue allowing actors to demonstrate the characters' abuse of power in an expressionistic style that represents the emotional content of their action rather than documenting it objectively as historical event. The technique prepares the audience for the events of the birthday party in which the idea of interrogation as a nightmare of intimidation is extended into a series of associatively linked visual images in which at first McCann turns off the lights and shines his torch in Stanley's eyes while Meg and later Goldberg propose toasts to him; subsequently, as the evening sky grows darker, the atmosphere becomes more and more sinister until the moment when the room is unaccountably plunged into darkness.[10]

The isolation and intimidation of Stanley provoke a change in his behavior. As he struggles to escape from victimization he reveals the potential of the peaceful social rebel for criminal activity. The effects of confusion, fear, and disorientation that occur under these conditions translate the stream of earlier verbal images into a bizarre series of sounds and visions that are apprehended in darkness or by torchlight. Although the motivation for the switching on and off of lights can be explained in realistic terms, the chiaroscuro effects of the lighting in this scene are disorienting in purely sensory terms as they transform a simple game like blind man's buff into horrifying images of violence, intimidation, and danger of the type conjured up in a forties film thriller. The combined effect of whisky, the darkness, and panic unleashes primitive feelings in Stanley and McCann; Stanley first appears to be trying to strangle Meg and later to assault Lulu sexually, while McCann deliberately smashes Stanley's glasses and uses the toy drum to trip him up.

A number of critics have interpreted the appearance of Goldberg and McCann as an externalization of Stanley's psychological state— a symbolic projection of his guilt. Although at some level the action can be viewed as directly expressive of his subjective consciousness, it appears to me an oversimplification to reduce the dramaturgical strategy to the explicitly allegorical narrative of Stanley's psychic process. In provoking various putative explanations of what the audience sees and hears, the montage of language and images invites both competing and complementary interpretations. Although the concrete details of the characters' behavior forms a complex mesh of interacting motives, drives, and feelings that could as well be explained in naturalistic terms, the deliberate hermeneutic indeterminacy constitutes the crux of Pinter's dramaturgical technique. What is distinctive in his work—apparent here even more overtly than in *The Room*—is his blurring of the boundary between naturalistic and expressionistic conventions of theatrical presentation. Exploiting a narrative motif popularized by film noir, *The Birthday Party* deploys the structural logic of a detective thriller as a frame for the investigation of subjective mental states, expressing through mood and tone the emotional intensity that characterizes social behavior in extreme situations. The detection of the alleged criminal is revealed more properly to be an exploration of the identity of the antisocial individual—the secret at the heart of the drama is the crisis of human vulnerability.[11] As Pinter himself has observed, "[P]eople fall back on anything they can lay their hands on verbally to keep away from the dangers of knowing, or being known" (Smith, 58).

Act 3 follows the climactic events of Stanley's interrogation and humiliation with a denouement constructed around a breakfast ritual similar to that in act 1. Although the conversation parallels the first scene of the play, a number of significant variations signal the aftermath of the party. McCann escorts Stanley downstairs to the dining room with his broken glasses. Goldberg and McCann employ a series of characteristic platitudes to reassure Stanley that they will take care of him and "make a man" of him (77), but Stanley has been reduced to a catatonic state and is incapable of responding.

The overall pattern of the play resembles an elaborate game of blind man's buff in which those who attempt to avoid detection by the blindfolded man are equally in the dark. The truth can only be apprehended by recognizing the complex web of playacting as an individual's battle to mask the secret of his or her private self. In this sense, Goldberg and McCann are as vulnerable as Stanley, McCann revealing his personal fears in anticipation of "doing the job" while in act 3, the self-defeating nature of Goldberg's victory over Stanley is exposed by his somewhat pathetic request that McCann blow in his mouth—an eccentric effort to restore his self-confidence. The language of authority is exposed as mere mumbo jumbo, disguising the brutal reality of power. A person's adherence to social norms is thus comprehended as a fear of exclusion from community, identity as a preassigned social role that masks the nakedness of authentic freedom. Stanley cannot escape his social destiny by hiding out in a holiday resort; he can only delay it. Goldberg and McCann repress the existential terror of self-knowledge by ignoring the dubious nature of the morality whose imperatives they administer, while Meg conceals the pointlessness of her existence in escapist and infantile delusions of being attractive and well-liked. Petey's dogged adherence to the banality of his daily work routine is likewise a vain attempt to evade the horror of confronting an existential void.

After Meg returns from shopping, she notices that "The car's gone" and, referring to Goldberg and McCann, asks Petey, "Have they gone?" Even though Petey confirms their departure, she still wonders, "Won't they be in for lunch?" Also, as in act 1, she wonders "Where's Stan?" and whether he's "down yet." Petey almost tells her ("No . . . he's"), but after she interrupts him to show that as in act 1, she thinks that Stanley must be "still in bed," Petey attempts to keep the truth from her: "Yes, he's . . . still asleep. [. . .] Let him . . . sleep." Clearly oblivious to what happened to Stanley during and after the party the night before, Meg describes it as a "lovely party" and herself as "the belle of the ball." As Petey remains silent, he continues to withhold his knowledge of Stanley's departure. Lulu's bitter accusation that Goldberg seduced her the night before also represents an evasion of the reality of her collusion in the act by flirting with him without taking responsibility for what might happen, while McCann and Goldberg's archetypally sexist response is to demand that she confess for her sin of sexual licentiousness. All of the characters are fundamentally dishonest or, at the very least, self-deceiving in denying their own complicity in realizing their personal destiny.[12]

The Birthday Party's manifold allusiveness is an invitation for the audience to explore and test a number of possible meanings connoted by the elaborate games played by the characters for a variety of hidden or equivocal motives, rather than to view it as a consistent allegory of Stanley's fear of punishment for attempting to escape the repressive obligations of society. It anticipates virtually all of Pinter's later plays by refusing to establish clear limits to interpretation. As in everyday life people are obliged to subject the language and behavior of others to microscopic scrutiny in attempting to understand the complex implications of their actions, so in *The Birthday Party* there is no easy explanation of the significance of the action. Interpretation is an activity in which members of the audience find themselves engaged from the beginning of the drama, the meaning of the play being apprehended in the process by which scenic context and represented behavior become signs to be interpreted by all the characters. The frustration at the failure unequivocally to interpret the meaning of these signs is, as in real life, an essential constituent of the dramatic experience. The power of *The Birthday Party* manifests itself in the way it engages an audience's empathy, so that although one may laugh at Meg's stupidity and Petey's passivity or criticize Stanley's mendacious cowardice, one nevertheless participates imaginatively in their experience of anxiety, terror, guilt, and shame.

As Stanley is escorted out of the house into the waiting automobile, Petey's line, "Stan, don't let them tell you what to do" (80), is the pathetic gesture of a defeated man who nonetheless retains a belief in the right of every individual to determine his own life. Yet Pinter has retrospectively suggested that Petey's line is a symbol of resistance to political oppression—indicating the political impulse that has motivated a great deal of his writing.[13] Petey is not an exemplary hero but a coward who fails to stand up to Goldberg and McCann's psychological destruction of Stanley's integrity. The dramatic potency of the line derives from its ironic ineffectiveness as a gesture of solidarity, allowing it to resonate with the awareness each member of an audience may have of his or her own helplessness in the face of the violations of human rights that have occurred in the modern world. In this manner, a Pinter play activates profound feelings about social and political realities rather than didactically advancing an ideologically motivated argument.

Although Pinter had early in his career refused to explain the meaning of his plays in explicitly political or ethical terms, he was later inclined—after advertising his own engagement with political issues, following upon the premiere of *One for the Road* (1985)—to extrapolate political significance from much of his earlier work:

> My earlier plays are much more political than they seem on the face of it [. . .] I think that the plays like *The Birthday Party*, *The Dumb Waiter* and *The Hothouse* are metaphors, really. When you look at them, they're much closer to an extremely critical look at authoritarian posture—state power, family power, religious power, power used to undermine if not destroy, the individual, or the questioning voice, or the voice which simply went away from the mainstream and refused to become part of an easily recognizable set of standards and social values. (Smith, 85)

The Hothouse was written in 1958, but not produced until 1980. More explicitly than they do, *The Hothouse* articulates political concerns manifest in *The Birthday Party* and *The Dumb Waiter* and, with the benefit of hindsight, it can be clearly seen to foreshadow Pinter's overtly political work of the eighties and nineties—*Precisely* (1983), *One for the Road*, *Mountain Language* (1987), *Party Time* (1991), and *Press Conference* (2002), all plays that reflect the personal commitment to political issues and causes to which Pinter devoted the greater part of the final two decades of his career. *The Hothouse* is set in the kind of mental institution one might imagine Stanley is being taken to in order that he might be "cured" of his antisocial impulses. While the function of the institution is never directly revealed, it appears to be a nightmarishly bureaucratic psychiatric hospital the inmates of which, although referred to only by numbers, are according to its director "not criminals. They're only people in need of help, which we try to give . . . to help them regain their confidence, confidence in themselves, confidence in others, confidence in . . . the world" (197).

The director, Roote, is a tyrant whose mad authoritarianism is challenged by the anarchic actions of certain of his staff, one or two of whom have killed one patient and raped another. (The evidence suggests that the culprit is in fact Roote himself.) The woman who has been raped has given birth on Christmas Eve, and the action takes place on Christmas Day, the investigation of staff misdemeanors taking place amid the desultory rituals of jollification aimed at pacifying the inmates, who end up massacring all but one of the staff. None of the so-called patients is ever present on stage, the play's anarchic humor arising from the maniacal power struggles among rivalrous members of the staff, who ironically have themselves become victims of the institutional machine designed to "correct" the patients' nonconformist behavior.

In a scene that develops the notion of interrogation as a form of mental torture explored in Goldberg and McCann's interrogation of Stanley, an ambitious but naive member of the staff, appropriately named Lamb, submits himself to a neurological experiment, during which he suffers torture by electric shocks and deafening blasts of sound in his ears, accompanied by a bizarre and threatening interrogation. *The Hothouse* is far less oblique than *The Birthday Party* in its satirical representation of the corruption of state bureaucracies by creeping totalitarianism, the comic English speech idioms of the characters insinuating that the occasional abuse of patients in psychiatric hospitals may without warning allow beneficent medical institutions to become Stalinist gulags or Nazi death camps, as a consequence of an endemic obsession with ordering and controlling individuals who do not conform in every respect to the social norm.[14] The comedy of *The Hothouse* is macabre and its satirical targets more obvious than either *The Birthday Party* or *The Dumb Waiter*, but it complements the earlier plays in exposing the risk to individual freedom posed by the potential oppressiveness of authoritarian institutions. What Pinter demonstrates over and over in these plays is the completely arbitrary basis for each institution's assertion of authority, and the ease with which such dubious authority can become corrupted by the mechanism of power itself.

CHAPTER 3

Questions of Identity:
The Caretaker

A Slight Ache

As a result of Pinter's rejection of the naturalistic convention of historical exposition ("backstory") many of his characters behave in
ways perceived by other characters and the audience as inexplicable,
the indeterminate nature of their motives evoking a sense of menace
that prompted the reviewer, Irving Wardle, to coin the phrase "comedy of menace" as a way of categorizing his early plays.[1] *A Slight
Ache* varies the recurrent theme of the intruder by exploring the
menacing import of a stranger positioned outside a suburban back
garden, selling matches. *A Slight Ache* was commissioned by BBC
Radio's Third Programme and broadcast in 1959. The fact that the
match-seller never speaks shows Pinter's masterful use of the peculiar property of sound radio to generate an ambiguity concerning the
putative identity of a silent character. Words and sounds evoke visual pictures and mental images in the mind of the listener, so that
the silent match-seller becomes as "real" as do Flora and Edward
who describe him, even though the listener can never be absolutely
sure of his identity or even of his actual existence. Nevertheless, his
virtual presence gradually undermines Edward's initial complacency,
eventually infiltrating the domestic environment so fully that he re-
places Flora's husband as the object of her affection.

   Is the unkempt match-seller gradually transformed from an unknown outsider into Flora's lover, or is this a projection of Edward's
paranoid fantasy? While the play works effectively on stage where

the audience can actually see the tramp-like figure of the silent match-seller, the peculiar power of the radio medium doubles the effect of the ambiguity, simultaneously keeping in play a number of meta-dramatic questions concerning his representational status in the drama. The ache in Edward's eyes constitutes a concrete image of sight that promotes interrogation of the underlying problematic of perception, the progressive deterioration of his eyesight to the point of blindness signaling the total loss of critical perspective concomitant on a close encounter with a disturbing reality. On radio the play problematizes the very basis of vision and insight, its form shaping the listener's aural experience of the radical subjectivity of perception and knowledge in order to promote such philosophical reflections.

A further device repeatedly employed by Pinter to convey the menace of the outsider or intruder is a bullying interrogation by such figures, whose authority can never be absolutely validated. While *The Caretaker* (1960) is not as overtly preoccupied with the pervasive threat to individual freedom posed by "authority" as are *The Dumb Waiter, The Birthday Party,* and *The Hothouse,* its central figure, Davies, is a tramp, whose whole existence appears to involve avoiding the real—or imagined—threat of authority. Questions of authority over the house of which he is invited to become caretaker by, respectively, Aston and his brother Mick, haunt Davies; and Aston himself bears the scars of having been incarcerated in a mental hospital where he was forcibly subjected to an operation on his brain

The Caretaker

In marked contrast to the disastrous reception of *The Birthday Party* in 1958, the production of *The Caretaker* in the West End two years later brought Pinter international recognition as the most original British playwright of his generation.[2] Even more so than any of Pinter's four earlier stage plays *The Caretaker* adheres scrupulously—if only in superficial terms—to the conventions of naturalistic theater. The setting is more detailed and the characters are no longer comic types vividly animated to fulfill the dramaturgical demands of a mystery plot, but are gradually revealed on stage in the manifold actual-

ity of their living human presence. From the start, the three characters' attitudes, their interior lives, their complex motivations and
mental processes are the focus of the drama.

The setting might at first be viewed as a clever variant of the
"kitchen-sink" environment of working-class bed-sitting rooms that
were after 1956 becoming a conventional substitute for the drawing
rooms of the well-made English drama in which Pinter had appeared
as a young actor in repertory.

> A room. A window in the back wall, the bottom half covered by a
> sack. An iron bed along the left wall. Above it is a small cup-
> board, paint buckets, boxes containing nuts, screws etc. More
> boxes, vases by the side of the bed. A door up right. To the right
> of the window, a mound: a kitchen sink, a step-ladder, a coal
> bucket, a lawn-mower, a shopping trolley, boxes, sideboard
> drawers. Under this mound an iron bed. In front of it a gas stove.
> On the gas stove a statue of Buddha. Down right, a fireplace.
> Around it a couple of suitcases, a rolled carpet, a blow-lamp, a
> wooden chair on its side, boxes, a number of ornaments, a
> clothes horse, a few short planks of wood, a small electric fire
> and a very old electric toaster. Below this a pile of old news-
> papers. Under ASTON's bed by the left wall is an electrolux,
> which is not seen till used. A bucket hangs from the ceiling. (4)[3]

Paradoxically, its random profusion of apparently unrelated clutter is
so overwhelming as to appear for a few moments to resemble the surreal scenographic symbolism of the French absurdist Ionesco whose
work was so fashionable in the late fifties; after a short while, however, the language and action of the play clarify that these are actual
household artifacts that have been acquired over time and stored by
Aston, who lives in the room. A number of them in fact play
significant parts in the onstage action, so this incredibly detailed list
of stage props is not intended merely to give an indication of a stage
crowded with junk but provides a specific set of instructions for the
placement of practicable stage props that will be used by the actors.
The overall impression of the peculiarly crowded stage space produces a kind of "hypernaturalistic" visual image that evokes the
jumbled content of Aston's confused mind.[4]

When Mick is discovered on stage at the opening of the play he
looks around the room, noting "each object in turn" (5). Before the
audience even knows who he is, this action specifically draws atten-

tion to the artifacts onstage, provoking curiosity as to their function and the nature of the environment. After Mick unaccountably exits, the audience is left to stare at the set in silence for a few moments before Pinter exploits its extraordinary clutter for the purpose of a joke. As they enter, Aston's first words to the tramp, Mac Davies, are "Sit down." The actor playing Davies will no doubt do a "take" in reaction to the fact that the only visible chair is lying on its side surrounded by piles of junk. Pinter's mastery of the craft of theater is absolute in *The Caretaker*. The dramatic economy of the writing is such that Aston's failure to order the objects in the room into a conventionally furnished living space does not simply reflect his own mental confusion; it represents a key to his difficult relationship with his brother Mick, which in its turn provides Davies with the opportunity to betray Aston's kindness by attempting to usurp his position as his brother's unofficial caretaker. The play maps a network of human relationships under a specific set of circumstances that illuminates for an audience the essential nature of what human relationships are. The history of its many productions around the world suggests that the situation of Mick, Aston, and Davies may be comprehended within the terms of a wide range of cultures.

The play's title offers an obvious clue to its central concerns, inviting an audience to view the implications of its characters' different attitudes to the notion of "taking care." From the outset, one witnesses Aston's innocent altruism toward Davies. He offers the tramp shelter from the winter weather, a little money to spend on essentials, and an unofficial job as caretaker of the house he himself looks after. At first Davies is constantly angling to insinuate himself into Aston's favor, agreeing to act as unofficial caretaker, but once he sees that Mick is the one who owns the house and therefore has real power in the situation, he switches his allegiance to Mick, offering himself as Mick's caretaker. In so doing he spurns Aston, who he understands is mentally handicapped, and therefore believes to be devoid of power in the running of the house. Davies fails to reckon with Mick's loyalty to his brother; in this respect, Mick is taking care of Aston, and has probably allocated to him the job of caretaker as a form of occupational therapy and as a way of allowing him a degree of dignity in the role.

The play can be read as a grimly ironic parable of brotherly love, with Mick and Davies in different respects exemplifying the jungle law of "eat or be eaten" and Aston's behavior representing adherence to a Christian notion of brotherhood in spite of his treatment at the hands of others as an injured animal to be exploited for their own purposes. Even Mick's loyalty to Aston manifests the instinctual self-interest of a jungle creature, as his halfhearted attempts to look after Aston are not purely altruistic but are a way of protecting himself by looking after his own. The ironic contrast in *The Caretaker* between the instinct for fraternal loyalty and the injunction of kindness to fellow man is equivalent to the opposition in *The Room* and *The Birthday Party* between the actuality of fractured or dysfunctional families and the authority of the family structure held as an ideal. The battle to secure and maintain one's territory in all three plays suggests the interrelatedness of the concept of self and the notion of "home." Riley's plea to Sal (Rose) in *The Room* to "come home" links home with her (former?) identity as Sal. Her identity as Rose seems to be linked with the room she is currently occupying, and this identity seems dependent on the legitimacy of her claim to the room as home. In *The Birthday Party,* Stanley has made a new home of his lodgings in Meg's boarding house, being adopted by Meg as a member of her pseudo-family in what Goldberg implies is an escape from his proper familial (social) obligations. Davies' attempts to secure some sort of lodging in the room that appears to be Aston's— and occasionally even Mick's—home, parallel the way in which the battle for a room of one's own[5] in the earlier plays is equivalent to a struggle to assert personal identity.

The instability of Davies' identity is symptomatic of the disorientation that is a consequence of the tramp's lack of a fixed abode. Pinter's reputation as the "poet of London transport"[6] owes much to his mythicizing of London place-names created in the litany of places, bus routes, and street names repeated by Mick and Davies in their various attempts to establish the authenticity of the autobiographical tales they tell. The potent image of Davies' homelessness is only intensified by his recurring attempts to situate his past experience in a number of anonymous locations that he evokes with an air of easy familiarity. In conversation with Aston in the first act, the places mentioned by Davies range from the "caff" nearby where the two met earlier in the day, to suburbs and satellite towns on the fringes of Greater London, such as a "monastery down at Luton" (11), the Great West Road (6), a public convenience at Shepherd's Bush

(11), a bootmaker's at Acton (12), Watford (13), the North Circular Road (13), Hendon (13), Sidcup (17), and Wembley (25). By referring to specific experiences in particular places, Davies constructs the fragmented topography of a past life, compensating for his sense of rootlessness by the repetitive naming of points of orientation in an itinerant existence. His identity is so unstable that he claims to be living under the assumed name of Bernard Jenkins and tells Aston the identity documents that would prove he is actually Mac Davies have been kept for him for fifteen years by an acquaintance in Sidcup.

Each character exploits a peculiar strategy aimed at reinforcing and authenticating the sense of identity projected in his behavior. Much of the play's comedy derives from Davies' transparent deceptions—his inability to supply a convincing account of himself and his itinerant circumstances. The tales he weaves of his peregrinations are eccentric fables of the outer London landscape. What is particularly funny is Davies' apparent inability to perceive how unconvincing and exaggerated the stories he repeats so insistently are to others, and how little they flatter the persona he wishes to project. His account of his attempt to cadge a pair of shoes from a monastery in Luton resembles a stand-up music hall sketch, the subtle intermingling of the tramp's stream of reflections and recollections ironically subverting his conscious intention to elicit sympathetic indignation:

> DAVIES: Shoes? It's life and death to me. I had to go all the way to Luton in these . . . You know what that bastard monk said to me? (*He looks over to the shoes*) I think those'd be a bit small . . . Can't wear shoes that don't fit. Nothing worse. I said to this monk, here, I said, look here, mister, I said, I come all the way down here, look, I said, I showed him these, I said, you haven't got a pair of shoes, have you, a pair of shoes, I said, enough to keep me on my way . . . I heard you got a stock of shoes here. Piss off, he says to me. Now look here, I said, I'm an old man, you can't talk to me like that, I don't care who you are. If you don't piss off, he says, I'll kick you all the way to the gate. (12)

The image of a monk swearing at the tramp is in itself funny and surprising, but it is made even richer because the audience might wryly sympathize with the way the tramp's long and difficult journey in broken shoes is rewarded only by the monk's lack of Christian charity, while laughing at the notion of how Davies' ungracious behavior might have provoked it.

In act 2, Mick matches Davies' inventive self-dramatizations with a series of audacious yarns aimed to unsettle and humiliate him, comically competing with the tramp by offering his own highly suspect autobiographical reflections as improvised variations on themes that mimic and mock the tramp's picaresque half-truths. His long speech about an acquaintance who is supposed to resemble Davies is a snide parody of his repeated attempts to authenticate his identity by referring to his acquaintances from around the outskirts of London:

> MICK: You know, believe it or not, you've got a funny kind of resemblance to a bloke I once knew in Shoreditch. Actually he lived in Aldgate. I was staying with a cousin in Camden Town. This chap, he used to have a pitch in Finsbury Park, just by the bus depot. When I got to know him I found out he was brought up in Putney. That didn't make any difference to me. I know quite a few people who were born in Putney. Even if they weren't born in Putney, they were born in Fulham. The only trouble was, he wasn't born in Putney, he was only brought up in Putney. It turned out he was born in the Caledonian Road, just before you get to the Nag's Head. His old mum was still living at the Angel. All the buses passed right by her door. She could get a 38, 581, 30 or 38A, take her down the Essex Road to Dalston Junction in next to no time. Well, of course, if she got the 30 he'd take her up Upper Street way, round by Highbury Corner and down to St Paul's Church, but she'd get to Dalston Junction just the same in the end . . . Dead spit of you he was. Bit bigger round the nose but there was nothing in it. (30)

Whereas Davies refers to places outside central London, Mick's surreal taxonomy of street and place-names establishes his insider knowledge of inner London. The mention of Putney and Fulham,[7] the only suburbs in southwest London named by Mick, turn out to be red herrings as his acquaintance was actually "born in the Caledonian Road." The point of Mick's bizarre narrative is to expose as fiction the hyperbolically presented details in Davies' string of autobiographical recollections. To anyone who knows London at all, the speech is extremely funny; Mick's exaggerated concern to authenticate every detail constitutes a hilarious parody of the confusion created by people who give over-elaborate street directions. Mick's pedantic insistence on verifying the truth of every particular by its connection with a place-name, implies that his whole story is a fabrication whose only purpose is to taunt Davies with an insinuation regarding the duplicity involved in his autobiographical ramblings.

In addition to his repetitious invocation of place-names, Davies accomplishes his self-affirmation by means of an aggressive racism that aims to assert his superiority as trueborn Englishman (the joke is that he is probably Welsh) over anyone who might seem foreign. Just as being known in a particular environment or neighborhood might be taken as proof of identity, so being a native rather than a foreigner implies the right to live in the area. Davies' fear and hatred of otherness is a symptom of his lack of a stable identity, of his sense of dispossession from his own country or race. Once again, Davies seems unaware that his appearance would seem repellent to the very "aliens" he affects to despise. Within the first two minutes of the play, Davies has expressed his vicious prejudice: "I couldn't find a seat, not one. All them Greeks had it. Poles, Greeks, Blacks, the lot of them, all them aliens had it . . . All them Blacks had it, Blacks, Greeks, Poles, the lot of them, that's what, doing me out of a seat, treating me like dirt" (6).

The chip on his shoulder that seems to motivate Davies' ingrained suspicion of others is the same impulse he manifests in irrational racism. Other people working in the café where he met Aston are "toe-rags," "gits," " a Scotch git," and the family of Indians living next door are referred to by him as "Blacks." In the middle of the meandering story about his trip to the monastery in Luton, Davies asks, "How many more Blacks you got around here then? . . . You got any more Blacks around here?" (12). When invited to share the use of Aston's lavatory, Davies asks, "I mean you don't share the toilet with them Blacks . . . do you?" (16), and when accused by Aston of making noises in his sleep, he accuses the Black neighbours of making the noises: "Maybe it were them Blacks making noises, coming up through the walls" (21). Such grotesque prejudice represents an extreme fear of otherness; in affirming his own self-worth, Davies projects the hostility and disgust habitually directed toward him as a tramp on to people of other races.

Language is the medium through which each of the characters constructs and performs a social identity. The image of self is not only unstable and unverifiable but the selfishness of Mick's and Davies' motives and their instinctive suspicion of others, causes them to mask the antisocial aspects of their intentions in order to manipulate others to behave as they would have them. This egoistical attitude is the opposite of Aston's, who in the first two acts offers shelter and kindness to Davies. Aston seems to have little capacity for authoring an acceptable persona through sophisticated manipulation of speech but even he is able to elaborate an autobiography that involves a complicated narrative of electric shock treatment administered against his will in hospital, by way of accounting for his present identity and circumstances:

> And . . . some kind of lie must have got around. And this lie went round. I thought people started being funny. In that café. The factory. I couldn't understand it. Then one day they took me to a hospital, right outside London . . . They . . . got me there. I didn't want to go. Anyway, I tried to get out, quite a few times. But . . . it wasn't very easy. They asked me questions, in there. Got me in and asked me all sorts of questions . . . Then one day . . . this man . . . doctor, I suppose . . . the head one . . . He called me in. He said . . . he told me I had something. He said they'd concluded their examination . . . And he showed me a pile of papers and he said that I'd got something, some complaint . . . And we've decided, he said . . . we're going to do something to your brain. He said . . . if we don't, you'll be in here for the rest of your life, but it we do, you stand a chance. You can go out, he said, and live like the others. (53)

As is often the case in Pinter's drama, Aston's autobiographical story is an implicit allegory of the individual's battle against the malign and repressive forces of social conformism. In his single sustained attempt at self-validation, Aston presents himself as an innocent victim of the violence and duplicity of others—his colleagues, drinking companions, the medical profession, even his mother, who have lied about his mental state in order to trick him into being mentally and emotionally neutered by the electric shock treatment. Aston's long speech has been criticized as out of keeping with the naturalistic conventions of the dramatic action, but it is completely convincing as the speech of someone whose lapse into monologue is a consequence of his inability to exploit the cut and thrust of ordinary conversation as a way of satisfactorily expressing his sense of self.

The form of the speech is entirely consistent with Pinter's positioning of dramatic action at the interface between consciousness and material reality, so that an audience responds to the directly subjective (expressionistic) presentation of an individual's interior experience of recollected feeling at the same time as it observes the social context within which the experience is communicated. The lighting effects indicated at the end evoke the conventions of film noir, in which the visual field is more and more narrowly focused until the face/eyes of the speaking actor fill the screen to evoke the character's act of recall or imagination:

> During ASTON'S speech the room grows darker.
> By the close of the speech only ASTON can be seen clearly . . . The fade-down of the lights must be as gradual, as protracted and unobtrusive as possible. (52)

Thematically the exploration of the existential foundations of social behavior has much in common with Beckett's theatrical evocation of people who are arbitrarily trapped in hostile or alien environments, but stylistically *The Caretaker* inhabits a different universe to that of *Waiting for Godot* (1953), or *Endgame* (1957). A detailed analysis of the comic strategies in *The Caretaker* exposes the way the poetic resonances of *Waiting for Godot* have been filtered through Pinter's very English assumptions about the craft and conventions of stage drama. Where Beckett's characters tend to inhabit an abstract and symbolic stage landscape and to speak an Irish-inflected English that tends toward lyrical self-dramatization or theatrical cross talk, the characters in Pinter's early plays speak in the flat conversational register of working-class London speech, only resorting to self-conscious rhetorical stylization as a calculated strategy of manipulating their listeners' perceptions. Notwithstanding the more realistic representation of milieu in Pinter, his intuitively filmic techniques of dramaturgical construction facilitate subtle fluctuations between the representation of interior experience and that of social environment, without a stylistic break in the performance.

On the surface, *The Caretaker* may appear not to share the overtly political preoccupation with authority central to *The Birthday Party*, *The Dumb Waiter*, or *The Hothouse*; nevertheless its concern with the operation of power in the social sphere provides a concentrated focus on the micropolitics of human relationships, and its dramaturgy is designed to expose the behavioral strategies and games of the three characters as a compulsive battle for dominance.[8] In this sense, all of Pinter's early stage plays are political in that they represent human interaction as power play. To this end the various possible combinations of characters in *The Caretaker* alternate in a structure comprising fourteen sections, the only pairing never shown, being that of the brothers, Aston and Mick.[9] Retrospectively, the opening image of Mick onstage alone might be seen to signify his sense of ownership of the place, but it also establishes a desire in the audience, unsatisfied throughout act 1, to question his relationship to Davies, Aston, and the room.

The first section (5–19) chiefly concerns Aston's offer to Davies of a bed for the night and it ends with a blackout of lights as each gets into bed to sleep. The interaction between the two consists chiefly of Davies' sly attempts to discover the underlying motives of the taciturn Aston, his obsequious behavior intended to elicit Aston's sympathy and exploit his unsuspecting kindness. The next section (19–24) begins the following morning with Davies' disorientation at waking up in a strange room followed by an argument over whether the tramp was making noises in his sleep, after which Aston's trusting nature is further demonstrated by his offer to Davies of a key to the room and house, while he leaves him alone. The final phase of act 1 is a brief and suspenseful scene (25–27) in which Mick enters surreptitiously to observe Davies nosing around the room searching for information about Aston, before violently interrupting the tramp and forcing him to the floor:

> DAVIES *starts to rise.* MICK *presses him down with his foot and stands over him. Finally he removes his foot . . .* DAVIES *remains on the floor, crouched.* MICK *slowly goes to the chair, sits and watches* DAVIES, *expressionless. Silence*
> MICK: What's the game? (27)

The moment provides a traditional cliffhanger as the curtain falls for the end of act 1, but it is the first clear indication of the ruthless power play that motivates Davies and Mick throughout the action. Here Mick uses his sheer physical strength to overpower the tramp completely, enacting a sadistic tableau of master and slave to express the reality of Davies' powerlessness as an intruder whose dubious intentions have been uncovered. The audience still knows nothing about Mick, however. Could this physically powerful young man also be an intruder, and what is his "game"?

Act 2 opens on the same tableau, a few seconds later. The fourth section of the action concerns Mick's attempts to force Davies to reveal his true intentions. The need for each to discover the identity of the other exposes one of the major dynamics of the play: the conflict between the need to know others while protecting oneself from being known by them. The audience has not been granted knowledge of the identity of either man:

> MICK: What's your name?
> DAVIES: I don't know you. I don't know who you are?
> *Pause.*
> MICK: Eh?
> DAVIES: Jenkins.
> MICK: Jenkins?
> DAVIES: Yes.
> MICK: Jen . . . kins.
> *Pause.*
>   You sleep here last night?
> DAVIES: Yes.
> MICK: Sleep well?
> DAVIES: Yes.
> MICK: I'm awfully glad. It's awfully nice to meet you. (28)

Power appears to derive from the ability to protect one's own true identity from being revealed while one exploits one's knowledge of the motives and strategies of others in order to manipulate them at will. By using physical force to render Davies completely powerless and then interrogating him like a criminal suspect, Mick enacts the real difference in social status between the tramp and the homeowner, but the audience can still not be sure that Mick has in fact any right to claim ownership of the space. Having reduced Davies to the humiliating position of the beggar he is, he then taunts him by treating him as the guest he pretends to be. Such humiliation is the opposite of the kindness of Aston, who in act 1 has treated Davies consistently as an equal.

Mick cunningly obscures his own motives and identity by teasing Davies with fanciful stories of his resemblance to, first, his uncle's brother and then a "bloke I once knew" (30). After deliberately disorienting Davies by asking him, "How do like my room?" Mick increases the tramp's sense of alienation by suggesting that he is a foreigner, the same insult that Davies habitually uses to valorize his own identity in contrast to that of strangers:

MICK: You a foreigner?
DAVIES: No.
MICK: Born and bred in the British Isles?
DAVIES: I was!
MICK: What did they teach you?
Pause.
    How did you like my bed?
Pause.
    That's my bed. You want to mind you don't catch a draught. (31)

After teasing Davies further by grabbing his trousers and waving them about in front of him, Mick projects a third unlikely resemblance on to Davies, reminding him again of his inability to verify his identity. Davies has no way of proving his right to be in the room as he does not even know Aston's name:

MICK: You know, you remind me of a bloke I bumped into once, just
    the other side of the Guildford by-pass—
DAVIES: I was brought here!
Pause.
MICK: Pardon?
DAVIES: I was brought here! I was brought here!
MICK: Brought here? Who brought you here?
DAVIES: Man who lives here . . . he . . .
Pause.
MICK: Fibber.
DAVIES: I was brought here, last night . . . met him in a caff . . . bloke
    saved me from a punch up . . . brought me here, brought me right
    here.

Pause.

MICK: I'm afraid you're a born fibber, en't you? You're speaking to the
    owner. This is my room. You're standing in my house. (32)

This is one of the few times in the play that Davies is completely helpless, an inversion of the situation in act 1 when his loquacious eagerness to explain his situation and define his identity was met by

Aston's puzzling taciturnity. Without any knowledge of who Mick is, or what relation Aston is to him, Davies can have no idea of the truth of Mick's seemingly extravagant claims. Mick plays a game with him, denying the tramp's desperate attempt to verify the truth of his situation by projecting a series of putative identities on him in a mockery of Davies' inconsistent autobiographical narratives in act I. By insisting on Davies' resemblance to a number of completely unrelated people, Mick insinuates his disbelief of the tramp's account of himself and challenges him to admit the truth of his scheming behavior. In another long speech Mick varies the game by first directly accusing Davies of being a liar and cheat ("You're stinking the place out. You're an old robber . . . You don't belong in a nice place like this" [33]), then immediately contradicting this characterization by casting him sarcastically as a wealthy potential purchaser who might either wish to rent the room for £400 a year or buy it outright ("Who do you bank with?" [34]).

Aston's entrance on this line interrupts Mick's game, introducing the fifth section of action, one in which all three characters are on stage for the first time and the hierarchy of power is masked by the complicated ambiguities that regulate manners among the three men together until Mick, in what appears to be a tacit warning to his brother not to trust the tramp, accuses Davies of trespassing:

> MICK: Watch your step, sonny! You're knocking at the door when no one's at home. Don't push it too hard. You come busting into a private house, laying your hands on anything you can lay your hands on. Don't overstep the mark, son. (36)

The audience still has no idea who Mick really is, so Mick's intimidation of Davies seems as arbitrary as Goldberg's victimization of Stanley, the tramp's situation reflecting the existential terror of being isolated in a hostile environment in which other people can be kind one minute and turn cruel the next. Unlike that of Stanley in *The Birthday Party*, Davies' status appears to depend on which of the two men he is talking to. Neither Mick nor Aston speaks in the name of an abstract conception of state or social authority, but Mick in particular asserts the authority of ownership and implicitly warns Davies of the ties of fraternity that bind him to Aston.

After Mick exits Davies tries to work out exactly who Mick is, in order to ascertain which of the two actually does have authority in the house. Aston confirms that Mick is his brother and there is no reason for the audience or Davies to doubt this, although given the equivocal nature of the situation as experienced thus far, there can be no absolute guarantee. Davies therefore reacts fairly circumspectly to Aston's offer to make him caretaker, his caution being attributed to the possibility that he might be attacked by one of his enemies while answering the door, or that he might be trapped by the authorities for not having enough stamps on his social security card:

> [T]hey'd find out I was going about under an assumed name. You see the name I call myself now, that's not my real name. My real name's not the one I'm using, you see. It's different. You see, the name I go under now ain't my real one. It's assumed.
> *Silence.*
> THE LIGHTS FADE TO BLACKOUT. (42)

The comic effect of Davies' fearful fantasies reinforces the apprehension of the hidden mysteries of human motivation introduced in Mick's suspicious and mocking exchanges with him, and its elaborate play on the notion of identity heightens the suspense at the end of the scene.

The opening of the next scene with Davies coming back into the darkened room repeats the shock effect at the end of act 1; this time Mick is lying in wait for Davies and exploits the sound of the electric vacuum cleaner to frighten and disorient him. Mick's insouciance as he explains that he was doing "a bit of spring cleaning" reflects his sense of owning the space. Davies now reverses his earlier attempts to find out the terms of Aston and Mick's relationship, trying this time to secure an explanation of Aston's eccentric and uncommunicative behavior from Mick, who repeatedly tricks him into making disparaging comments about Aston that Mick then challenges, using the privilege of a brother to criticize Aston, but closing ranks in fraternal loyalty whenever Davies goes too far in agreeing with him. In what seems almost a parody of Aston's offer in the previous scene, Mick now invites Davies to be caretaker on his behalf. Davies' growing realization of Mick's power initiates a switch in his allegiance from Aston to Mick that is discernable in his more aggressive attitude to Aston in the final section of act 2.

Act 3 takes place two weeks later, the opening stage tableau evoking a relationship of familiarity between Mick and Davies as employer and employee that has developed in the interim:

> MICK *is lying on the floor, down left, his head resting on the rolled*
> *carpet, looking up at the ceiling.*
> DAVIES *is sitting in the chair, holding his pipe. He is wearing the*
> *smoking jacket. It is afternoon.*
> *Silence.* (56)

Davies is intent on turning Mick against Aston, ingratiating himself with Mick by feeding his fantasies of transforming the flat into "a palace" (58). Here each character's contrasting motives becomes clearly focused in their attitudes to the stage environment. Aston's cluttering of the room with dislocated household objects represents his failed attempt to create a comfortable living space, his aim of fixing the garden shed as a workshop in which he can repair his furniture a naive pipe dream of bourgeois domestic respectability (38–39). Mick's fantasy of home improvement is more ambitious—a vulgar adman's notion of redecorating in the slick modern style of a trendy interior design magazine:

> I could turn this place into a penthouse . . . You could have an off-
> white pile linen rug, a table in . . . in afromosia teak veneer, side-
> board with matt black drawers, curved chairs with cushioned
> seats, armchairs in oatmeal tweed, a beech frame settee with a
> woven sea-grass seat . . . (58)

To Davies, the room is a shelter from inclement weather, a place of rest and security that protects him from the vagaries of an itinerant existence. He will ingratiate himself in whatever way he believes will allow him to stay, and is only concerned that the room keeps out the cold and enables him to feed himself.

Aston's apparent failure to maintain and improve the house in the way that Mick desires becomes the key to Davies' scheme to supplant Aston as caretaker of the property. Mick encourages Davies in his delusion by suggesting that the tramp may, as a "friend" of his brother, be able to persuade him to realize Mick's plans for redecorating, but Davies' uncertainty about the true nature of the brothers' relationship prompts him to insist that Mick should do this, and his obsessive image of himself as a victim provokes Davies to complain persistently about Aston's management of the house without himself offering to help.

The next two sections of the third act reveal the deterioration in the relationship between Davies and Aston. As a result of Davies' miscalculation of the extent to which he has ingratiated himself with Mick, he becomes overconfident in his attitude to Aston, quarrelling rudely and taunting him with insults about his lack of mental stability, until Aston tells him to leave: "I . . . I think it's about time you found somewhere else. I don't think we're hitting it off" (66). This brilliant moment of comic understatement exposes the power that Aston has in fact always had over Davies, a power his kindness has up to now prevented him from exploiting. When Davies returns after approximately twelve hours, he has brought Mick with him, presumably hoping that Mick will restore his position in the house. Mick however continues the devious game by means of which he has misled the tramp from the start:

> DAVIES: . . . This is your house, en't? You let him live here!
> MICK: I could tell him to go, I suppose . . .
> DAVIES: That's what I'm saying.
> MICK: Yes . . . I mean, I'm the landlord. On the other hand, he's the sitting tenant . . . So what it is, it's a fine legal point, that's what it is.
> DAVIES: I tell you he should go back where he come from!
> MICK (*turning to look at him*). Come from.
> DAVIES: Yes.
> MICK: Where did he come from?
> DAVIES: Well . . . he . . . he . . .
> MICK: You get a bit out of your depth sometimes, don't you? (68–69)

As before, Mick's tricky behavior is intended to remind Davies of his status as a menial whose role is to follow the rules laid out by his master and to try to adapt to any changes dictated by his master's whims. Mick now deliberately misremembers Davies' earlier suggestion that he should give him a hand with the redecorating as an offer to act as a professional interior designer, humiliating Davies once more by showing him up as a fraud. Mick interprets Davies' demurral as a betrayal concomitant on the tramp's assumption of a false identity:

MICK: How could I have the wrong man? You're the only man I've spoken to. You're the only man I've told, about my dreams, about my deepest wishes, you're the only one I've told, and I only told you because I understood you were an experienced first-class professional interior and exterior decorator . . .
You're a bloody imposter, mate! (70)

The strategy by means of which Mick has projected a series of imagined identities onto Davies, who has never contradicted him, is abruptly ended as Mick now blames the tramp for having willfully deceived him. In response to Davies' attempt to blame the confusion on Mick's "nutty" brother, Mick unexpectedly asserts his fraternal loyalty and circles Davies physically as an animal moving in for the kill:

MICK: Did you call my brother nutty? My brother. That's a bit of . . . that's a bit of an impertinent thing to say, isn't it? [. . . . . .
. . . .]
MICK: . . . Ever since you came into this house there's been nothing but trouble. Honest. I can take nothing you say at face value. Every word you speak is open to any number of different interpretations. Most of what you say is lies. (71)

Mick's blunt accusation constitutes a reversion to his naked aggression toward Davies when they first met, refusing the possibility of any further social maneuvering by exposing all social intercourse with the tramp as based on falsehood. In fact Mick here cynically applies an epistemological analysis that conceives all forms of social interaction as dishonest, since the accusation could apply equally to any of the three characters—or, indeed in Pinter's view to any social communication. The action has shown each pair constructing a social relationship that to an extent excludes the third, and Mick chooses finally to revert to the fraternal allegiance that pertained before Aston introduced Davies to the house, thereby repeating a pattern that must throughout his life have left the tramp devoid of society. Mick's rage at Davies culminates in his smashing of Aston's plaster Buddha against the gas stove. The gesture suggests that his anger and disappointment may also be directed at Aston for his inability to live up to his expected role as caretaker and decorator, a failure of intelligence that has effectively permitted Davies' intrusion into the household. Mick may also be angry that he has been deluding himself about the possibility of accomplishing Aston's rehabilitation by giving him some responsibilities in the house; it has taken Davies' devious manipulations to disabuse him of his own illusions.

When Aston enters in the next section, there is a momentary non-verbal exchange between the brothers, suggesting that they may previously have agreed to expel Davies from the house, before Mick exits ("*They look at each other. Both are smiling, faintly*" [73]). Davies is now forced to beg to be reinstated as Aston's assistant, but Aston rejects all his pleas and the tramp's condition of alienation and desperation is revealed for what it is:

DAVIES: But . . . but . . . look . . . listen . . . listen here . . . I mean . . .

ASTON *turns back to the window.*

What am I going to do?

Pause.

What shall I do?

Pause.

Where am I going to go?

Pause. (75–76)

The comedy of the cunning intruder who has been hoist with his own petard is intermingled with the Lear-like specter of a vulnerable old man, alone in a hostile universe. In contrast with Pinter's preceding plays, it is character rather than narrative structure or incident that generates the sense of mystery in *The Caretaker*. It is not that there is no suspense built up in Pinter's typically ambiguous presentation of exposition, and no surprise at some of the unexpected turns of narrative, but that *The Caretaker*'s plot is manifest as a direct expression of the characters' interrelated intentions. Elaborated in fits and starts, the action alternates between progress and stasis or conflict in the various permutations of relationships possible among the three characters, creating a complex rhythm of anticipation, revelation, and reversal that intermingles comic moments with moods of bleakness and despair.[10] The characters' idiosyncratic actions and responses demand to be interpreted as symptoms of their condition rather than symbols in a coherent moral allegory.

Such naturalism in terms of character is potentially present in each of the earlier stage plays, but conventional naturalistic plotting is always subverted by the oddly inexplicable behavior of intruders or traitors, whose mysterious actions or appearances demand that audiences resolve whatever is immediately incomprehensible by interpreting the superficial incoherence of narrative or behavior in symbolic terms. Everything in *The Caretaker*, on the other hand, can ultimately be explained with reference to the social manipulation of one character by another. The battle for possession of territory is more overtly presented as the motivation for the characters' complicated interactions than in any of the earlier stage plays; here the action is shaped by the assumption shared by Davies and Mick that life is a dangerous and unceasing struggle for dominance. Ironically it is only the simpleminded Aston who behaves as though kindness to another might elicit an honest and humane response, and even he believes that it was a crucial betrayal of his trust by friends and family that affected his mental well-being and his capacity to relate normally to others. In avoiding the resort to extraneous plot devices to heighten mystery and terror, Pinter achieves full mastery of a form in constant development from *The Room* onward, succeeding in basing the dramatic structure entirely on human motivation.

CHAPTER 4

Family Voices:
The Homecoming

The Collection and *The Lover*

The relationship between "home" as a concept and as physical territory that motivates the action of *The Room* and *The Caretaker* is elaborated in *The Homecoming* in a more complex form. In *The Caretaker* the gradual revelation of an unspoken familial bond between two brothers can ultimately be seen to explain a great deal of what happens in the play, in spite of an apparent ambivalence in Mick's attitude to Aston and to the house that in different respects is their home. In *The Homecoming* the ideology of the family as social unit is conceived as itself the source of profoundly ambivalent emotional attitudes. In both plays, the right to inhabit the physical territory in which the action is located signifies the psychological sense of being home. In the later play, the territory that individual members of the family fight to possess is represented scenically by the living room of a typical Victorian house, with the significant alteration of the wall that was removed some time after the death of the matriarch to leave the main hallway and staircase visible. While all four characters living in the house may have the right to inhabit it, at least three of them are engaged in a Darwinian battle to control the household in a way that would ensure their dominance in the family; thus home itself constitutes the battleground of an internecine war for power.

The element of experience that constitutes a significant new focus in *The Homecoming* is its disclosure of the complications introduced into the war for possession of territory by the erotic impulse. While a patriarchal mother/whore dichotomy characterizes the misogynistic sexual attitudes of both Stanley and Goldberg to the two female characters in *The Birthday Party*, that play's exploration of sexuality and gender is limited. In this respect Pinter's formal experimentation in *The Collection* (1961) and *The Lover* (1963) prepares him directly for a complex articulation of the power of the erotic and the erotics of power—a key dynamic of human interaction in *The Homecoming*.

The Collection ritualizes a Pirandellian[1] drama of competing subjective viewpoints around a supposed infidelity perpetrated by two fashion designers, Stella (married to James) and Bill, who lives with his older lover, Harry. Originally written for television—and brilliantly exploiting a convention of alternating locations that made economical use of studio-based TV drama—the play's completely unprejudiced representation of the equivalence of heterosexual and homosexual feelings was avant-garde when it was first produced, and its exploration of masculinity in a middle-class milieu still stands as a textbook illustration of a number of significant issues in men's studies.[2] The psychological rivalry between the apparently homosexual Bill and Stella's supposedly heterosexual husband James is emblematized by the divided space of the play's setting in two upper-middle-class neighborhoods of London—Harry and Bill in Belgravia and James and Stella in Chelsea—with a neutral space in which telephone calls are made by James from a public telephone. Stock conventions of the detective thriller are used to generate tension, as Harry and Bill receive an anonymous phone call, followed by a further unsettling visit from a man who refuses to leave his name. The mystery at the heart of the drama concerns the question of whether Stella and Bill had a one-night stand while away on business in Leeds. When James calls on Bill at Harry's house, it becomes apparent that he is the anonymous caller and the unexpected visitor. James confronts Bill with Stella's confession that she slept with Bill in Leeds. At first Bill claims Stella's story is an invention. While admitting that they "kissed a bit," he asserts that what James claims "never happened," but when James insists that Bill was "sitting on the bed, next to her" when he phoned, Bill changes his story to render the account more ambiguous: "Not sitting. Lying" (137).[3]

The mock duel with household knives initiated by James reveals a strongly homoerotic undercurrent, Bill's slight scarring causing Harry to intervene with an account of Stella's alleged admission that she has invented the whole story and that the two never really met (she claims that James was the one who "dreamed it up"). Bill confirms that nothing happened, and Harry sarcastically denigrates him as a "slum slug." As James is about to leave, Bill suddenly changes his story for the final time:

> BILL: [. . .] we sat . . . in the lounge, on a sofa for two hours [. . .] talked [. . .] we talked about it . . . we didn't move from the lounge [. . .] never went to her room . . . just talked about what we would do . . . if we did get to her room [. . .] two hours . . . we never touched . . . we just talked about it. (138)

James then goes back home and confronts his wife with this final version: "You didn't do anything, did you? [. . .] (*Pause*) That's the truth . . . isn't it?" (141). Stella's response is equivocal: she "looks at him, neither confirming nor denying. Her face [. . .] friendly, sympathetic" (141). Typically, Pinter leaves the mystery unresolved, with the woman seemingly in control of a situation in which two men appear to be jousting over her like medieval knights, a situation that in many ways anticipates the ending of *The Homecoming*.

The Lover tricks the audience into assuming that there are three characters in the play—the middle-class husband Richard, his wife Sarah, and her lover. The opening shock tactic of the play is created by the contradiction between the setting of a detached house near the salubrious commuter town of Windsor as Richard leaves for work on a summer morning and the insouciant immoralism of the opening lines:

> RICHARD (*amiably*): Is your lover coming today?
> SARAH: Mmnn.
> RICHARD: What time?
> SARAH: Three.
> RICHARD: Will you be going out . . . or staying in?
> SARAH: Oh . . . I think we'll stay in.
> RICHARD: I thought you wanted to go to that exhibition.
> SARAH: I did, yes . . . but I think I'd prefer to stay in with him today.
> RICHARD: Mmn-hmmn. Well, I think I must be off.

A moment later a man knocks on the door raising expectations that he is the lover, but he turns out to be the milkman. In fact the man who calls on the wife in the afternoon *is* her husband, who performs the role of her lover while she plays the role of his whore. On the surface, the play stages a Genet-esque game of transgressive sexual behavior that appears to challenge suburban norms of bourgeois respectability. Here Pinter undermines the misogynistic patriarchal construction of woman as both virgin and whore, by showing the woman deliberately role-playing these two archetypes at her husband's behest.

Most subversively, it is the woman who is shown to be more sexually adventurous than the man; when Richard wishes to call a halt to the game of pretended adultery, Sarah is dismayed until he is eventually seduced into switching back to the role of lover to satisfy her sexual needs, so that she is seen to be the stronger of the two in the battle for sexual satisfaction within the marriage.[4] Sarah's assumption of power through the manipulation of masculine desire in complex role-play directly anticipates the pattern through which Ruth turns the tables on the male family members in *The Homecoming*, and the last lines of the play suggest that in a patriarchal and sexist world, the woman achieves power only by playing the whore:

> SARAH: Would you like me to change? Would you like me to change my clothes? . . .
> RICHARD: Yes . . . Change . . . Change . . . Change your clothes . . . you lovely whore. (196)

The Homecoming

The Homecoming explores both the erotic power play of *The Lover* and the conflict of subjectivity evinced in *The Collection* to create a much more complex battle of the sexes. In place of the fragmented or pseudo-families of *The Room*, *The Birthday Party*, and *The Caretaker*, *The Homecoming* represents the conflict between two interrelated family units, and alludes to the influence of a third family—Max's parents and their offspring—on the behavior patterns of the two families represented on stage. Before returning from a holiday in Venice to his home in America, Max's eldest son Teddy brings his wife Ruth to visit the family home in North London. Teddy's homecoming problematizes the overlapping concepts of home and family, revealing clearly the network of intense masculine rivalries that constitutes Max's family life in its present dysfunctional state. It is not specified when exactly Max's wife, Jessie, died, but the absence of wife and mother is discernible in the dissatisfaction expressed by both the retired butcher Max and his son Lenny, over Max's assumption of the role of cook and housekeeper, as well as in the sarcastic bickering between the crudely masculine Max and his waspishly asexual brother Sam. The rude competitiveness existing in the London household before the arrival of Ruth and Teddy can be seen to typify the aggressive camaraderie of an entirely male milieu, but it can equally be interpreted as the compulsive acting out of corrosive and long-standing family hostilities.

If the refinement and emotional warmth of Jessie's femininity are occasionally identified as the catalyst for the past transformation of the family environment into a proper home ("That woman was the backbone to this family" [54]),[5] not all memories of this matriarch are entirely pleasant. When meeting Ruth for the first time before she is introduced to him as Teddy's wife, Max accuses Teddy of bringing a "filthy scrubber" into the house, saying, "I've never had a whore under this roof before. Ever since your mother died" [50]. The afterthought is surely a Freudian slip. Does Max remember his wife Jessie as a whore? Sam does insinuate later that she was unfaithful to Max with his friend MacGregor, and there are possible imputations of marital infidelity in Sam's claim that he often drove Jessie around London in his taxi, so the nostalgic image of a happy marriage that Max occasionally promotes in his role of paterfamilias may well be a sham. Or are such suspicions merely products of the perverse imagination of a pathologically jealous husband? At times his ambivalent feelings toward Jessie are expressed in crudely misogynistic terms ("Mind you, she wasn't such a bad woman. Even though it made me sick just to look at her lousy, stinking face, she wasn't such a bad bitch" [17]), and at others his resentment of his family responsibilities seems so overwhelming that he himself calls into doubt the paternity of his sons:

MAX: . . . A crippled family, three bastard sons, a slutbitch of a wife— don't talk to me about the pain of childbirth—I suffered the pain, I've still got the pangs . . . and here I've got a lazy idle bugger of a brother won't even get to work on time. (55)

In some situations, Max regards the family as dysfunctional or even diseased—a center or source of corruption in all personal relationships:

SAM: Our father's house.
MAX: Look what I'm lumbered with. One cast-iron bunch of crap after another. One flow of stinking pus after another. (27)

At other moments, however, Max conceives the family as a social organism enabling the mutual exchange of loving care that nurtures each individual member:

MAX: Well, it's a long time since the whole family was together, eh? If only your mother was alive. Eh, what do you say, Sam? What would Jessie say if she was alive? Sitting here with her three sons. Three fine grown-up lads. And a lovely daughter-in-law. The only shame is her grandchildren aren't here. She'd have petted them and cooed over them, wouldn't she, Sam? . . . Mind you, she taught those boys everything they know. She taught them all the morality they know . . . And she had a heart to go with it. (53–54)

His nostalgic and clichéd memory of the family as it was when his wife was alive, is in context savagely ironic, not only as a result of the doubts already cast on Jessie's fidelity to Max, but because Lenny's and Max's demonstrations of naked aggression towards one other, Teddy's sly detachment, and the intimations given by Lenny's evasive language and manipulative behavior that he is a pimp, imply that the "morality" the three sons may have learned from Jessie is extremely dubious. The Judeo-Christian notion of the family unit as source of personal identity and moral authority is shockingly undermined by the vicious and predatory behavior actually shown on stage.

The fact that the characters' actions are indistinguishable from the marauding habits of jungle animals reveals the concept of the family home as domestic haven to be an illusion. With the possible exception of the youngest son Joey, who although the least assertive of the men is *literally* a fighter, each of the male characters attempts to assert his own masculinity by symbolically castrating another. Max's ironic assessment of Joey's limitations as a boxer typifies this attitude to masculine behavior:

MAX: I'll tell you what you've got to do. What you've got to do is you've got to learn to defend yourself, and you've got to learn to attack. That's your only trouble as a boxer. You don't know how to defend yourself and you don't know how to attack. (25)

His advice on boxing provides an emblem of human interaction as the equivalent of a blood sport, rationalizing the characters' instinctive attitudes toward others in the Hobbesian terms of a "war of all against all."[6]

Some of the comic moments in the play derive from the spectacle of chauvinistic men being obliged to perform the traditional roles of women. "Who do think I am, your mother? [. . .] Go and find yourself a mother" (24) is Max's response when Joey remarks that he is hungry. In deflecting his own rage at being reduced from heroic breadwinner to abject housewife, Max projects onto Sam the misogynistic stereotype of the resentful wife that he himself has assumed in retirement:

MAX: You resent making my breakfast, that's what it is, isn't it? That's why you bang round the kitchen like that, scraping the frying-pan, scraping all the leavings into the bin, scraping all the plates, scraping all the tea out of the teapot . . . that's why you do that, every single stinking morning. I know. Listen, Sam. I want to say something to you. From my heart.

He moves closer.

I want you to get rid of those feelings of resentment you've got towards me. (47)

In context, the last line is hilarious, as the audience has in fact been witnessing Max's resentment of Sam for at least half an hour! Max's misogynistic projection of femininity onto Sam—and, at other times, his sons—is a result of the absence of a woman in the family that is highlighted by the shock of Ruth's arrival. Max calls Sam, Lenny, and Teddy "bitch," and he taunts Sam at various moments about not having married, not having the grit to follow his father into the butcher's trade, not having fought in the war, and not even being heterosexual ("You'd bend over for half a dollar on Blackfriar's Bridge" [56]). In Max's hierarchical view of masculinity the virility implied by his own career as butcher and father of three sons valorizes his superior position as patriarch while Sam's job as taxi driver or chauffeur reduces him to the lowest level. Throughout the play, however, Max's view of himself is challenged by Lenny's contemptuous treatment of him (early in the play he calls the retired butcher a "dog cook" [19]), by Teddy's patronizing superciliousness, and even by Joey ,who remarks that he is an "old man," thereby situating Max below the demeaning position of a housewife in a hierarchy that completely diminishes the status of old people.

The fact that Ruth and Teddy have three sons implies a direct parallel between the structure of the younger American family unit and Max and Jessie's family, the primacy of the older, English family being threatened in the same way that a modern American lifestyle might in 1965 have challenged the vanishing traditional culture of imperial Britain.

> TEDDY: . . . It's a great life, at the University . . . you know . . . it's a
> very good life. We've got a lovely house . . . we've got all . . . we've
> got everything we want. It's a very stimulating environment.
>
> *Pause.*
>
> *My department . . . is highly successful.*
>
> *Pause.*
>
> We've got three boys, you know.
> MAX: All boys? Isn't that funny, eh? You've got three, I've got three.
> (58)

After six years away from home, Teddy is an outsider. Not only has he has gone outside the family circle to create a new home in America, but his profession as an academic has also alienated him from his inherited family and class values. Max recognizes that Teddy's adult identity as professor of philosophy and father directly threatens his own position as patriarch, appearing to resent the fact that his son's university education has distanced him from his working-class family as decisively as the geographical separation has done, while Teddy himself condescendingly boasts of the gulf that his intellectual training has created between the family and himself:

> TEDDY: You wouldn't understand my works. . . . You'd be lost. It's
> nothing to do with the question of intelligence. It's a way of being

able to look at the world. It's a question of how far you can operate on things and not in things . . . I'm the one who can see. . . . You're just objects. You just move about. I can observe it. I can see what you do. It's the same as I do. But you're lost in it. You won't get me being . . . I won't be lost in it. (69–70)

Teddy's study of philosophy has taught him to assume a distance from his experience in order to view it objectively, but it has alienated him from his own instinctive feelings and made him a stranger in the family home.[7] Once again in a Pinter play outsiders intrude upon a household; but in *The Homecoming* the outsiders are also in fact members of the family. Teddy's intention to distance himself from his experience in order to operate upon the world with detachment parallels other characters' deliberate efforts to mask their feelings in order to achieve success in accomplishing their ends. Although Teddy exhibits his professional expertise in achieving such distance, Ruth is capable of equally rational self-reflexivity, while Lenny is an intuitively cunning strategist. Sam is certainly capable of distancing himself from his strong instinctive feelings in scheming to disconcert Max and get Teddy on his side against him, and even the aggressive and volatile Max displays a degree of self-conscious deliberation in conducting tactical battles with Sam, Lenny, and Teddy.

The shifting allegiances and ambivalent feelings of the individual members of the family render the apparent irrationality and contradictory nature of their behavior even more difficult to comprehend than that of characters in the earlier plays. As in the earlier plays, however, the excessive intensity of certain characters' reactions seems to reflect their psychic disequilibrium. Having been kept in ignorance of Teddy's marriage, Max's reaction to meeting Teddy and Ruth at breakfast is not merely an expression of his understandable surprise, but a projection of his own misogynistic sexual fantasy[8] and attendant guilt onto Teddy's relationship:

MAX: . . . (*To* JOEY.) Have you ever had a whore here? Has Lenny ever had a whore here? They come back from America, they bring the slopbucket with them. They bring the bedpan with them. (*To* TEDDY.) Take that disease away from me. Get her away from me.
TEDDY: She's my wife.
MAX (*To* JOEY). Chuck them out. (50)

The dichotomous image of woman as mother or whore underlies the men's inability to resolve their attitude to Jessie, whose memory remains alive to Max and Sam as both mother and whore, and it motivates Max's ambivalent view of Ruth. The most shocking twist of the plot is created by Ruth's cool acceptance of the patriarchal construction of her femininity by Max, Lenny, and Joey as mere object of desire; this is rendered even more disquieting because Ruth herself sexualizes her relationship with Lenny on their first meeting and may be thought to encourage such a sexist view of her by her insinuation that she was a prostitute (in her own words, "a model for the body") before marrying Teddy and giving birth to their sons. During the last phase of the action, Ruth's cool poise as she negotiates the terms of an arrangement whereby she will live in the house in exchange for servicing three of the men and earning money as a part-time prostitute is profoundly unsettling to any audience. When Ruth chooses to remain in the household rather than return to America with Teddy, the title of the play can ironically be understood to refer to *her* homecoming as she apparently prepares to resume a career as prostitute.

Much critical controversy has been provoked by the representation of her self-assured sexual game-playing. In the covert battle for power that occurs when Lenny and Ruth meet for the first time, Ruth startlingly turns the tables on him by performing the role of sexual aggressor traditionally reserved for men. She outmaneuvers him by exploiting her own sexual assertiveness to combat the threat he intends in relating two tales of his own violence against women. The conflict is enacted as a petty quarrel:

> LENNY: Excuse me, shall I take this ashtray out of your way?
> RUTH: It's not in my way.
> LENNY: It seems to be in the way of your glass. The glass was about to fall. Or the ashtray . . . I'm sure you won't object if I move the ashtray.
>
> *He does so.*
>
> And now perhaps I'll relieve you of your glass. (41)

After a brief argument in which Ruth speaks as though she were a mother reprimanding her child, Lenny continues:

Just give me the glass.
RUTH: No.

Pause.

LENNY: I'll take it, then.
RUTH: If you take the glass . . . I'll take you.

Pause.

LENNY: How about me taking the glass without you taking me?
RUTH: Why don't I just take you? (42)

She then teases Lenny by saying, "Sit on my lap. Take a long, cool sip," after which she stands and undermines him completely by ordering him to "Lie on the floor. Go on. I'll pour it down your throat" (42). The relationship between gender and sexuality is observed with an anthropologist's scrupulous attention to detail in this surprising reversal of the conventional view of men as typically sexually assertive and women as passive partners.

Is the play's presentation of Ruth as both mother and whore in itself an endorsement of the sexism of patriarchal society? Does Ruth collude in the homosocial[9] male fantasy of women as sexually available, or does her exploitation of the power of her physical attractiveness over sexually driven men represent a kind of personal liberation? On a few occasions Pinter has himself reminded critics that the ending of the play provides no guarantee that Ruth genuinely intends to meet her part of the bargain. The only unequivocal interpretation of her behavior that may be derived directly from the context of the action is that she is manipulating the men's need for her as mother and/or lover in order to maneuver herself into a position in the household that she finds more acceptable than living in America as Teddy's wife. That Ruth is clearly aware of the homosocial nature of the men's competition for her is made apparent a short while after the start of the second act:

> RUTH: You've forgotten something. Look at me. I . . . move my leg. That's all it is. But I wear . . . underwear . . . which moves with me . . . it . . . captures your attention. Perhaps you misinterpret. The action is simple. It's a leg . . . moving. My lips move. Why don't you restrict . . . your observations to that? Perhaps the fact that they move is more significant . . . than the words which come

through them. You must bear that . . . possibility . . . in mind. (60–61)

In refocusing the terms of Lenny and Teddy's philosophical discussion, Ruth does not merely interpellate herself into the men's abstract argument, she reminds them that the self-conscious philosophical debate is not merely another expression of the mutual hostility between Teddy and his family but a fight for the possession of a woman. Not only does her speech startle the men into recognizing the atavistic desires and fantasies that determine their interaction at this moment, it also undercuts the abstract logic of Lenny's verbal sparring by pointing out the importance of its context of enunciation. Ruth thereby self-reflexively defamiliarizes her own act of speaking, visually prompting the audience to contextualize the meaning of the verbal exchange so that a spectator views her speaking body as an object being sexualized by a roomful of gazing men. Theatrically, the moment offers a striking visual illustration of the point Ruth is making, since an audience may find the physical charm of the actress performing the speech act even more persuasive than the witty content of the words themselves.

Ruth's decision to live in the London household reinforces earlier hints in the play that her relationship with Teddy is wholly unsatisfying to her. The marriage restricts her freedom to define her identity as an individual, confining her within the stereotypically sexist role of supporting her husband and taking care of her sons. Jessie's desire to be driven around London by Sam and his imputation of a sexual liaison between her and MacGregor may well indicate that the domestic role of wife and mother did not satisfy her any more than it does Ruth. In this respect the play offers no moral judgment of Jessie's or Ruth's behavior but instead exposes the traditional institution of marriage as preventing women from satisfying their personal needs. The ironic mode of the play's dramaturgy obviates the presentation of moral or political argument, so that it cannot be judged to be either directly reinforcing or overtly attacking patriarchal ideology.[10] Instead *The Homecoming* lays bare the contradictions experienced by individuals obliged to order their lives according to this ideology and exposes the psychological effects of doing so. Pinter's ambition to be scrupulously honest in observing human behavior may explain the paradoxical co-existence of such intensely contradictory feelings within members of the family:

> I think there's a good deal of love about in some of my plays. But love can very easily go down the wrong path and be distorted as the result of frustration in all kinds of different ways. In *The Homecoming* . . . the violence of the family towards their son when he comes back from America, using his wife to embody their own rage . . . comes about because they don't know where to put their love. I think there's a great deal of love in that play but they simply don't know what to do with it. (Smith, 73–74)

Structurally, *The Homecoming* is more subtle and more elaborately plotted than any of Pinter's previous plays. The multiple networks of relationships include all of the six characters represented and, additionally, four who are absent from the stage; their allegiances shift and transform themselves in surprising ways according to the various contexts created by different moments in the action. The unique stylization of speech and action that allows the drama to shift imperceptibly between oneiric experience—the realm of the unconscious states, memory, dream, or fantasy—and the material plane of social interaction, suggests the influence of cinema that is detectable in Pinter's theater as early as *The Room*. The boldness of the stylistic experiment in *The Homecoming* may also reflect a new confidence in the writer's ability to subvert the dramaturgy of the well-made West End play. Typical of his drama are abrupt and occasionally alarming switches in mood and tone; these often resemble the surreal logic of a dream, directly juxtaposing disconnected or contradictory ideas and feelings that normal social conventions would function to disguise or repress. This is especially so in *The Homecoming*. Although its characters maintain a semblance of socially coherent discourse and may be understood as exploiting the familiarity of long-standing family relationships to express a range of socially unacceptable feelings in a brutally frank manner, the irrational self-contradictions and inexplicable changes of mood and attitude repeatedly suggest that the drama may be a projection of unconscious states upon a framework of social situations. At the same time social interaction can be seen to be consciously expressed in a series of strategies that disguise the will to power motivating each character's pursuit of an offensive or defensive plan. The intricate negotiations of the characters in *The Homecoming* hark back to the cunning social manipulations represented in the tradition of English comedy of manners exemplified at its most complex and savage by William Congreve's *The Way of the World* (1700).

The sphinx-like characterization of Ruth as the play's sole female figure radically problematizes gender relations as a key concern in the play. In Pinter's earlier work, the older female characters (e.g., Meg in *The Birthday Party*, Rose in *The Room*) are invariably presented as wives and mothers while the younger ones are conceived almost entirely in terms of their sexuality (Lulu in *The Birthday Party*, Stella in *The Collection*, Sarah in *The Lover*). Subsequent developments in his dramaturgical approach confirm the idea that *The Homecoming* indicates a crisis in Pinter's representation of women. The "realist" presentation of Ruth as the only female character renders her position as outsider to the family of men doubly problematic from the perspective of gender. Notwithstanding the fact that Ruth's desires are never allowed direct expression, she appears to outmaneuver all the men—including her husband—in negotiating a position in the household that she finds preferable to her life in America. Within the "objective" mode of naturalistic representation that prevents a character's motives from being inferred other than from the context of stage action, Ruth is portrayed without paternalistic bias as the potential victim of a sexist society. Given the patriarchal society represented in the play, it is ironic that she may be seen under the circumstances to make the best possible compromise available to a woman. Since this is the last time Pinter portrays a woman in an all-male milieu as *other* in terms of gender, the final scene of *The Homecoming* may be seen to test the potentially sexist representation of women as objects of male fantasy by exposing it at its most extreme.

Fantasy can be seen to determine the shape of the stories narrated by Max and Lenny that pretend to illustrate topics under discussion but are actually calculated performances, which interrupt the cut-and-thrust of social conversation with exaggerated descriptions of bizarre events intended to enhance the speaker's self-image. Some of the chief examples are Max's long digression on his understanding of horses (17–18), his uncharacteristic homily on the joys of family life (53–55), Lenny's horrifyingly matter-of-fact narrative about the prostitute he punched and kicked senseless (38–39) followed by the equally callous story of the old woman he tried to help and ended up punching in the belly (40–41), and his vindictive recounting of the time when Joey forced a prostitute to have sex without "contraceptive protection" (74–76). The rendering of unconscious patterns of feeling and thinking in the form of such overtly rhetorical narratives is an obvious example of the stylization of speech to mimic the forms of fantasy.

The stylized use of speech, tableaux, and movement together with the more filmic approach to tempo anticipates the exploration of a more overtly non-naturalistic dramaturgy in his next two plays.[11] Although the intended objectivity of the single naturalistic location in *The Homecoming* is once again derivative of the scenic convention of the well-made stage play, a dreamlike rhythm of experience is created by a temporal scheme that subtly conveys the flow of twenty-four hours from the first evening to the last by dividing the action of the two acts into six segments separated by time shifts as follows: act 1, evening (15–27); blackout; night (27–45); blackout; morning (45–52); curtain; act 2, afternoon (53–70); blackout; evening (70–90); curtain. Within each segment the rhythm created by breaks, indicated as usual in the script by three dots (momentary), "pause" (longer), or "silence" (longest), promotes a musical conception of the tempo of its performance. While Pinter's stage directions habitually express the precision of the expert actor-director in visualizing the action on stage, the script's directions for characters grouped in tableaux in *The Homecoming* invite a visual stylization that complements the musical patterning of speech with a rhythm of movement and stillness in space that may reflect his newfound expertise as a writer of film screenplays.[12]

Most of the directions in the first act prescribe precise but minimal stage movement, schematizing significant moments of the characters' interactions in spatial/kinetic terms. Approximately five minutes after the start of the play, for example, the indifference of Lenny toward his father is signified in their proxemic relationship ("MAX *sits hunched.* LENNY *reads the paper*" [19]), while the tableau of Teddy and Ruth in the doorway provokes bafflement at their unexpected arrival and simultaneously in visual terms foreshadows their disruption of the status quo of the London household:

BLACKOUT.
LIGHTS UP.
Night. TEDDY *and* RUTH *stand at the threshold of the room.*
[. . . . .]
Two suitcases are by their side.
They look at the room. (27)

These directions for stage blocking are extended in a series of more complex sculptural tableaux or movement sequences that visually express unspoken feelings and attitudes. Occasionally these reinforce the meaning of the characters' utterances; at other times they counterpoint or even contradict what is spoken.

The strange appearance of people perceived in dreams is evoked in the sequence when lights are successively turned off and on, as Teddy goes up to bed after his initial meeting with Lenny:

TEDDY *goes into the hall with the cases.*
LENNY *turns out the light in the room.*
The light in the hall remains on.
LENNY *follows into the hall.* (34)

Pinter's stage directions convey the eerie play of light and darkness that evokes both the surprise of Teddy's night-time arrival and the uncanny appearance of the house he grew up in, while Lenny's control of the lights signals his sense of being in charge of the territory:

LENNY *turns out the hall light and turns on the first landing light.*
[. . . . .]
TEDDY *goes upstairs.*
LENNY *goes off L.*
Silence
The landing light goes out.
Slight night light in the hall and room.
LENNY *comes back into the room, goes to the window and looks out.*
He leaves the window and turns on a lamp.
He is holding a small clock.
He sits, places the clock in front of him, lights a cigarette and sits.
RUTH*comes in the front door.*
She stands still. LENNY *turns his head, smiles. She walks slowly into*
   the room. (35)

As in the nightmarish party scene in act 1 of *The Birthday Party* or the sequence in the dark in *The Caretaker* in which Mick uses the sound of the vacuum cleaner to frighten Davies, atmospheric effects of sound and light, silence and darkness transform the scene as normally apprehended into a space in which unconscious fears, dreams, and desires are heightened. Lenny's remarks on the clock he brings into the living room amount to a haunting evocation of the effect of night on the imagination:

> There are a lot of things which tick in the night, don't you find that? All sorts of objects, which, in the day, you wouldn't call anything else but commonplace. They give you no trouble. But in the night any given one of a number of them is liable to start letting out a bit of a tick. (36)

The moment of shocked silence when Teddy and Ruth come downstairs after having slept in the house without Max, Sam, and Joey knowing, is reinforced by the stillness on stage that effectively creates a visual moment in which the two "outsiders" face the stares of the three men (48). At the beginning of act 2, the masculine ritual of smoking an after-dinner cigar constitutes a comic tableau of false bonhomie as Joey and Ruth serve coffee. In performance, this is invariably a highly effective moment of slightly stylized action that depicts the complacent paternalism of patriarchal culture (53). A little later, the most ambitious deployment of movement and sound occurs when Lenny, seeming to challenge Teddy's decision that Ruth should leave with him, puts on a "record of slow jazz" and invites Ruth to dance, the music providing a "soundtrack" accompanying the succeeding conversation and action:

> RUTH *stands. They dance, slowly.*
> TEDDY *stands, with* RUTH'S *coat.*
> MAX *and* JOEY *come in the front door and into the room.*
> *They stand.*
> LENNY *kisses* RUTH. *They stand, kissing.*
> JOEY: Christ, she's wide open.
>
> *Pause.*
>
> She's a tart.

Pause.

Old Lenny's got a tart in here.

JOEY *goes to them. He takes* RUTH's *arm. He smiles at* LENNY. *He sits with* RUTH *on the sofa, embraces and kisses her.*
He looks up at LENNY.

Just up my street.

He leans her back until she lies beneath him. He kisses her. He looks up at TEDDY *and* MAX.

It's better than a rubdown, this.

LENNY *sits on the arm of the sofa. He caresses* RUTH's *hair as* JOEY *embraces her.*

MAX *comes forward, looks at the cases.*

MAX: You going. Teddy? Already!

Pause. (66–68)

While Joey, Lenny, and Ruth continue to engage in heavy petting, Max with studied indifference reassures Teddy that he does not object to his having married "a woman beneath him" (67) since she is "a woman of quality . . . a woman of feeling" (68).

After Joey and Ruth have rolled off the sofa onto the floor, Ruth stands up and demands a drink, switching the mood from that of a male sexual fantasy in order to enact a rather different "whore" scenario of a spoiled and domineering sex goddess demanding service from her male attendants. The counterpoint of the jazz music with the cool lack of concern shown by Teddy, Max, and Sam over an overtly sexual exhibition of marital infidelity provokes voyeurism and shock at the same time. How is this sequence to be understood? Is it actually happening or is it a dream? If it is a dream, who is dreaming? After Lenny and Ruth agree on the terms of an arrangement by which Ruth will live with Teddy's father and brothers and be set up in a flat to earn some money as a prostitute, Sam blurts out, "MacGregor had Jessie in the back of my cab as I drove them along," then "croaks and collapses" (86). A few minutes later Teddy leaves as if nothing much has happened, and the play closes on a tableau of Ruth enacting the dual role of mother and sex object that is desired by Max, Lenny, and Joey, but now Joey kneels in front of Ruth like a child with his head on her lap and she comforts him by stroking it (88) while Lenny stands beside the chair and Max falls to his knees beside her, groaning:

MAX: I'm not an old man.

Pause.

Do you hear me?

He raises his face to her.

Kiss me.

She continues to touch Joey's head, lightly.
LENNY *stands, watching.*

Curtain. (88)

Sam still lies inert on the floor, having possibly suffered a stroke. The spectacle of the formerly domineering and abrasive old man physically begging a younger woman for a sexual favor while she pets his younger son, watched by the elder one, is a disturbing image of the voyeurism and sexual desperation of loveless men that unmasks the condition the men have fought so aggressively to deny.

Since the playwright appears to make no effort to distinguish between what is actually happening in the living room of the family home and what is dream or fantasy, it is left to the audience to make sense of what it has witnessed. Decisions about the narrative coherence of the drama are irrelevant to an understanding of the play as no clear distinctions are made between events actually taking place and characters' dream or fantasy versions of that reality.

Quite possibly Pinter's radical deconstruction of the spurious objectivity of naturalistic dramaturgy confronted him simultaneously with the difficulty of representing women in patriarchal society as independent agents and with the problems it poses in representing the consciousness of thinking and desiring subjects per se; certainly the sequence of quasi-expressionistic plays that follow *The Homecoming* (*Landscape, Silence,* and the less easily categorizable *Old Times*) conceive women and men as occupying potentially interchangeable subject positions. It is also possible that Pinter believed his own particular subversion of English "kitchen sink" naturalism, in which social interactions are the primary engine of the drama, to have run its course, thereby leaving the form in danger of becoming mannered. For whatever reason, *Landscape* and *Silence* employ structures most obviously modeled on the form of radio drama, employing a type of voice-over technique as a mode of representing the "stream of consciousness"; in these two plays oneiric states are directly presented in a more Beckettian theater language that represents the subject's consciousness as the medium through which material reality is grasped.

CHAPTER 5

New Conceptions of Gender and Memory: *Landscape, Old Times*

After *The Homecoming*, Pinter began for the first time to employ a stream-of-consciousness technique redolent of expressionistic dramaturgy. In his own words, "[I] couldn't any longer stay in the room with this bunch of people who opened doors and came in and went out" (Gussow, 18). The one-act play *Landscape*, marked the first clear departure from the dramaturgical approach of Pinter's early drama, as it directly represents a mental rather than a material universe. Neither Beth nor Duff moves from the chair each occupies, thereby intensifying the concentration on the psychological nature of their relationship by focusing the senses of an audience almost exclusively on the verbal play of memories. It is as though we were "watching" a radio play, listening to the thoughts of the characters, but with the addition of a visual image of their shared environment. Such a tension between a static visual image and the verbal drama of consciousness is most likely to have been inspired by Beckett's plays from *Happy Days* (1961) onward.

The stage directions of *Landscape* locate the present action in the material world, yet the frozen quality of the image created by the peculiar positioning of each actor vis-à-vis the other, subverts both the historical and geographical certainties promised by the spare naturalism of the scenography to produce instead a direct evocation of an interior mindscape of each character's thoughts and memories:

The kitchen of a country house.
A long kitchen table.

BETH *sits in an armchair, which stands away from the table, to its*
  left.
DUFF *sits in a chair at the right corner of the table. The background,*
  of a sink, stove etc., and a window, is dim.
Evening. (166)[1]

Furniture in the foreground is concrete and material, while the image
of the surrounding kitchen is "dim," rendering it metonymic of the
domestic milieu referred to in Beth's and Duff's intercut monologues. The positioning of Duff and Beth indicates the emotional distance between them. Separated by the long kitchen table, each exists
in a private world of reverie:

DUFF *refers normally to* BETH, *but does not appear to hear her voice.*
BETH *never looks at* DUFF, *and does not appear to hear his voice.*
  (166)

The audience can never be sure the two are married, although this
seems to be implied by Duff's speeches to Beth. Their physical placement in the kitchen suggests they inhabit the same environment,
but, given that Beth never refers to Duff, there is no certainty either
that their interwoven monologues are being "thought" simultaneously or that they are only positioned in the kitchen at the same moment as a emblem of their relationship as retainers in the household
of their deceased employer, Mr Sykes. The evocation of remembered
incidents is prompted by the vivid particularity of their recollection
of material objects. This Proustian representation of involuntary
memory foreshadows Pinter's pleasurable engagement with his adap-
tation of *A la Recherche du Temps Perdu* in the year (1971–72) that
he spent adapting the novel into a screenplay.

It has been remarked by scholars that, by comparison with Ruth
in *The Homecoming*, Pinter creates a female character in *Landscape*
whose subjectivity is as fully expressed as that of the male characters[2] rather than employing a representation of women's behavior
from the "outside" in a perspective determined by men.[3] The dramaturgical form of the play necessitates for the first time in his career Pinter's full imaginative investment in the interior life of a female character who possess a degree of complexity equal to that of
Aston and Mick in *The Caretaker* and Max in *The Homecoming*. As
in *Night*, *Silence*, and *Old Times* (1970), *Landscape* exhibits a ten-

dency to represent gender archetypically so that Duff's masculinity is the psychological counterpart of Beth's femininity.[4] In his repetition of technical jargon, Duff's obsession with the mundane pragmatic details of storing and drawing beer ("give the drayman a hand with the barrels," "down the bunghole," "spile the bung," "hammer the tap in," "feed the slops back to the ullage barrel" [183–84]), feeding the ducks, walking the dog, dusting and polishing items of furniture, and the aggressive bluntness of his speech ("This beer is piss," "someone's used this pintpot instead of the boghole" [173], "its bullshit," "fuck all," "I booted the gong down the hall," "I would have had you in front of the dog, like a man," "mind you don't get the scissors up your arse" [186–87]) seems crudely masculine.

Duff is unable to express tender feelings for Beth; he speaks of his need for her as a companion who will share a life of manual labor and social activity, while she speaks in a lyrical register of the romantic tenderness of her lover. Her speech evokes the rapt reminiscence of a woman whose memories and desires have become indistinguishable. Beth's language as she remembers lying on the beach with her lover is sensuous and musical: "I would like to stand by the sea," "people move so easily, men move," "my man slept in the dune," "snoozing, how lovely," "I am beautiful," "rested in the water," "touched the back of my neck," "underneath I was naked," "would you like a baby?" "body drawn in sand, head on his arm," "darting red and back flecks under my eyelid," "put his arm around me, cuddled me." Images of the sea, sand, dunes, sun, and sky conjure the idyll of pure romance, but Beth's retrospection also reflects the sadness of irretrievably past experience. Another poignant occasion is evoked by images of the beauty of a natural landscape ("lightness of your touch," "lightness of your look," "your eyes," "the silence," "the loveliness of my flowers," "misty morning, sun shining, wetness all over the ground," "beautiful autumn morning" [182–84]), while the evanescence of the moment of joy is implied in reflections on how shadow threatens to obscure the vision of beauty ("basic principles of shadow and light," "shadow is the deprivation of light," "sometimes the cause of the shadow cannot be found" [185–86]). These less pleasant recollections seem by the end of the play to impel a return to Beth's memories of the earlier time on the beach: "[he] lay above me, supported my shoulder," "So tender his touch on my neck. So softly his kiss on my cheek," "Tiny the sand on my skin," "So silent the sky in my eyes," "Gently the sound of the tide," "Oh my true love, I said" (187–88). It is never certain, however, whether her lover is imagined or real, or whether he may in fact have been Mr Sykes or Duff at an earlier time in their relationship.

Whatever the case, the pain of Duff's emotional exclusion by Beth is represented as both pathetic and comic in his desperate appeal to her completely unresponsive presence: "Do you like me to talk to you?" (179). *Landscape* succinctly traces the process of romantic disillusionment, interweaving fragmentary images of the failure of a married couple to establish an emotional bond with intimations of the husband's petty infidelity and the wife's nostalgic reverie of a doomed or imaginary romance. *Landscape* is a minor masterpiece—an entirely successful experiment in a form of dramatic writing that represents a complete break with Pinter's previous dramaturgical approach and leads to the more abstract if less fully achieved form of *Silence.*

Presented by the Royal Shakespeare Company in a double bill with *Landscape* in 1969, the thirty-minute *Silence* is Pinter's most radical attempt to evoke the sheer experience of remembering in a fractured postmodern form reminiscent of Beckett's short dramas from *Play* (1966) to *What Where* (1984). Not as well received critically as *Landscape,* the play has an implicit narrative structure that can only be tentatively pieced together by the audience from echoing shards of memory that suggest Ellen ("in her twenties") has known Rumsey (a forty-year-old farmer) and Bates (who seems to be a farmhand "in his middle-thirties") as a young girl who later fell in love with Rumsey before having an affair with—and possibly even marrying—Bates. The characters sit on chairs in three separate areas, the premier reproduction by the Royal Shakespeare Company seeming to suspend them in a space of consciousness, indicated by a mirrored back wall and floor. In performance, the play enacts an obsessive ritual of remembering in the form of intercut soliloquies, the three characters repeatedly recalling the key experiences of their intertwined emotional lives, albeit from radically different perspectives. Each character appears on stage at what appears to have been his or her age when these events occurred, yet all of their speeches indicate that these selves are now only memories, that what the audience sees is long past, while what it hears is the continuous present of consciousness. Rumsey's speech characterizes him as more refined and contemplative than Bates, whose idiolect is cruder and more rooted in direct sensuous perception. Ellen not only recounts conversations about her "wedding" with a female acquaintance who she meets in a pub, but also soliloquizes poignantly on having been in love with an older man (Rumsey?) and having rejected a somewhat younger suitor (Bates?). Emotionally, the drama revolves around loneliness and loss, each character seemingly haunted by his or her failure to make a permanent connection with another. The language is achingly lyrical, evoking the most intimate feelings of each character in an intense interplay of speech and silence that expresses the corrosive sadness of time passing and past.

Written for inclusion in the West End revue *Mixed Doubles*, the brief play *Night* (1969) advances Pinter's exploration of the processes of memory by combining an evocation of the involuntary flow of reminiscence with the rudiments of a naturalistic situation to produce an original dramaturgical form that is exhaustively employed in his next full-length drama, *Old Times* (1971). The stage directions for *Night* imply the presence of two chairs and—possibly, but not necessarily—a coffee table: "*A woman and a man in their forties. They sit with coffee*" (214). The action taking place in the present within this fragmentary location is restricted to a minimum, constituting merely the vague image of a domestic environment in which context the characters voice contradictory memories of their first meeting. As in *Landscape*, the play reveals the power of memory to create a mental world at odds with the material environment in which the characters are located; unlike *Landscape* however, the later play represents a genuine conversation between a husband and wife, who do listen to each other but whose memories of the occasion of their first meeting are opposed. His version is obsessively concerned with the physical expression of his desire for her, whereas hers is gently romantic. Each of them condenses the entire history of their marriage into a brief and fragmented series of images, in which each both acknowledges and rejects the other's construction of their relationship. The economy of the play is remarkable, evoking in a matter of minutes the progress of a marriage from romantic courtship to middle-aged compromise as an archetypal battle of the sexes redolent of lovers in a novel by D. H. Lawrence.

Like *Night*, *Old Times* does not directly exploit the stream-of-consciousness technique; nevertheless its focus on the function and effects of memory represents a continuation of the thematic concerns of *Landscape* and *Silence*. The reunion of two close female friends in the company of one of the women's husband occurs in a material environment—the living room of a converted farmhouse. As in *The Homecoming* the relationships among the characters are defined by their power struggles, but now memory is identified as the chief weapon in the war for psychological dominance over others. The archetypal Pinterian battle over territory is transmuted in *Old Times* into a ruthless competition for the emotional and spiritual possession of a person. While Kate's husband Deeley and her friend Anna each attempt to define her as the object of their affection and desire, she remains not only resolutely independent but also enigmatic, resisting all their efforts to fix her image in the memories they construct of her. For the first time in Pinter's stage drama, women onstage outnumber men; as in *The Homecoming*, the victor in the battle for power is a woman, although unlike Ruth in the earlier play the figure of Kate is never in danger of being mistaken by an audience for her image as constructed in male fantasy, and she has no need to resort to the exploitation of her sexuality in order to wield power over the other two characters.

Old Times is the shortest of the full-length plays Pinter had so far written. Lasting approximately eighty minutes if performed without an intermission, it reflects his tendency after 1965 to create shorter pieces for the theater. Although in most respects *Old Times* observes the scenic conventions of naturalism, there are a few stylized moments of action, the first at the start of the play when Anna is present in shadow at the rear of the stage before she is supposed to enter the living room in the represented location of the drama. She may not be physically present in Kate and Deeley's living room but she is present as the subject of their conversation, her uncanny "ghost" image initiating the doubleness of the play's representation of the simultaneous existence of past (in memory) and present (in the presence of the characters who are engaged in acts of remembering). In this sense Pinter is able to superimpose an epistemological drama that conveys the subtle workings of the conscious and unconscious mind upon the frame of a well-made West End play of middle-class sexual intrigue and betrayal.

Deeley's excessive curiosity about the details of Kate's friendship with Anna betrays a degree of insecurity in his own relationship with his wife that motivates what soon begins to appear as obsessive jealousy. While he repeatedly pressures Kate to analyze every detail of Anna's life and personality, she employs a series of evasive strategies to resist his compulsive desire to rationalize all aspects of their past relationship. After having been the subject of conversation for some ten minutes, the silent figure of Anna turns, the action resembling a filmic jump cut to present the reunion of the two women who had shared a room when they were young secretaries in London twenty years previously. Anna's opening speech is a flood of nostalgic images of her past life with Kate in London, conjuring an impression of a bohemian world of cultural activity and shared anticipation of future happiness:

> I mean the sheer expectation of it all, the looking-forwardness of it all, and so poor, but to be poor and young, and a girl, in London then . . . and the cafés we found, almost private ones, weren't they? Where artists and writers and sometimes actors collected, and others with dancers . . . and does it still exist I wonder? do you know? can you tell me?

> *Slight pause*

> DEELEY: We rarely get to London. (256)

Although Anna seems to address her breathless questions to Kate, it is Deeley whose reply closes down the possibility of exploring the extent to which some aspects of the London life of the fifties might still exist twenty years later. His words imply that London holds no interest for himself and Kate—that it constitutes no part of their social or cultural landscape—as if to demonstrate that his marriage to Kate has divorced her from her past life with Anna. After a brief hiatus in which coffee and brandy are offered, Anna initiates a conversation about the present situation of Kate and Deeley, introduced by her remarking on the silence of the surrounding countryside. Simply yet vividly, an audience is made to feel the calm atmosphere of the present in contrast with the bustle of the past invoked by Anna's memories—"You can hear the sea sometimes if you listen very carefully," says Deeley (257).

Underlying the apparently random flow of the conversation are signs of the rivalry that exists between Anna and Deeley as each instances her or his own knowledge of Kate's habits as definitive proof of "possessing" her. Deeley's remark to Anna, "You live on a different coast," and her reply, "Oh, very different. I live on a volcanic island" (260), hints not only at the gulf between their different mentalities, but also at Deeley's apparent need to possess knowledge of Anna's milieu as a way of protecting his relationship with Kate. "I know it [. . .] I've been there" (260) reveals a competitive desire for power. For a moment the two appear to collude in criticizing Kate, as Deeley opines, "We're forcing her to think. We must see you more often. You're a healthy influence" (263), before embarking on a song competition in which, through nostalgic prism of classic American love songs, they memorialize Kate as the object of their affection, who herself often listened with Anna to recordings of these old hits twenty years previously.

This concise and powerful theatrical sequence mobilizes the play of sentimental associations evoked by popular songs in the individual and collective memories of an audience, thereby foregrounding the subjective process of remembering itself:

> KATE: (To ANNA.) I don't know that song. Did we have it?
> DEELEY: (Singing, to KATE.) You're lovely to look at, delightful to know . . .
> ANNA: Oh we did. Yes, of course. We had them all.
> DEELEY: (Singing.) Blue moon, I see you standing alone . . .
> ANNA: (Singing.) The way you comb your hair . . .
> DEELEY: (Singing.) Oh, no they can't take that away from me. (265)

Significantly, both Anna and Deeley misremember some of the lyrics. Deeley sings "I see you" instead of "You saw me standing alone," which indicates not merely the fallibility of memory but also suggests his desire to identify Kate in the present as isolated rather than to acknowledge his own weak position in the past ("standing alone"), denoted by the correct lyric. Anna substitutes "comb your hair" for "wear your hat," possibly indicating that the song arouses her specific memories of Kate combing her hair. Both Anna and Deeley try to control the form through which the past is captured in musical and lyrical reminiscence, ignoring Kate herself in their determination to fix their own images of her in song. A few moments later each sings a lyric that signifies desire rather than memory. Deeley's "I've got a woman crazy for me. She's funny that way" (265) reflects his need to believe that Kate is still passionate about him. By singing, "They asked me how I knew / My true love was true. / I of course replied, / Something here inside / Cannot be denied" (266), Anna reiterates her parallel insistence that Kate's love for her has not died, while Deeley's "When a lovely flame dies" (266) is a maliciously competitive yet witty riposte that continues the song, "Smoke Gets in Your Eyes," while playfully denying the validity of Anna's claim to a significant relationship with Kate.

Deeley ends the sequence of remembered lyrics with the platitude, "They don't make them like that any more," and the stage direction "Silence" (267) denotes an extended moment of reverie during which the audience will assume the three characters are absorbed by their memories. Deeley himself interrupts the silence with an abrupt change of topic, speaking as if he were merely continuing the stream of memory, but in fact jumping to a completely new train of thought in recalling the time he first met Kate after seeing the film *Odd Man Out*.[5] In parallel with the way songs have been used to emblematize nostalgia for old times, Deeley may be romanticizing his own situation by association with the film's depiction of a revolutionary figure alienated from a world without compassion; nonetheless, he recalls the bug house in which he saw the film at a summer matinee screening by way of some sordid details, remembering two female usherettes who may have been masturbating in the foyer (is this entirely his fantasy?), as well as the figure of Kate seated in the auditorium:

> And there was only one other person in the cinema, one other person in the whole of the whole cinema and there she is. And there she was, very dim, very still, placed more or less I would say at the dead centre of the auditorium. I was off centre and have remained so. (267–68)

Again, Deeley conflates Kate's image in memory with her contemporaneous presence ("and there she is") before correcting himself to refer to the past only, and he positions her symbolically as central to his experience, while he was—and still is—off-center, expressing his frustration at being peripheral to her world, an odd man out. Meeting Kate in the street after the film, he invited her for coffee and they concurred in their admiration for Robert Newton's perfor-

mance. Kate remembers the film, as does Anna, but does not corrob-
orate Deeley's story of their meeting. Deeley's account of his first
sexual encounter with Kate ("our naked bodies met") is presented in
homosocial terms as a betrayal of Robert Newton and an exhibition-
istic challenge to his own rival, Anna—"What do you think he'd
think?" Deeley asks her (269). In response to the question Anna,
without missing a beat, constructs a paradoxical commentary on the
constitutive power of memory to (re)create past experience:

> I never met Robert Newton but I do know I know what you mean.
> There are some things one remembers even though they may
> never have happened. There are things I remember which may
> never have happened but as I recall them so they take place.
> (269–70)

Deeley's shocked reply of "*What?*" (270) possibly indicates a mix-
ture of surprise, incomprehension, and indignation at the implication that he has invented the particulars of the meeting to suit his
need in the present moment; whatever the case, Anna is quick to
take the upper hand by recalling her discovery of a man—presumably
Deeley—crumpled in an armchair in their flat, crying, while Kate sat
on the bed, silent. Or is she remembering an incident that never happened—as she implies Deeley has just done? During her narration of
the event, she corrects herself concerning the detail of the man walking over to her bed and looking at her, claiming in both versions, "I
would have absolutely nothing to do with him, nothing" (270). Although he left the flat, she remembers waking later to find him "lying across [Kate's] . . . lap on her bed" (271). At this point Deeley
seems to deny any involvement in the event by expressing disapproval of Kate's behavior with a stranger: "A man in the dark across
my wife's lap?" (271). Anna's desire to claim possession of Kate appears to motivate her remark that after he had left in the early morning, "It was as if he had never been," implying that the man (Deeley?)
was not important to Kate (271). Whereas Anna had obliquely cast
doubt on the veracity of Deeley's account of meeting Kate, he is
cruder in his sarcastic rejection of Anna's putative memory as a
fiction ("Well, what an exciting story that was. / *Pause.* / What did he
look like this fellow?"), pretending not to realize that Anna intended
to implicate him as the man in her account (272).

At this point in the battle between Anna and Deeley to impose on the other his or her own version of their past relationship with Kate, she rejects their attempts to manipulate her past—"You talk of me as if I were dead" (272)—before Anna's flirtation with Kate provokes Deeley's crude demand that she desist:

KATE: I said you talk of me as if I am dead. Now.
ANNA: How can you say that? How can you say that, when I'm looking at you now, seeing you so shyly poised over me, looking down at me—
DEELEY: Stop that!

Pause. (273)

Deeley then talks of Kate in typically sexist terms as a "classic female figure" (274), employing the language an art connoisseur would of a sculpture, while Anna's subsequent maneuver to keep control of Kate's image is to say how happy she was when she heard that Kate, who "had always been interested in the arts" (275), had married a filmmaker. Her speech recalling Kate's absorption in the arts ends with an account of how Kate had taken Anna "on a bus, to some totally obscure, some totally unfamiliar district and almost alone, [we] saw a wonderful film called Odd Man Out" (276).

Without appearing to react in any way to Anna's claim that *she* attended *Odd Man Out* with Kate, which contradicts Deeley's story of meeting Kate alone, Deeley clumsily but tactically changes the subject: "Yes, I do quite a bit of travelling in my job" (276). His attempt at glamorizing his image as film director leads to a discussion about how both Anna's husband and Kate cope when left alone by their respective spouses. The conversation betrays Deeley's pathetic envy of Anna's Sicilian lifestyle: "I had a great crew in Sicily. A marvelous cameraman. Irving Schultz. Best in the business. We took a pretty austere look at the women in black . . . I wrote the film and directed it. My name is Orson Welles" (280). The calculated absurdity of Deeley's claim to be Orson Welles is perhaps a strategy aimed at ridiculing what he imagines is Anna's pretentious cosmopolitanism but it merely serves to expose his own lack of self-esteem, his naked malice and uncontrollable jealousy of Anna's married life.

After a break in the discussion of Sicily indicated in the script as a silence, Anna acts as though the time has changed to the fifties, when Deeley was no longer part of her life with Kate. Behaving as if they have not eaten the casserole cooked by Kate (it has been mentioned twice already), Anna suggests that they stay in and relax, that she cook something and they listen to records. In response, Kate suggests that they go out ("We could walk across the park") to which Anna replies, "The park is dirty at night, all sorts of horrible people [. . .] and there are policemen [. . .] and you'll see all the traffic" (281–82). The conversation would only make sense if it were a flashback to the women's life in London, yet this is not a viable interpretation as Deeley is still present in the isolated farmhouse surrounded by countryside, and once interjects, "Hungry? After that casserole" (282), suggesting that Kate's meal has been eaten, even though this action has not been shown on stage. Are Kate and Anna deliberately acting out a scene from their past life in order to exclude Deeley, or are they so rapt in memory that they are behaving as though past and present have become conflated in a continuous present? As Kate exits to take her bath and the light fades on the first act, Deeley and Anna look at each other, the only certainty being that the two are locked in a psychological battle over Kate.

Old Times began by seeming to concentrate straightforwardly on the triangular relationship of a husband, his wife, and her female chum—a typical subject of bourgeois commercial drama. As usual, with Pinter's theater, however, the seemingly banal dramaturgical conventions are subverted almost from the outset, in this case by a structure that utilizes the property of the film medium to alternate the subjective viewpoint of Deeley with that of Anna; the associative flow of their memories and fantasies—these are never clearly distinguished—being interrupted at intervals by Kate's contradictory assertions or cryptic reminders of her presence in the room. As the drama intensifies, an audience becomes progressively disoriented by the complex series of contradictions and counterpoints that arise from the contrasting experiences of hearing the past remembered in words and observing the characters' behavior as they manipulate their memories of it. It is as though the writer has intercalated both Anna's and Deeley's streams of consciousness into a naturalistic play. In the last five minutes of act 1, the play begins to resemble a séance for a past life, the ghostly appearance of the past evoked in visual terms by means of minimal stage furniture that provides a spectral image of the room inhabited by Kate and Anna twenty years before. That past life, however, is itself in question. Whose memory of it is authentic? To what extent is each version a product of imagination or dream? And what is at stake now for the characters who seek to impose their image of the past in the present?

Act 2 is set in Kate and Deeley's bedroom, furnished as a mirror image of the living room, with a door to the bathroom up left, a door to the living room up right, and an armchair, while two divans are set in the place of the sofas from the previous act: *"The divans and armchair are disposed in practically the same relation to each other as the furniture in the first act, but in reversed positions"* (285). Whereas at the beginning of the first act Anna was standing upstage in shadow, the second act begins with Kate's offstage presence invoked by a *"faint glow from the glass panel in the bathroom door"* (285). After serving Anna coffee, Deeley delivers an odd and patronizing speech about the beds that suggests a psychological obsession with the many potential variations of sexual or romantic conjugation:

> We sleep here. These are beds. The great thing about these beds is that they are susceptible to any amount of permutation. They can be separated as they are now. Or placed at right angles, or one can bisect the other, or you can sleep feet to feet, or head to head, or side by side. It's the castors that make all this possible. (286)

Without any conversational transition, he continues, "Yes, I remember you quite clearly from The Wayfarers," thereby imbricating Anna as "the darling of the saloon bar" in his memory of a pub frequented by "poets, stuntmen, jockeys, stand-up comedians" (287). Although she denies any knowledge of the pub, Deeley insists upon the accuracy of his memory, producing a number of putative circumstances as evidence that they have met and talked before, and that he has bought Anna drinks. The memory of their acquaintanceship is further complicated by his account of going to a party afterward "somewhere in Westbourne Grove" (289) at which he sat opposite her and looked up her skirt—"You didn't object, you found my gaze perfectly acceptable" (289)—before a girl friend of hers (Kate?) arrived and they left together. Anna's response ("I've never heard a sadder story," is a conversational put-down reinforcing Deeley's image as odd man out, and the silence which follows ends this episode of remembering. (290)

What now follows is Deeley's voyeuristic description of the way Kate luxuriates in her bath and of her inability to dry herself properly, his suggestion that Anna help him to dry Kate being intended to identify Anna as a sexual rival who, as a woman, has an intimate knowledge of the procedure: "Listen. I'll tell you what. I'll do it. I'll do the whole lot. The towel and the powder. After all, I am her husband. But you can supervise the whole thing. And give me some hot tips while you're at it" (294). When she comes back into the bedroom from bathing, the voyeuristic objectification of Kate continues, stimulated by her own sigh of pleasure as she stands, looking out of the upstage window in the same position as Anna had occupied in the first ten minutes of the play. While Deeley and Anna watch her, they sing snatches of the Gershwins' "They Can't Take That Away from Me" again—this time remembering the lyrics correctly. As Kate sits on a divan, she forms a picture of the beauty they both desire to possess; their idealization of her achieves its apotheosis when Anna asks rhetorically, "Doesn't she look beautiful?" and Deeley concurs, "Doesn't she?" (297).

Instead of resisting their aestheticization of her as she has repeatedly done in act 1, Kate alters her strategy, choosing to treat their reduction of her person to the status of an admired object simply as a spontaneous compliment, and substituting her immediate impressions of the present moment in place of their memories:

> Thank you. I feel fresh. The water's very soft here. Much softer than
> London. I always find the water very hard in London. That's one
> reason I like living in the country. Everything's softer. The water,
> the light, the shapes, the sounds. There aren't such edges here.
> And living close to the sea too. (297)

In response to Kate's focus on present experience, Anna tries to effect a return to their past life in London, while Deeley, presumably feeling threatened, tries to revert to his memory of meeting Kate: "That's the same smile she smiled when I was walking down the street with her, after Odd Man Out, well, quite some time after" (299). Anna and Kate persist in behaving as if he were not present, talking of old friends as if they existed in the present moment. When Kate speaks affectionately of Christy ("He's so gentle, isn't he? [. . .] And I think he's . . . so sensitive. Why don't you ask him round?") Deeley jealously interrupts for the second time to neutralize the image of Christy as masculine competitor: "He can't make it. He's out of town" (301).[6]

Another silence precedes Deeley's attempt to change the subject by asking Anna if she intends to visit friends or relatives while she is in England, reinforcing his wish to remain focused on the present, but when he asks whether Anna finds Kate changed, she exploits the opportunity to recall Kate as she was, remembering in minute detail an occasion when she "borrowed" some of Kate's underwear to go to a party where a man looked up her skirt. This memory is a game in which Anna for the first time corroborates the fact that she was at the party Deeley has described (although she still doesn't identify him as the man who looked up her skirt), teasing Deeley with the notion that he may have seen Kate's underwear on her body. For the first time, Deeley explicitly acknowledges his envy of Anna and Kate's putative relationship as "a perfect marriage," but Anna quizzically admits only that they "were great friends" (304). He betrays the intensity of his jealousy by sarcastically agreeing with Anna's suggestion that Kate's passion is his "province": "I'm glad someone's showing a bit of tact at last. Of course it's my bloody province. I'm her husband. / *Pause.* / I mean I'd like to ask a question. Am I alone in beginning to find all this distasteful?" (304). Deeley continues to play the cuckolded husband by launching into an absurdly sexist rant in which he purports to be concerned about Anna's husband "rumbling about alone in his enormous villa living hand to mouth on a few hardboiled eggs and unable to speak a damn word of English," to which Kate replies that if he doesn't like Anna being with them he can go—"To China. Or Sicily" (306). In his speech, Deeley crudely expresses the archetypal misogyny of the paranoid male, self-righteously aligning himself with Anna's husband as a masculine victim of Anna's and Kate's supposed infidelity.

Anna's gesture of pouring oil on troubled waters is hypocritical, as her disingenuous assurance actually insists on the priority of her claim on Kate: "I came here not to disrupt but to celebrate [. . .] a very old and treasured friendship that was forged between us long before you knew about our existence" (306). The speech beginning "I found her" (307) reveals Anna's belief that she was responsible for Kate's cultural education, reinforcing her suggestions that Kate's sensibility has been shaped by her influence. Deeley's only possible tactic is to try to surprise his wife with the information that he had an affair with Anna after meeting at the Wayfarers' Tavern before he knew her: "She took a fancy to me. [. . .] We had a scene together. She was pretending to be you at the time. Did it pretty well. Wearing your underwear she was too, at the time" (307). Deeley's inability to separate desire, fantasy, and memory may be indicated by his uncertainty as to whether the woman he had an affair with was Anna or Kate, but Kate now joins the game, boldly collaborating in his fantasy by insisting that Anna fell in love with Deeley because, unlike most other men, he was not crass or brutish. For the first time, Anna fully corroborates Deeley's story: "Oh, it was my skirt. It was me. I remember your look . . . very well. I remember you well" (309).

Now, Kate turns the tables on the other two, creating a startling dramatic reversal as she verbalizes her own conflicting memory of Anna—"But I remember you. I remember you dead" (309)—as the action moves into a final phase in which Kate commemorates the ending of her relationships with first Anna, then Deeley, by describing a vision of Anna's face covered in dirt as she lies dead on her bed, succeeded in her memory by an occasion some time after Anna's body had gone from the room, when a man (Deeley?) lay with her on Anna's bed, until one night she "plastered his face with dirt":

> He would not let me dirty his face, or smudge it, he wouldn't let me.
> He suggested a wedding instead, and a change of environment.
>
> *Slight pause.*
>
> Neither mattered.
>
> *Pause*
>
> He asked me once, about that time, who had slept in that bed before him. I told him no one. No one at all.
>
> *Long silence.* (311)

Kate's narrative is not only bizarre but baffling. It appears to express her feeling that her past life with Anna is dead and buried, and furthermore that she regards her relationship with Deeley as existing only in the past. What is the implication of "Neither mattered"? Kate appears to be suggesting that it would have made no difference whether she married Deeley or whether they moved away from London, since in her mind he was already dead (she had plastered his face with dirt so that it resembled Anna's). An audience understands at this moment that, contrary to what has seemed to be the case throughout the play, Kate has been manipulating both relationships from its start. Deeley has been engaged with Anna in a pointless battle to win back the affection of his wife that had already died before they were married, while Anna has been laboring under the illusion that Kate harbored fond memories of a past life of mutual happiness with her.

Putative memories unexpectedly take corporeal form in the final minutes of the play. Anna and Deeley perform a mimed reenactment of the central events of the story Anna has narrated in act 1 concerning her discovery of Deeley in an armchair in their flat; there is no sound other than Deeley's quiet sobbing at the start of the mime sequence. In what appears as an uncannily ritualistic performance, first Anna, then Deeley moves toward the door as if to leave the room, but they both seem unable to do so. Anna switches off the lamps, leaving the stage in half-light, before lying on "her" divan; Deeley lies across Kate's lap on her divan before returning to sit, slumped in the armchair. The characters remain in these postures to compose a final tableau as the lighting suddenly becomes "very bright" (313). The final image appears to evoke the hell of three people trapped in an unending cycle of reminiscence in which they are forced to replay perpetually the key events that constitute the pattern of their ménage à trois—a scenario that bears a striking resemblance to the situation of Sartre's existentialist classic, *Huis Clos*.[7] In retrospect, act 2 appears to represent the mechanisms by which people compulsively engage in revising or remaking their past as experience changes their lives. Tragically, Deeley and Anna are unable to leave the past behind. Their obsessive desire to reassemble their memories suggests that for some reason neither of them can overcome the devastating reality that Kate has moved beyond them emotionally. Kate herself remains something of an enigma at the end, but the fact that her rejection of the others motivates the final ceremonial game intimates that she possesses emotional reserves that neither of the other two has ever discovered.

In its assumptions about gender, *Old Times* represents a distinct advance on *The Homecoming*. Pinter proves more than capable of representing heterosexual conflicts and fantasies on stage from the subject positions of both male and female characters. While the femininity of Kate and Anna may paradoxically attract and disturb Deeley, and Kate's unwillingness or inability to exhibit her feelings and thoughts for the benefit of others may render her behavior opaque or enigmatic, Anna is every bit as much the subject of the drama as Deeley, and Kate proves herself more than a match for both of them in the surprising reversal she engineers at the close of the action. When Deeley constructs sexualized images of Kate or Anna, these are clearly shown as his creation, and the projection of his subjective version of reality upon their figures is revealed as a function of dream, fantasy, or memory—and this is equally true of the way the two women manipulate their subjective experience. *Old Times* explicitly focuses on the actual process by means of which people rearrange the raw data of experience to create memories. Throughout the play, an audience is as conscious of the mechanisms through which the faculty of memory functions as it is of the content of the memories. In this way, Pinter succeeds in drawing into the ambit of the commercial theater the form of an epistemological drama pioneered by Beckett.

CHAPTER 6

Ghost Lives:
No Man's Land

Of all Pinter's plays *No Man's Land* (1975) is probably the one that audiences find most difficult to comprehend. On the surface, the plot is entirely baffling. There is no discernable framework of exposition that might enable a spectator to decipher the many puzzles presented by the fragmentary action being witnessed on stage. Having met at Jack Straw's Castle, a pub on the northwestern edge of Hampstead Heath, two old men retire to the Hampstead home of Hirst. who, it later emerges, is a distinguished man of letters. His guest Spooner is somewhat raffish and down-at-heels, claiming to be a poet who clears the tables at the Bull's Head pub in Chalk Farm as well as organizing regular poetry readings in a room upstairs.[1] Halfway through act I two men named Foster and Briggs turn up unexpectedly and begin to behave as though they were Hirst's guardians, interrogating Spooner in a rude and insinuating manner. Other than the consumption of large amounts of alcohol, virtually nothing happens in the play The characters inhabit a large and decorous reception room containing a bar, and drink whisky and champagne while engaging in rather self-conscious conversations in which they introduce themselves in deliberately obscure and equivocal ways; they make ambiguous or contradictory assertions and tell brief autobiographical stories that seem intended to intrigue, mystify, or intimidate rather than to enlighten the listener.

The apparently static nature of the action is designed to provide a close-up focus on themes first articulated in *Old Times*, the later play experimenting with alternative methods of representing the interrelated functions of memory, dream, imagination, fantasy, and immediate sensory perception in the production of what philosophers have called the *lebenswelt* (lived experience of the world).[2] At times the play itself seems almost to be a discourse on the very possibility of representing life in dramatic form, the *reductio* of exposition, character, and plot to a level of skeletal abstraction where virtually nothing can be known for certain except the bare fact that the audience actually witnesses two older and two younger men enter and exit a particular room at particular times, and engage in a series of conversations that occasionally seem to cohere in the construction of a fictional world, before seeming completely to negate that fiction in the elaboration of a different one. The play seems at times to be a self-referential joke about the typical incoherence of a Pinter play.[3]

Hirst, who in the first scene has fallen down drunk and crawled out of the room to bed before returning later that night in a maudlin and depressed state, bounds into the drawing room the following morning (act 2), brimming with joie de vivre and greets Spooner as Charles Wetherby, an old friend whom he has known since his student days at Oxford. Spooner seemingly accepts the new identity projected onto him and joins in a game of mutual reminiscence. The situation presented in act 1 is completely contradicted by the picaresque backstory narrated with histrionic flourish by Hirst in act 2 and the audience is left to unravel the meaning of a series of disconnected autobiographical episodes, many of which seem to comprise improbable literary narratives that are not wholly credible as accounts of the characters' lives or motives. The people in the play seem impelled to spin intriguing stories of their past experience in order to construct personae that, while satisfying their own present needs, nevertheless constitute inadequate or incoherent accounts of the causal relationship between past and present. In the world evoked by *No Man's Land*, individual identity appears impossible to ascertain, personality serving as a mask to protect one from being known by others. Indeed, the very possibility of integrated selfhood is challenged by the way in which the conventional dramaturgical notion of character is deconstructed.

With the exception of the mysterious Hirst, every character is instinctively pretentious; it is as if each were manufacturing an exotic persona in order to dignify his position or glamorize his self-image. This aspect of the play in some respects parallels the way characters in *Old Times* seem to be inventing the past in order to maintain or enhance their present position; however the later play involves not merely each individual's manipulation of memories but the invention of a persona as an emblem of sensibility—potentially a new theme in Pinter's work. Spooner and Foster in particular seem self-consciously determined to project images of themselves as intelligent and sophisticated. In Spooner's case, this involves an extreme literary preciosity; he is continually half-quoting the poetry of T. S. Eliot or making a pastiche of literary references to demonstrate an easy familiarity with the language of an aristocratic high culture that is not his own by right of birth:

> SPOONER: I'm a staunch friend of the arts, particularly the art of po-
> etry, and a guide to the young. I keep open house. Young poets
> come to me. They read me their verses. I comment, give them
> coffee, make no charge [. . .] But with the windows open to the
> garden, my wife pouring long glasses of squash, with ice, on a
> summer evening, young voices occasionally lifted in unaccompa-
> nied ballad, young bodies lying in the dying light, my wife mov-
> ing through the shadows in her long gown, what can ail? I mean
> who can gainsay us? What quarrel can be found with what is, *au
> fond,* a gesture towards the sustenance and preservation of art,
> and through art to virtue? (333–34)[4]

When he is left alone on stage by Hirst, Spooner somewhat portentously generalizes the relation between present and past experience, alluding to T. S. Eliot's *The Love Song of J. Alfred Prufrock* in evoking the process by which memory enables the interpretation of an equivocal present: "I have known this before. The exit through the door by way of belly and floor" (340). This pseudo-poetic commentary is repeated with variations at the beginning of the second act.[5] Such self-conscious literary and philosophical posturing reveals Spooner as a cheap snob, someone whose rhetorical style is so polished that it unwittingly exposes his deliberate characterization of himself as "a man of intelligence and perception" (323) to be a parody of the real thing:

Although wives and mistresses are spoken of, it is remarkable that after a series of plays that focus almost exclusively on the differences between masculine and feminine cultures of romantic love (*Landscape, Silence, Night, Old Times*) there are no female characters in *No Man's Land.* By way of compensating for the absence of women, Foster and Spooner both at times adopt passive feminine positions in their interaction with others, Foster teasing the older men with the nubile pliability of a prostitute desirous to give pleasure and Spooner offering to be Hirst's secretary-companion in a manner that echoes his earlier intimations of a repressed but romanticized homosexual predisposition. In *Monologue* (1973), the representation of conflicting perspectives created by a difference of gender is replaced by a man's obsessive recollections of his rivalry with a friend for possession of a woman. A significant aspect of the man's relentless battle to repair his injured sense of masculinity is his accusation that his friend has, in adopting the bourgeois aspirations of the middle class, compromised the integrity of his working-class roots. Such a remaking of self is portrayed by the man (who has lost the woman to his friend) as the betrayal of their shared culture resulting from the pretentious effort to achieve higher social status. A similar observation of the effect of class in the formation of cultural values is present in *No Man's Land,* but here it has become central to the rhetorical and theatrical argument of the play. The setting of the action in the upper-middle-class environment of an expensive Hampstead home and the fact that all the characters are men, gives especial prominence to differences in English class and culture characterized by Pinter's razor-sharp observations of social behavior. Whereas he had earlier in his career shown a remarkable facility in reproducing a variety of working-class and middle-class English dialects,[6] Pinter now for the first time presents a direct clash of cultures through the contrasting speech idioms of four men.

This new theme surely reflects Pinter's pleasurable year working on a screenplay for Marcel Proust's *À la recherche du temps perdu* commissioned by the film director Joseph Losey. Clearly Proust's extensive detailing of the decadent beauty of an aristocratic culture seen through the eyes of a middle-class observer (Marcel) has influenced Pinter's portrayal of the infiltration of Hirst's world of traditional elegance and classic beauty by Spooner—a pretentious connoisseur whose voyeuristic appreciation of its pleasures is matched by his jealousy of its owner. Many of the comic moments in the play are provided by the confrontation of the expert pretensions of Spooner with the crude and clumsy efforts of the servants Foster and Briggs, to act up to the cultural ethos of their master. Another opposition of cultures in the play is created by the age difference between

Hirst and Spooner (both in their sixties), Briggs (in his forties), and Foster (in his thirties). This is indicated through their deliberately contrasted manners and rhetorical styles, reflecting the way tastes and fashions effect changes in "lifestyle" over time.

Unlike Spooner, the younger Foster and Briggs, although they seem to be paid to minister to Hirst's needs, are incapable of empathizing with their master's past experience or appreciating the traditional literary and esthetic values that bespeak high culture. The limits of their education and age prevent them from seeing him as anything other than an important man whose wealth buys him power and status—"class" in the egalitarian American sense of the word. On the other hand, Spooner's ability to comprehend the complex and subtle signifying systems of a sophisticated culture is a mode of interpretation akin to that of aesthetic or literary analysis. With the trained eye of an art critic, Spooner deciphers and analyzes every nuance of speech or behavior, every item of clothing or décor that he encounters. Foster attempts to compete with him—albeit crudely—in this respect; however, Briggs's naive inability to interpret cultural signs and attitudes with appropriate subtlety, makes him the butt of theatrical jokes:

> FOSTER: You've just laid your hands on a rich and powerful man. It's not what you're used to, scout . . . This is another class. It's another realm of operation. It's a world of silk. It's a world of organdie. It's a world of flower arrangements. It's a world of eighteenth-century cookery books. It's nothing to do with toffeeapples and a packet of crisps. It's milk in the bath. It's the cloth bellpull. It's organization.
>
> BRIGGS: It's not rubbish.
> FOSTER: It's not rubbish. We deal in originals. Nothing duff, nothing ersatz, we don't open any old bottle of brandy. (355–56)

Although clearly intended to diminish Spooner's cosmopolitan posture as one of the cognoscenti, Foster's crude warning to the older man to keep off his territory is couched in the grossly materialistic language of the social climber. Its unintentional travesty of the typical jargon of television commercials for expensive liquor or an estate agent's catalog of houses for sale to the nouveaux riches, reveals him as a callow and uneducated young boor. While lacking the social sophistication of Spooner, Foster is nevertheless quite as capable of deliberate mystification in order to confuse the visitor as to the precise nature of the relationships in the Hampstead household. Although not explicit, the hints at a homosexual element in the relationships among the men add another layer to the game of detecting hidden motives; Briggs and Foster certainly appear to entertain the possibility that they or the other men conceal a homosexual interest in one or other of the four, as indeed does Spooner in his initial attempts to discover Hirst's domestic circumstances in act 1. After his long and ingratiating speech to Hirst near the start of the play, Spooner asks a blunt question that always gets a huge laugh in the theater, "Do you often hang about Hampstead Heath?" (323). This is funny, partly because its directness is in sharp contrast with the florid rhetoric of Spooner's pretentious introductory speech, but also because the area of Hampstead Heath behind Jack Straw's Castle (the pub where the men later confirm they have met) had by 1975 become fairly well known in London as a gay cruising ground.

Not only does the idea of two highly cultivated old men "hanging about" such an area produce comic incongruity, it also introduces some doubts about their motives:

> SPOONER: I often hang about Hampstead Heath myself, expecting nothing. I'm too old for any kind of expectation. Don't you agree? . . . But of course I observe a good deal, on my peeps through twigs [. . .] I do feel it incumbent upon me to make one thing clear. I don't peep on sex. That's gone forever. You follow me? When my twigs shall I say rest their peep on sexual conjugations, however periphrastic, I see only whites of eyes, so close, they glut me, no distance possible. (324–25)

Referring to a need to maintain a distance from one's own emotional experience in terms similar to those of Teddy in *The Homecoming,* Spooner shows an awareness that Hampstead Heath is a regular location for sexual assignations of all kinds, and entertains the possibility that Hirst may have invited him home for the purpose of a sexual liaison:

> SPOONER: I have gone too far, you think?
> HIRST: I'm expecting you to go much further.
> SPOONER: Really? That doesn't mean I interest you, I hope?
> HIRST: Not in the least.

SPOONER: Thank goodness for that. For a moment my heart sank.
(326)

Spooner then tries to ascertain whether Hirst is involved in an intimate relationship by asking "Is there another?" (327) and talks, lovingly, of his own friendship with a Hungarian émigré he met years before at Jack Straw's Castle, as though his putative relationship with Hirst might turn out to be comparable:

SPOONER: It is not what he said, but possibly the way he sat which has remained with me all my life and has, I am quite sure, made me what I am.

Pause

And I met you at the same pub tonight, although at a different table. (331)

The extended cat-and-mouse game by means of which Spooner attempts to make Hirst clarify his motives for bringing him back to his home, can be seen as a kind of platonic seduction, revealing Spooner's willingness to mold his own identity to any form according with Hirst's needs.

In context, the louche nonchalance exhibited by Foster in his introductory encounter with Spooner can be interpreted as the insolent familiarity assumed by a slick young gangster or a rent boy whose identity is unstable and whose sexual orientation ambivalent:

FOSTER: What are you drinking? Christ, I'm thirsty. How are you? I'm parched [. . .] I'm worn to a frazzle. This is what I want. (*He drinks.*) Taxi? No chance. Taxi drivers are against me. Something about me. Some unknown factor. My gait perhaps . . . Or perhaps because I travel incognito [. . .] How are you? What are you drinking? Who are you? I thought I'd never make it [. . .] I'm defenceless. I don't carry a gun in London. But I'm not bothered. Once you've done the East, you've done it all. I've done the East. (341)

Possibly because Foster is discomposed by the solitary presence of a stranger in Hirst's living room, he chatters relentlessly to mask his surprise without giving Spooner a chance to speak; however he soon asserts his proprietorial rights to the territory by casually claiming—although this is an obvious untruth—to be Hirst's son:

FOSTER: Have you met your host? He's my father. It was our night off
tonight, you see. [. . .] Who are you, by the way? What are you
drinking?
SPOONER: I'm a friend of his.
FOSTER: You're not typical. (341–42)

The final put-down insinuates either that Spooner is too old to be
a homosexual pickup, or that he is too shabby to be a suitable friend
to the distinguished man. Foster's presumption that Spooner is lying
or exaggerating the case is further elaborated when Briggs enters and
Foster continues insultingly, "His name's Friend. This is Mr Briggs.
Mr Friend—Mr Briggs. I'm Mr Foster. Old English stock. John Foster.
Jack. Jack Foster. Old English name. Foster. John Foster. Jack Foster.
Foster. This man's name is Briggs" (342). The aggressive and sarcastic parody of old-fashioned gentility is intended to humiliate Spooner
by casting doubt on the veracity of his claim to be Hirst's friend, and
to advertise Foster's own credentials; it also elaborates the motif of
friendship that preoccupies Hirst throughout the play, drawing attention to the distinction between the unselfish generosity of true
friendship and the self-interested trading in affection that characterizes most social relationships. Although the insult is spun out for
some minutes, Spooner is imperturbable and, instead of being
shocked by Briggs's lewd implications that Foster is "loved at first
sight" by Siamese girls, he counters with his own deliberately mystifying account of a visit to Amsterdam:

SPOONER: I've been to Amsterdam.

FOSTER and BRIGGS stare at him.

I mean that was the last place . . . I visited. I know Europe well. My
name is Spooner, by the way. Yes, one afternoon in Amsterdam
. . . I was sitting outside a café by a canal. The weather was superb.
At another table, in shadow, was a man whistling under his
breath [. . .] I decided to paint a picture of the canal, the waiter, the
child, the fisherman, the lovers, the fish, and in background, in
shadow, the man at the other table, and to call it The Whistler.
The Whistler. If you had seen the picture, and the title, would the
title have baffled you? (345)

In some respects Spooner's obscure narrative is a tactic designed
to neutralize Foster's impertinent insinuations that he is an oppor-

tunistic exploiter of Hirst's loneliness who operates according to the same low morality as Foster does. Foster responds with a crude denial of the imputation that he lacks the sophistication of the true connoisseur: "Well, speaking for myself, I think I would have been baffled by that title. But I might have appreciated the picture [. . .] A good work of art tends to move me . . . I'm not a cunt you know" (346). Foster's story of a naked beggar "out East" who played a trick on him while soliciting a coin is an attempt to outdo Spooner, responding to Spooner's emblematic puzzle on the oblique relationship between reality and its representation in art by parodying Spooner's pretentiousness in the form of a meretricious conundrum. In spite of Spooner's patronizing assertion of superiority as an art critic and savant, Foster reveals himself to be every bit as cunning in recognizing the games Spooner plays and inventing his own strategies to outmaneuver him:

> SPOONER: You would be wise to grant the event no integrity whatso-
> ever.
> FOSTER: You don't subscribe to the mystery of the Orient?
> SPOONER: A typical Eastern contrick.
> FOSTER: Double Dutch you mean? (348–49)

Foster's story implicitly casts Spooner in the role of the Eastern beggar, insinuating that he is trying to penetrate Hirst's defenses by tricking his way into his confidence through intellectual sleight-of-hand ("Double Dutch" is a snide jibe at Spooner's Amsterdam story). Both autobiographical episodes are presented in the form of symbolic narratives that demand interpretation of the kind normally required by complex works of art. Just before the close of act 1, Foster describes his uncanny sighting of a man carrying two umbrellas in the Australian outback and, near the beginning of act 2, Briggs continues this peculiar series of accounts of unexpected incidents in odd places with his memorable and often-cited story of how he directed Foster to Bolsover Street in the West End of London on their first meeting:

> BRIGGS: It was a one-way system easy enough to get into. The only
> trouble was once in you couldn't get out. I told him his best bet,
> if he really wanted to get to Bolsover street, was to take the first
> left, first right, second right, third on the left, keep his eye open
> for a hardware shop, go right round the square, keeping to the in-

side lane, take the second Mews on the right and then stop. He will find himself facing a very tall office block, with a crescent courtyard. He can go round the crescent, come out the other way, follow the arrows, go past the two sets of traffic lights and take the next left indicated by the first green filter he comes across. He's got the Post Office Tower in his vision the whole time. All he's got to do is to reverse into the underground car park, change gear, go straight on, and he'll find himself in Bolsover Street with no trouble at all. I did warn him though that he'll still be faced with the problem, having found Bolsover Street, of losing it. (366)

The virtuoso comic speech is not only a delightfully exaggerated depiction of the real difficulties of driving in the rabbit warren of one-way streets in central London but also a metaphor for the obfuscation created by the failure of systems originally intended to aid human commerce and communication that emblematizes the puzzles created by the characters in defense of their privacy.

Hirst and Spooner belong to a generation that grew to maturity in the heyday of the British Empire between the two world wars. If one believes Hirst's account of his youth in the second act, then he experienced an idyllic life in the company of Spooner (Charles Wetherby?) and others as a student at Oxford in the thirties. This extended sequence of actual or assumed memories, signified by Hirst's nostalgic fondness for his photograph album, portrays the tendency of older people to memorialize the past as a period of vitality and youthful expectation, by contrast with the prospect of stasis and decay that appears to constitute the "no man's land" of an unchanging present. The images that both Hirst and Spooner adduce in remembering past experiences and customs, and the style in which they represent them, creates a pastiche of the literature that has mythicized the romantic image of prewar England to the point where history is indistinguishable from fiction:

> HIRST: When did we last meet? I have a suspicion we last dined together in '38 at the club. Does that accord with your recollection? Croxley was there, yes, Wyatt, it all comes back to me, Burston-Smith. What a bunch. What a night, as I recall. All dead now, of course. No, no! I'm a fool. I'm an idiot. Our last encounter—I remember it well. Pavilion at Lord's in '39, against the West Indies, Hutton and Compton batting superbly, Constantine bowling, war looming. Surely I'm right? We shared a particularly fine bottle of

port. You look as fit now as you did then. Did you have a good war? (372–73)

By contrast with Hirst, however, Spooner is not living in a no man's land of fixed memories that are "all in my [photograph] album" (350), for he regards his invitation to Hirst's home as an opportunity to gain a foothold in the realm of upper-class culture that he has been educated to appreciate without being wealthy enough to afford. While Hirst seems lost in memories and dreams, Spooner is operating tactically in the present, studying the situation that confronts him and adapting his own behavior and personality to fit what he perceives to be Hirst's requirements and to combat the danger represented by Foster and Briggs.

Significantly, Spooner does not reply to any of Hirst's questions, allowing him to prattle for almost five minutes while he tries to make sense of the unexpected scenario that Hirst appears to be constructing. This section of the drama is so unlike what has gone before and what follows that it appears almost as though a Terence Rattigan comedy from the thirties has been inserted as a play-within-a-Pinter-play. An audience is delightfully but wholly disoriented by the theatrical conceit, enjoying the witty style of the thirties pastiche, while completely baffled as to how it could relate to the situation of the characters they have hitherto witnessed. Spooner himself is clearly taken aback but as usual, he strives to appear nonchalant before permitting himself to collaborate in performing Hirst's blimpish variations on the theme of English upper-middle-class life in the thirties and forties:

HIRST: You did say you had a good war, didn't you?
SPOONER: A rather good one, yes.
HIRST: How splendid. The RAF?
SPOONER: The Navy.
HIRST: How splendid. Destroyers?
SPOONER: Torpedo boats.
HIRST: First rate. Kill any Germans?
SPOONER: One or two.
HIRST: Well done. (375)

Without at first appearing to adopt a different persona, Spooner responds with the typical clichés concerning military service that would signify in generic terms the experience of any educated or upper-class Englishman of his generation. A few moments later, however, he appears to play his own variation on Hirst's game, inserting himself subtly into Hirst's nostalgic memories of Oxford by adopting his own impeccable pastiche of the style:

SPOONER: Do you ever see Stella?

Pause.

HIRST: Stella?
SPOONER: You can't have forgotten.
HIRST: Stella who?
SPOONER: Stella Winstanley.
HIRST: Winstanley?
SPOONER: Bunty Winstanley's sister.
HIRST: Oh, Bunty. No, I never see her.
SPOONER: You were rather taken with her.
HIRST: Was I, old chap? How did you know?
SPOONER: I was terribly fond of Bunty. He was most dreadfully annoyed with you. Wanted to punch you on the nose.
HIRST: What for?
SPOONER: For seducing his sister. (376–77)

Quite early in this play-within-the-Pinter-play, it becomes apparent that the bucolic prewar life summoned up in memory is in fact corrupted by the same duplicity, competitiveness, and malicious compulsion to betray friendships that typifies the men's relationships in the present. The charming facade of lost gentility is merely an illusion, and no moral distinction can be drawn between time present and time past. Whether or not Hirst and Spooner were actually the friends conjured up in Hirst's memories hardly matters because the golden time of his memory is exposed as a myth by Spooner's revelations of secret infidelity. Hirst is forced to recognize that his "true" friendships were false, and the action returns to the situation represented in act 1.

Which of the play's two versions of reality is "real"—that presented in act 1 in which Hirst and Spooner have just met? Or the version in act 2 in which Hirst recognizes Spooner as his old friend, Charles Wetherby? In some ways one can make sense of *No Man's Land* without finding a solution to the puzzle of these contradictory narratives. In psychological terms, the play portrays the gulf between the nostalgic memory of the past—which may be indistinguishable from a cherished fiction—and the historical fact of what happened. Both versions challenge an audience to discriminate love or true friendship from self-motivated sexual interest and the habitual bartering of flattery and affection consistent with everyday social intercourse. As usual in Pinter's drama, the four characters' motives appear ambivalent and their behavior mystifying. Any interpretation that can be made is subsequently contradicted, so the effort to identify genuine feelings beneath equivocal social surfaces is rendered entirely problematic. Exceptionally, however, Hirst exhibits true politesse in his speech and manners. His sophisticated response to Spooner's behavior, reveals both refinement and intelligence, even though his bluff and disinterested attitude—perhaps a consequence of his heavy drinking throughout the play—suggests that he has lost his curiosity regarding other people or new experiences, and no longer possesses a need to compete with other men: "Tonight . . . my friend . . . you find me in the last lap of a race . . . I had long forgotten to run" (338).

Although his companions appear to be either paid carers or self-serving strangers, Hirst's desire for genuine friendship is implied in various ways throughout the play, forming a leitmotif that expresses the essentially human need for the gentility, kindness, affection, and charity that characterize proper friendship. His own references to having been depressed and lonely reflect a desperate need for the comfort of others:

> HIRST: How nice to have company. Can you imagine waking up, finding no-one here, just furniture staring at you? Most unpleasant. I've known that condition, I've been through that period—cheers—I came round to human beings in the end. Like yourselves. A wise move. I tried laughing alone. Pathetic. (350)

His subsequent request for another drink is couched as a plea for kindness: "Who is the kindest among you? . . . Thank you. What would I do without the two of you? I'd sit here forever, waiting for a stranger to fill up my glass" (351). In offering to help Hirst when Briggs is manhandling him, Spooner insists, "He has grandchildren. As have I. As I have. We both have fathered. We are of an age. I know his wants. Let me take his arm. Respect our age [. . .] There's no pity in these people [. . .] I am your true friend" (353–54). Spooner's empathy with Hirst at this point appears as one of the few occasions when he is genuinely concerned for Hirst's well-being, yet it is interpreted as guileful manipulation by Foster, whose speech concerning his own role and Briggs's as Hirst's carers characterizes them as thuggish minders: "Listen, chummybum. We protect this gentleman against corruption, against men of craft, against men of evil, we could destroy you without a glance, we take care of this gentleman, we do it out of love" (355).

Exploiting Hirst's perceived need for friendship, the other three characters behave as rivals in an ambivalent courtship to secure Hirst's favor. Hirst seems to have given up seeking to establish lasting friendships, choosing instead to pay Briggs and Foster to assist him in maintaining his world of images—memories, dreams, and photographs. Instead of trying to disorient his companions by the construction of a mystifying mask, Hirst shares with them his enigmatic dream images of a waterfall or lake, and a figure running through trees, who then seems to drown in the water. The dream is recounted most clearly in the final minutes of the action:

> HIRST: I am walking towards a lake. Someone is following me, through the trees. I lose him, easily. I see a body in the water, floating. I am excited. I look closer and see I was mistaken. There is nothing in the water. I say to myself, I saw a body drowning. But I am mistaken. There is nothing there.
>
> *Silence*
>
> SPOONER: No. You are in no man's land. Which never moves, which never changes, which never grows older, but which remains forever, icy and silent.
>
> *Silence*
>
> HIRST: I'll drink to that.
>
> *He drinks* (399)

"No man's land" itself is a term dating from medieval times that indicates a strip of unoccupied land whose ownership is in dispute; its modern meaning derives most especially from its use in World War I to indicate the land left empty between the boundaries of two enemy forces. In such a no man's land, only the dead or dying might be found. The image provides a haunting metaphor for the ghostly experience of an existence between life and death, where no action occurs, but people wait—either to die or to go on merely waiting.

The dream is difficult to interpret, and its various reiterations in the play tease the audience with the idea that any reading of it involves a degree of subjective introjection. Does Hirst perceive an image of himself drowning in the lake—a symbol of his imminent death? Is the figure a life partner who has already died? If there was ultimately no one drowning, was the image merely a product of his own desire or fear? Earlier, Spooner has interpreted the man in the dream as himself, possibly an opportunistic strategy to demonstrate his potential significance as Hirst's friend. Spooner's image of no man's land—repeated with slight variations from Hirst's speech in the first act—can refer to the transitional state between life and death, to the perfect stasis of an artwork; to photographs that fix each subject in an eternal instant in time, freezing particular moments as unchanging memories; to the alienating state of clinical depression; to the haze of alcoholic torpor, which blots out the individual's sense of responsibility for action; or it could represent the purgatorial stasis of old age, when all expectations of growth and change give way to a state of retrospective contemplation. Each of these interpretations can be fairly applied to Hirst's condition, yet although he believes he is an inhabitant of no man's land, ironically at the end of the play he perceives that in old age it may still be possible to experience the present in a creative way, albeit without the great expectations of youth. A conversation shortly before the above excerpt concerns the implications of having changed the subject for the last time, yet the fact that Hirst hears birds suggests that this is not so, for the fact that he remains aware of life continuing, negates the total sense of spiritual and emotional death emblematized by the idea of no-man's-land:

HIRST: It's night.
FOSTER: And will always be night.
BRIGGS: Because the subject—
FOSTER: Can never be changed.

Silence.

HIRST: But I hear the sounds of birds. Don't you hear them? Sounds I
  never heard before. I hear them as they must have sounded then,

when I was young, although I never heard them then, although they sounded about us then. (398–99)

Significantly, old age brings Hirst a more sensitive awareness of phenomena as they exist around him, for the simple reason that he is no longer engaged in the youthful struggle to act upon the world around him. Old age may not be a purgatory, but a time to live more deeply in the world by savoring phenomena without the compulsive need to manipulate them in achieving self-definition.

Perception of the phenomenal world includes deciphering the appearances encountered in both the natural and cultural realms. This requires the ability to interpret every social persona and every sensory phenomenon as if it were a work of art. Such a focus on the act of interpretation is particularly apposite in a play whose two central characters are themselves creative writers and professional critics. Although never overtly expressed by any character, the relationships between art and criticism and between the experience of life and its expression through art, dream, or fantasy underpin the action of the entire play, motivating the inexplicable shifts from one topic of conversation to another. Rather than developing in a cause-and-effect pattern, the action follows the associative flow of conversation, spiraling continuously back upon itself, without any real sense of progression. The situation in the household is a paradigm of social existence—a series of puzzling appearances and alienating fragments of narrative to be interpreted by Spooner as an art critic analyzes a work of art. By representing characters who are connoisseurs and critics of art, No Man's Land self-reflexively offers the ambiguous surfaces of Pinter's own dramaturgy as the basis for a series of metatheatrical reflections on the demand made by brute reality for the kind of explication necessitated by postmodern theater.

A number of reviewers criticized the play in its original production as too self-consciously Pinteresque, as if, lacking inspiration, the playwright was merely recycling earlier motifs and styles. With the benefit of hindsight, No Man's Land can be seen as a highly original experiment. As always with Pinter's drama, the play models for the audience an experience of how it feels to be in world of bewildering surfaces, rather than supplying a straightforward allegorical meaning. The play itself is about the problem of how we construct meaning from the shards of our raw experience, employing the process of interpreting art as a paradigmatic illustration of that problem. While it recapitulates the core motifs that run through Pinter's oeuvre, it produces a metadramatic reflection on the epistemological drama that every person experiences in trying to ascribe meaning to existence.

CHAPTER 7

"The Art of Taking Away": *Betrayal*

Years after *Betrayal* (1978) was written Pinter admitted that it was based on his affair with the journalist and broadcaster Joan Bakewell that took place between 1962 and 1969. It is unique among his stage plays in being based directly and in detail on autobiographical experience.[1]

> *Betrayal* . . . is about my relationship with Harold . . . It's accurate in its chronology and in its events. Often quite tiny events like that in which Jerry talks about picking up this little girl . . . and throwing her in the air. Harold actually did that with my three-year-old daughter. (Billington, 264–65)

Although the triangular relationship of Emma, Robert, and Jerry corresponds in most particulars to the situation of Joan Bakewell, her husband, and Pinter himself, there are differences, the chief one being that Michael Bakewell and Pinter were never intimate friends. As a radio producer he had been an early champion of Pinter's work, who had encouraged the fledgling playwright in 1958 to write *A Slight Ache* for the BBC radio drama department, but, although on good terms professionally, they had never been close personal friends. Pinter himself believes that a writer inevitably draws on his own experience:[2]

> I think every writer does that in one way or another. Otherwise what are we writing about? We're writing about something to do with ourselves and observable reality about us . . . If you're true to that, then

you're not doing any harm . . . What can I say about *Betrayal?* . . . I did that. (Billington, 258)

The overt metatheatricality that in *No Man's Land* expresses the relationship between raw experience and its representation as literature is elaborated in different ways in *Betrayal.* After ten very brief lines of dialogue, Emma's quip, "Just like old times" (4),[3] must have struck the play's first audiences as a teasingly Stoppardian pun on the title of Pinter's last full-length play but one, reminding them that a Proustian conception of the remembrance of past times had been a key motif in his stage drama and screenplays since 1966. Such an arch joke about the way in which life imitates art is entirely appropriate to the literary and artistic milieu depicted in *Betrayal,* and it signals the reciprocal parasitism of art and life that is a thematic leitmotif in the play. During the course of the action Emma becomes the successful curator of an art gallery; Robert is a publisher, while Jerry is a literary agent who works as representative for one of the play's two chief "offstage" characters, a writer called Casey who in 1974 moved from Hampstead to live "alone round the corner" from Robert and Emma and is "writing a novel about a man who leaves his wife and three children and goes to live alone on the other side of London to write a novel about a man who leaves his wife and three children" (53). Emma thinks Casey's previous novel "about the man who lived in a big house in Hampstead with his wife and three children and is writing a novel . . . about" (53) was "bloody dishonest" (54), invoking a distinction between artistic truth and verisimilitude that is a consistent theme of *Betrayal.*

If any Pinter play demonstrates his inventiveness in the constant experimentation with form to enable new perspectives on abiding thematic preoccupations, it is *Betrayal.* Although the development of its plot proceeds in reverse chronology from 1977 to 1968, thereby allowing the experience of old times to be incrementally retrieved, the play is less preoccupied with the vagaries of memory in constructing the past than it is with the nature of betrayal. In the clockwork precision of its plotting the play is a tour de force that has little in common with *Old Times* or *No Man's Land.* While being as deeply concerned with the relationship between present and past as these two plays, its extreme economy in the deployment of action and speech represents a wholly new departure for Pinter. Whereas past time is evoked entirely through the agency of memory in the earlier plays, *Betrayal* employs the cinematic device of extended flashback that Pinter had so successfully exploited in his screenplays for *Accident* (1967), *The Go-Between* (1969), and *À la recherche du temps perdu* (written 1972) in order to stage past events as they are actually happening. The play offers no serious examination of the problematic effect of memory in inventing or transforming the events of the past. Its scenic scheme is designed to expose the ways in which Emma's marriage, Jerry and Robert's friendship, and Jerry and Emma's clandestine love affair become progressively corrupted by the necessity of lying. In promoting each audience member's reflection on the causal process through which the future is constituted by present actions, the backward movement of the plot emphasizes the pattern of intricate deceptions and complex jealousies that proceed from a romantic infatuation in a relentless chain of causes and effects.

By successively peeling away layer on layer of deceptions that have accreted during nine years of secret lovemaking from the first adulterous impulse to a reunion of the lovers two years after the end of their affair, *Betrayal* anatomizes the progress of their relationship, revealing its cost in emotional terms, without ever adopting a glib moralistic attitude. When they were students, Robert and Jerry had edited poetry magazines at Oxford and Cambridge respectively; their betrayal of high art in favor of the pragmatic choice of earning a living by the buying and selling of novels is equivalent to the manifold betrayals of the ideals of undying love and faithful friendship signified by the title of the play:

JERRY: [Casey is] over the hill
ROBERT: Is he?
JERRY: Don't you think so?
ROBERT: In what respect?
JERRY: His work. His books.
ROBERT: Oh his books. His art. Yes his art does seem to be falling away, doesn't it?
JERRY: Still sells.
ROBERT: Oh, sells very well. Sells very well indeed. Very good for us. For you and me. (35–36)

It is not improbable to speculate that this exchange reflects Pinter's experience with the first production of *No Man's Land,* which although a popular success at the Old Vic and on its transfer to the West End in 1975, had provoked the criticism that a failure of artistic imagination was causing the writer to repeat his own mannerisms. The accusations of self-parody suggest that certain reviewers mistook the subtly critical presentation of Spooner's literary pretentiousness for a failed attempt by the playwright to achieve poetic resonance, and also missed the point of the pastiche of interwar theater in the second act. In the case of *Betrayal* three years later, a few journalists mistook Pinter's conscious deconstruction of the well-made theater of Rattigan and Coward for uncritical imitation. It is true that if one ignores the ingenious deployment of reverse chronology, the play comes closer to evoking the bourgeois world of the well-made play than anything Pinter has written, its style and subject matter deriving from the conservative English tradition of comedy of manners and the elegant patterning of its nine scenes showing little obvious affinity with the more overtly postmodern mode of Pinter's previous plays. Pinter's biographer, the long-serving *Guardian* critic Michael Billington, admits to being among those who missed the full significance of the play in 1978. While conceding that it "was technically original," he felt the play represented a retrogressive step from the originality of *The Homecoming* and *No Man's Land* to an outmoded form of "smart-set adultery" drama:

> What distresses me is the pitifully thin strip of experience it explores and its obsession with the tiny ripples on the stagnant pond of bourgeois-affluent life [. . .] Harold Pinter has betrayed his immense talent by serving up this kind of high-class soap-opera (laced with suitable brand-names like Venice, Torcello and Yeats) instead of a real play. (Billington, 258)

Pinter's familiarity with the work of Rattigan (a number of whose plays he had appeared in as an actor) and Coward (he had directed a highly successful revival of Coward's *Blithe Spirit* at the National Theatre in 1976) certainly allowed him to exploit a polished style of mannered reticence with such skill as to suggest surprising surface resemblances between *Betrayal* and the well-made drama of its antecedents.

A superficial comparison between *Blithe Spirit* and *Betrayal*, however, is enough to indicate the profound philosophical differences between Pinter's drama and Coward's. The Coward play illustrates the impossibility of a man being entirely faithful—at least on a mental/emotional plane—to one woman. Its comic device of the accidental materialization of the ghost of Elvira, Charles Condomine's glamorous deceased wife, engineers a situation in which a man is simultaneously plagued by the jealousies of both his bourgeois wife and his bohemian former wife, to the point where he eventually feels compelled to murder his second wife and walk out on both of their ghosts. By switching the gender of the people in this ménage à trois so that it is Emma Downs who walks out, first on her lover Jerry, and later on her husband, Pinter avoids the potentially misogynistic implications of *Blithe Spirit*. His literal presentation of multiple infidelities—as opposed to Coward's farcical ghost scenario—radically subverts the bourgeois ideology of such plays, while the reverse chronology calls into question the very possibility of absolute honesty in any human relationship, exposing the pain suffered in experiencing betrayal. The clipped, rhythmic dialogue utilized to portray the emotional reticence typical of the English upper middle class invokes a subtext of complex and ambivalent feelings that Coward's comedy only hints at in jest.

In comparison with other Pinter plays, the comparatively brief scenes, lack of extended monologues, and absence of the ubiquitous stream-of-consciousness narratives that are so unsettling in most of his full-length plays, reflect a deliberate intention to mimic the mode of drama popularized by Coward, while paradoxically challenging its philosophical perspective. At a deeper level, *Betrayal* seems to have been inspired by the cyclical form of a haunting eight-minute "dramaticule" by Samuel Beckett called *Come and Go* (1966), in which three women are seated on a bench recalling past events. As each in turn leaves the lit area of the stage, the other two betray her by whispering something about her state of being that they assume she does not know. The audience never hears what is being whispered, but in witnessing the three successive instances in which a confidence about the absent woman is shared, the play reduces a whole lifetime of human friendships to a pattern of betrayals connected by the shared experience of time passing. The scandalous "secret" that each pair withholds from the other apparently consists of the truism that as she ages, she is inevitably approaching death.

Even if the uncharacteristically symmetrical shaping of the plot from the triangular configuration of the characters' relationships does not directly mirror the skeletally spare structure of *Come and Go*, the wry melancholy of Pinter's comedy of manners has profound affinities with Beckett's darkly comic observation of the duplicity endemic in social existence. Both writers reveal the polite practice of social reticence among middle-class people as a habit of lying. As each character in both plays deceives one of the others, so are they in their turn deceived by another, the history of any trio of friends forming a palimpsest of betrayals built upon the foundations of secrets and lies. For once Pinter incontrovertibly exposes the lies that obfuscate truth and create the equivocal appearances so disturbing to both characters and audiences in his other plays. The successive movements of the plot backward in time unambiguously reveal the truth beneath each pretense. In place of the typically Pinterian epistemological drama that depicts the impossibility of attaining true knowledge, *Betrayal* excavates both the motivation and the context for each lie in order to examine the fundamental function and process of social role-playing. For the first time in his career Pinter assumes authorial omniscience regarding the gradual unraveling of dramatic exposition in a relentless regression to the moment when Jerry first declares his infatuation for Emma in 1968.

Ruby Cohn was the first critic to map the symmetrical arrangement of the play's nine scenes leading to and issuing from the one scene outside London in which Robert discovers Emma's affair with Jerry:

1. 1977—Emma and Jerry in a pub.	6. 1973—Emma and Jerry in a flat.
2. 1977, later—Jerry and Robert at Jerry's house.	7. 1973, later—Jerry and Robert in a restaurant.
3. 1975—Emma and Jerry in a flat.	8. 1971—Emma and Jerry in a flat.
4. 1974—Emma, Jerry, and Robert in Robert's house.	9. 1968—Emma, Jerry, and Robert in Robert's house.
5. 1973—Emma and Robert in Venice	

(In Lois Gordon, 24)

The emotional fallout from the doomed love affair is counterpointed against an image of domestic paradise by means of the repetition at various moments of the one important memory represented in *Betrayal*. In scene 1 Emma remembers Jerry throwing her daughter Charlotte up in the air during a Sunday luncheon, a joyful moment shared by both families. (Ironically, Jerry's memory of the incident is somewhat inaccurate, obliging Emma to point out that the incident actually took place in *his* kitchen, not hers.) The nostalgic realization that this happy moment can never be reexperienced is ironically counterpoised by the inevitable advance of the plot toward the final scene, disclosing Jerry's reckless impulse to betray Robert with Emma at their party in 1968. The reverse chronology of the plot creates a pervasive irony. At the same time as they recall their shared memory of the prelapsarian experience of joy, Emma and Jerry's somewhat melancholy reunion in the pub (scene 1) reveals their sober realization that Emma's marriage to Robert is about to end two years after her affair with Jerry did, Emma having found out the previous night that Robert had "betrayed . . . [her] for years . . . [with] other women" (18). Emma's outrage is qualified by Jerry's reminder that they "betrayed him for years" (18), so that each of the three characters has betrayed another—the male friends as well as the married couple. As Jerry's wife Judith never appears on stage, it might be assumed that she knows nothing about her own betrayal by the ménage à trois. Emma's line ("It's all all over" [23]), which sounds ironically like the ending of a play that has just begun, is contradicted by the following scene.

Scene 2 deliberately misleads an audience into expecting the play to proceed in normal chronological order; after the scene in the pub Jerry has invited Robert to his house, presumably to discuss the issues raised by Emma's confession to Robert the previous night of her infidelity with Jerry. Robert's revelation that Emma had already informed him four years earlier is a shock to both Jerry and the audience, exposing Emma's version of events in scene 1 as at least partly untrue.

> ROBERT: I thought you knew.
> JERRY: Knew what?
> ROBERT: That I knew. That I've known for years. I thought you knew that.
> JERRY: You thought I knew?
> ROBERT: She said you didn't. But I didn't believe that.
>
> *Pause.*
>
> Anyway, I think I thought you knew. But you say you didn't?

[. . .]

JERRY: But we've seen each other . . . a great deal . . . over the last four
    years. We've had lunch.

ROBERT: Never played squash though.
JERRY: I was your best friend. (29–30)

Jerry's self-righteous outrage at Robert's and Emma's conceal-
ment of the fact that Robert knew about his affair is comically exposed as sheer hypocrisy as he himself had been betraying Robert
with Emma for seven years. His distress regarding Robert's betrayal
of their friendship is as disturbing to him as the thought that if
Emma could lie about not having told Robert about their affair until
the previous night, she might well have been deceiving Jerry
throughout their relationship. Indeed Robert appears to confirm his
suspicion of Emma's habit of deception by informing Jerry a few minutes later that Emma and Casey are having an affair—something
Emma had refused to admit to Jerry in the pub. From this perspective
Jerry, who for seven years betrayed his wife Judith with Emma, re-
ceives his comic comeuppance when he realizes that he himself has
been deceived for four years ("No, you didn't know very much about
anything, really, did you?" [33]). One further deception is revealed to
the audience at the close of scene 2:

JERRY: Don't you remember? Years ago. You went over to Torcello in
    the dawn, alone. And read Yeats.
ROBERT: So I did. I told you that, yes. (37)

Significantly, Robert qualifies his "so I did" with "I told you that,"
implying that he lied to Jerry about events in Venice, so as to conceal
his discovery of Emma's affair.

The conventional sequence in which scene 1 is followed in
chronological order by scene 2 creates the normal expectation that
this sequence will continue; therefore the switch from 1977 to 1975
(scene 3), which initiates the retrogressive series of scenes with the
moment when Emma and Jerry agree to end their liaison, provokes
genuine surprise. Emma's final line, "Listen. I think we've made absolutely the right decision," is startlingly contrasted with Robert
shouting "Emma! Jerry's here" (47–48), as scene 3 gives way to

Robert's living room in the previous year (1974)—the first occasion when the play stages a meeting of all three characters. (The introduction of the principle of successive reversions to earlier times appears to be confirmed by the dating of scene 5 a year earlier than scene 4.) One might attribute the slight tension implied in the stilted conversation about the difference between male and female babies (Jerry asserts that boy babies cry more because "boys are more anxious" [50]) to Robert's guilt at having been unfaithful to Emma. At this juncture Jerry does not know about Robert's adulteries; neither can he know that Robert is making small talk to mask his knowledge of Jerry's affair with Emma.

The discussion of the men's squash ritual is vintage Pinter, providing a characteristic instance of the way he envisages the archetypal pattern of homosocial behavior. When Robert invites Jerry for a game of squash, Emma interposes:

EMMA: Can I watch?

Pause.

ROBERT: What?

EMMA: Why can't I watch and then take you both to lunch?

ROBERT: Well, to be brutally honest, we wouldn't actually want a woman around, would we, Jerry? I mean a game of squash isn't simply a game of squash, it's rather more than that. You see, first there's the game. And then there's the shower. And then there's the pint. And then there's lunch. After all, you've been at it. You've had your battle . . . You really don't want a woman buying you lunch [. . .] You see, at lunch you want to talk about squash, or cricket, or books, or even women, with your friend, and be able to warm to your theme without fear of improper interruption. (56–57)

Robert exaggerates the necessity of excluding Emma from the friends' masculine ritual in order to pretend that he does not know that Emma has had an affair with Jerry, while Jerry colludes with him on the mistaken assumption that such an assertion of friendship will prevent Robert from harboring any suspicion of the affair. Both men spontaneously exploit a misogynistic stereotype of masculine bonding to assert loyalty to a friendship that each has betrayed. This friendship is sentimentally portrayed as equal or superior in value to heterosexual love in its romantic conjunction of physical and intellectual competition/admiration. After Jerry leaves, Robert kisses her, and she cries on his shoulder: Emma does not know at that point that Robert has been unfaithful to her, but the audience will notice his hypocrisy in seeming to forgive her for a betrayal that he has paid back in kind.

The turning point of the plot occurs when Robert deliberately provokes Emma's terse admission in scene 5, "We're lovers" (69), the whole scene representing one of the most complex and sophisticated deployments of subtext in modern English drama. Robert and Emma negotiate a minefield of equivocal conversational ploys. Robert starts by affecting an attitude of nonchalance to conceal his fearful suspicions, while Emma demonstrates the accomplished duplicity learned during years of pretending:

> ROBERT: Book good?
> EMMA: Mmn. Yes.
> ROBERT: What is it?
> EMMA: This new book. This man Spinks.
> [. . .]
> ROBERT: I must read it again myself, now it's in hard covers.
> EMMA: Again?
> ROBERT: Jerry wanted us to publish it.
> EMMA: Oh really?
> ROBERT: Well, naturally. Anyway, I turned it down.
>
> EMMA: Why?
> ROBERT: Oh . . . not much more to say on that subject, really, is there?
> EMMA: What do you consider the subject to be?
> ROBERT: Betrayal. (61–63)

Although the real issue in the scene is Robert's suspicion of Emma's affair with Jerry, Robert's literary discussion of Spinks's latest novel euphemistically skirts the topic of betrayal, as does his detailed cross-questioning about Emma's receipt of a letter from Jerry and his pompous affectation of moral disapproval of the Venetian postal service for suggesting he deliver her letter ("I've a good mind to write to the Doge of Venice about it" [65]). Robert's response to Emma's disclosure of her long-standing adultery reveals the stereotypical "stiff upper lip" of English middle-class manners; he may be trying to avoid the embarrassment of an emotional scene, but the fact that he himself is unfaithful to Emma may make him reticent to express any sense of injury. Robert may indeed be more wounded by Jerry's betrayal of their friendship than by Emma's infidelity. At the end of the scene, he comes as close to declaring his love for Jerry as any of Pinter's male characters ever do. Ironically, he does this vindictively with the aim of hurting his wife:

> I've always liked Jerry. To be honest, I've always liked him rather more than I've liked you. Maybe I should have had an affair with him myself.
>
> *Silence*
>
> Tell me, are you looking forward to our trip to Torcello. (72–73)

After the emphasis on the suppressed emotions indicated by the silence, the calculated insouciance of the final line expresses cynical acceptance of the continual duplicity to which an imperfect marriage has accustomed both parties. The scene appears to come full circle, ending as it has begun with a polite reference to the trip to Torcello that Robert mentions in scene 2.

Emma's reunion with Jerry in their flat in Kilburn (scene 6) after the summer holiday comprises the second significant disruption of the overall principle of backward movement in time, confounding audience expectation once more because it is part of a sequence of two scenes that follow scene 5 in chronological order. Emma and Jerry's affectionate chatter chiefly revolves around three issues. First, she tells Jerry that they did not go to Torcello because the speedboats were on strike, thereby contradicting what the audience remembers Robert telling Jerry in scene 2. Jerry's disclosure that he is meeting Robert for lunch on Thursday causes Emma a great deal of anxiety, reminding the audience that she is deliberately concealing from Jerry the fact that Robert has found out about their affair; this is ironically reinforced by the story he tells about two recent occasions when he had panicked that his wife Judith had found out. Set against all this worry about the possibility of multiple deceptions being discovered is the memory of shared happiness invoked for a second time by Jerry of picking Charlotte up in the air in his kitchen (again, he gets this point wrong, and has to be corrected by Emma).

Scene 7 takes place in an Italian restaurant on the Thursday after scene 6, once more transgressing the convention that the plot is moving backward in time. The setting is a witty reminder of Robert's recent holiday (the waiter even points to a picture of Venice on the wall) and Robert now talks about taking a speedboat to Torcello, contradicting Emma's story in scene 6 that the speedboats were on strike, and causing both Jerry and the audience to wonder whether it is Emma or Robert who is lying:

> ROBERT: Incredible day. I got up very early and—whoomp—right across the lagoon—to Torcello. Not a soul stirring.
> JERRY: What's the "whoomp"?
> ROBERT: Speedboat.
> JERRY: Ah, I thought—
> ROBERT: What?
> JERRY: It's so long ago, I'm obviously wrong. I thought one went to Torcello by gondola.
> ROBERT: It would take hours. No, no—whoomp—across the lagoon in the dawn.
> JERRY: Sounds good.
> ROBERT: I was quite alone.
> JERRY: Where was Emma?
> ROBERT: I think asleep.
> JERRY: Ah. (93–95)

In the context of the fake "Italy" evoked by the décor of the restaurant, the conversation elaborates a mannerist game of truth and pretense, stimulating an audience to try to disentangle real experience from fictional mimesis. Jerry politely plays along with what he suspects is an elaborate fiction, even to the extent of pretending that he thought one traveled to Torcello by gondola when Emma has recently told him this is not so. During the remainder of a scene interspersed with farcical miscommunications with an Italian waiter, Robert seems to drink in order to pluck up courage to engineer a confrontation with Jerry, the intensity of his feelings being somewhat excessive in a conversation about Spinks (he says Emma "seems to be madly in love with" Spinks's novel), Casey, and being alone on Torcello:

> ROBERT: You know what you and Emma have in common? You love literature. I mean you love modern prose literature. I mean you love the new novel by the new Casey or Spinks. It gives you both a thrill.

JERRY: You must be pissed.
ROBERT: Really? You mean you don't think it gives Emma a thrill?
JERRY: How do I know? She's your wife. (97–98)

Robert's telling repetitions of the words "love" and "thrill" are inappropriate signifiers of a fondness for modern novels, his language revealing to the audience if not to Jerry his reaction to his recent discovery of the affair. Jerry's guilt makes him evasive, complex currents of unexpressed feeling being implied by the contradiction between what each character says and what the audience knows they know. Toward the end of the scene the wine seems to encourage Robert to become more emotionally open, and his account of reading Yeats on Torcello expresses his feeling of having betrayed his earlier literary ideals:

> ROBERT: . . . I can't bear being back in London. I was happy, such a rare thing, not in Venice, I don't mean that, I mean on Torcello, when I walked about Torcello in the early morning, alone, I was happy, I wanted to stay there forever.
> JERRY: We all . . .
> ROBERT: Yes, we all . . . feel that sometimes. Oh you do yourself, do you?
>
> *Pause.*
>
> I mean there's nothing really wrong, you see. I've got the family. Emma and I are very good together. I think the world of her. (99)

Robert's attempt to reassure himself that he is content in his life with Emma is another lie. Both characters weave a web of equivocation and self-deception throughout the scene, ending in Robert's cool pretense that all is well: "You must come and have a drink sometime. She'd love to see you" (100).

Jerry does indeed see Emma in the next scene, but the surprise is that it takes place two years earlier (1971) in the flat rented as the venue for their afternoon assignations. The flashback to the past in scene 8 ends the chronological progression in time from scene 5 to scene 7, showing the lovers two and a half years after the start of their relationship. The opening of the scene in an empty flat is a reminder of the banal practicalities of an adulterous affair that were initially represented in scene 3: lovers require a venue for clandestine meetings. *Betrayal* ironically details the mechanics of keeping the infidelity secret by means of the conversations about renting, furnishing, and disposing of the Kilburn flat. The sparse appurtenances to a meal in the flat (the chairs, table, "crockery, glasses, bottle of wine" [101]) contrast starkly with the clichéd atmosphere of Venice simulated by the restaurant and with the exotic atmosphere of the city itself, echoing the conversation in which Jerry and Emma decide what to do about the disposal of the flat and its effects at the end of their affair (winter, 1975). To Emma the stark materiality of the room furnished only with bare necessities has become a symbol of absence:

> EMMA: Nobody comes here. I just can't bear to think about it actually. Just . . . empty. All day and night. Day after day and night after night. I mean the crockery and the curtains and the bedspread and everything. And the tablecloth I brought from Venice. (*Laughs.*) It's ridiculous.
>
> *Pause.*
>
> It's just . . . an empty home.
> JERRY: It's not a home.
>
> *Pause.*
>
> I know . . . I know what you wanted . . . but it could never . . . actually be a home. I have a home. You have a home. With curtains, etcetera. And children. Two children in two homes. (43–44)

Jerry's inventory of effects in each of their homes, reduces the complex network of human feelings and relationships that constitutes each family to a collection of artifacts ("curtains, etcetera") that are the merely material contents of a house. In emptying the notion of a home of its powerful emotional aura, Jerry's language betrays his sense of alienation from his own life, exposing his attachment to his home as a mere convention or convenient habit. In contrast, Emma is troubled by the empty flat as she has wanted to see it as a home; indeed it did once permit them to create an alternative universe in which to live together momentarily, but she believes that Jerry's motivation may have been merely sexual:

> JERRY: You didn't ever really see it as a home, in any sense, did you?
> JERRY: No, I saw it as a flat . . . you know.
> JERRY: For fucking.
> JERRY: No, for loving. (44)

Emma speaks of the flat as "our home" (81) in scene 6, and brings back a tablecloth from Venice. The romantic private life created by Emma and Jerry is reflected in their imaginative transmutation of the "empty" flat as Emma perceives it in scene 3 into a bohemian pied-à-terre in scene 8. An image of life lived fully in the present in excited anticipation of future joy, is evoked by Jerry's description of his journey to the flat after a walk in the mist through Hyde Park:

> JERRY: Then I got a taxi to Wessex Grove. Number 31. And I climbed the steps and opened the front door and then climbed the stairs and opened this door and found you in a new apron cooking a stew.
>
> EMMA *comes out of the kitchen*
>
> EMMA: It's on.
>
> JERRY: Which is now on. (103)

As Emma enters on cue Jerry incorporates her cooking in his pastiche of a romantic narrative about the journey to his secret assignation, enacting in speech the process of time passing as a progression from past into present tense, while the stage action ironically shows the dissolution of future into present and present into past. This is perhaps the only occasion in the play in which a causal sequence motivating the straightforward progression of dramatic action is instantly recalled as narrative. Significantly, Jerry's anticipation of the future does not involve authorial manipulation of the audience's conventional expectation of what might occur next but is provoked through immediate retrospection on how what has just happened leads to what is now happening. His reflection on the contribution of his autobiographical narrative to the plot deploys a metadramatic device to depict the process of time passing—a key preoccupation throughout the play.

The news that Emma "ran into Judith yesterday" (103) while lunching with a female friend at Fortnum and Mason's causes them to speculate on the possibility that Judith might know about Jerry's infidelity; his claim that "she has an admirer" (107) implies the perpetual threat of infidelity to any relationship—even their own affair. The anxiety observed early on in their relationship that one of the four partners may betray another in the same way that she or he has

been betrayed is portrayed as a specter of one betrayal mirroring another in a series to infinity. As a response to this fear of reciprocal betrayal, Emma's question, "Have you ever thought . . . of changing your
life?" (108) together with Jerry's reply, "It's impossible" (108), provokes an audience to reflect on the reasons why people conduct clandestine affairs rather than living more honestly in a state of serial
monogamy. Jerry's repeated assertion "I adore you" (110) indicates
the paradoxical state of wishing to possess a stable relationship at the
same time as desiring the immediacy of romantic passion. When
Emma informs Jerry that she is pregnant by Robert, Jerry's somewhat
ambivalent response at the end of the scene ("I'm so happy for you"
[111]) suggests that he may jealously experience her sexual relationship with her own husband as a kind of betrayal. The contradictory
thoughts and feelings that are evoked as a subtext to scene 8 provide
a concentrated focus for all the ambivalence and conflicted emotions
the audience has witnessed in *Betrayal*, illustrating how early in any
clandestine affair the fantasy of living simultaneously in two parallel
universes starts to undermine the personal sense of integrity achieved
by living one's life with uncompromising honesty. The playwright
never moralizes about adultery; he merely exposes its impact on the
people involved.

Scene 9 is the occasion in 1968 when in the bedroom during
Robert and Emma's party, Jerry first conceives the possibility of a liaison with Emma. The final scene of the play thereby represents the
earliest chronological moment of the action, revealing that the corrosive conflict between the romance of spontaneous sexual attrac-
tion and the rational norm of marital fidelity was already manifest at
the start of the affair. Jerry's declarations of passion ("You're beautiful . . . You're incredible" [113]) contrast with Emma's sensible good
manners ("My husband is on the other side of that door" [115]) to
heighten the intensity of feeling caused by the combination of the
clandestine nature of the situation and his drunken state. From its
origin, however, a disturbing impulse can be perceived as unconsciously motivating Jerry's flatteringly clumsy wooing of Emma. She
herself appears to understand that Jerry's wish to besmirch her on her
wedding day is not simply an uncomplicated moment of pure desire
but also an envious wish to hurt his best friend by betraying him
with his bride.

JERRY: I should have had you, in your white, before the wedding. I should have blackened you, in your white wedding dress, blackened you in your bridal dress, before ushering you into your wedding, as your best man.

EMMA: My husband's best man. Your best friend's best man. (114)

Positioned at the end of the play, this betrayal of friendship is the climax of an incremental revelation of the homosocial basis of male friendship represented more systematically in *Betrayal* as a motivation for masculine behavior than in any of Pinter's other stage plays. Jerry's final—though chronologically first—betrayal of Robert is a lie that tells the truth. Pretending complete fidelity to his friendship with Robert, Jerry informs him that he has been telling his wife how beautiful she is:

JERRY: As you are my best and oldest friend and, in the present instance, my host, I decided to take this opportunity to tell your wife how beautiful she was. [. . .] And how wonderful for you that this is so, that this is the case, that her beauty is the case.

ROBERT: Quite right.

JERRY *moves to* ROBERT *and takes hold of his elbow.*

JERRY: I speak as your oldest friend. Your best man.

ROBERT: You are, actually. (116–17)

As is so often the case in Pinter's theater, gesture or movement expresses the truth of people's feelings less equivocally than speech. As Robert leaves the bedroom, he "clasps Jerry's shoulder," and seconds later, as Emma is about to follow her husband, "Jerry grasps her arm. She stops still. They stand still, looking at each other" (117). Deploying the simplest of theatrical means at this point, the playwright evokes the most complex feelings. The audience is made to experience the paradoxical conflict between Robert and Jerry's complex love for each other as friends and the homosocial rivalry between two men in the company of a woman: Robert is proud that Jerry envies him his wife, his cool assurance of Emma's fidelity possibly sparking Jerry's desire to seduce her virtually in front of his friend. *Betrayal* transforms the conventional curiosity about what comes next generated by the kind of plot tension typical of a stage thriller into the Proustian fascination with the retrieval of old times.

Ironically, the instant before Emma makes the decision to embark on an affair is moving precisely because the audience already knows the outcome. For one brief instant, time stands still as an audience contemplates the way that the happiness of Robert and Emma's married life hangs in the balance. The curtain falls on a frozen moment in which the audience understands on what arbitrary impulses human destiny can turn.

CHAPTER 8

States of Catatonia:
Family Voices, A Kind of Alaska,
Moonlight

> I won't walk, I'll be a cripple, I'll descend, I'll diminish, into to-
> tal paralysis, my life is in your hands, that's what you're ban-
> ishing me to, a state of catatonia, do you know the state of cata-
> tonia? do you? do you? where the reigning prince is the prince
> of emptiness, the prince of absence, the prince of desolation.
> (115)[1]

Jerry's speech from the final scene of *Betrayal* not only reformulates
the key trope of *No Man's Land*, it also prefigures the title and subject matter of *A Kind of Alaska* (1982); Jerry visualizes the absence of
romantic love as a psychological no man's land, a state of being suspended between life and death. The proper diagnosis of the mental
paralysis or comatose state in which Deborah appears to have been
suspended for twenty-nine years—her kind of Alaska—is *encephalitis lethargica,* but it is not the scientific explanation of the medical
condition that most interests Pinter. What appears to engage him
imaginatively is its affinity with the frozen landscape of depression,
an absence from self that anesthetizes a person's normal emotional
faculties. This state of mind is to some degree represented in Stanley's depression and breakdown in *The Birthday Party*, but becomes
a leitmotif of *Silence, No Man's Land, A Kind of Alaska,* and *Moonlight* (1993). Although at first glance *Family Voices* (1980) appears to
have little in common with the above plays, its focus on the experience of absence as a metonymic sign of the emotional alienation of a
son from his parents, creates subtle variations on the connected

themes of geographical and emotional separation that are apparent in Pinter's drama as early as *The Room* and constitute the primary thematic motif of *Moonlight.*

Broadcast initially on BBC Radio by the cast of its National Theatre premiere production, *Family Voices* exploits the paradoxical play of close proximity and alienating distance that is a property of sound radio as a medium. The voices seem to sound in each character's head as imagined moments of intimacy contradicted by the decorum of their epistolary form, the poignant separation of son and mother as he grows up and moves away being paralleled by the complete absence of the father who speaks at last from beyond the grave. In exploring the restrictions created by the familial expectations imposed on every individual, the drama reveals the respective failure of each to break through socially constructed patterns of behavior and share feelings freely. The father is alienated from any positive connection with his family, his "glassy grave" evoked as a landscape of frozen emotion—"absolute silence everywhere, absolute silence throughout all the hours [. . .] occasionally a dog barking" (146).

Mother (Voice 2) and son (Voice 1) speak their thoughts in the form of letters to each other, with an intervention by the dead father near the end. The comic drama of maternal possessiveness and intrafamilial jealousy, rivalry, and resentment at the same time parodies the preciosity of literary letters:

VOICE 1: I am having a very nice time.

The weather is up and down, but surprisingly warm, on the whole, more often than not.

[. . .]

Do you miss me?

I am having a very nice time and I hope you are glad of that.

At the moment I am dead drunk. (131)

Voice 1's letters home are full of the euphemisms and evasions that suggest the cautious duplicity of a dutiful son who is reassuring his mother of his well-being while at the same time determined to assert his newfound freedom. The paradoxical attitude of mother to son comically represents the impossibly possessive demands of an Oedipal relationship:

VOICE 2: Darling. Where are you? The flowers are wonderful here. The blooms. You so loved them.

I think of you and wonder how you are. Do you ever think of me? Your mother? Ever? At all?

Have you changed your address?

[. . .]

I often think that I would love to live happily ever after with you and your young wife. And she would be such a lovely wife to you and I would have the occasional dinner with you both. A dinner I would be happy to cook myself, should you both be tired after your long day, as I'm sure you will be.

[. . .]

Darling. I miss you. I gave birth to you. Where are you? (133–34)

The ontological status of each speaker is ambiguous: every speech may be construed as the utterance of a letter actually being written or as the verbalizing of a letter conceived by the intended recipient in the imagined voice of the other. The son's gradual attempts to unravel the grotesquely complicated structure of the Withers family, whose matriarch owns the house in which he has rented a room, comprises the key narrative element; it is written as a burlesque bildungsroman[2] of sexual and social awakening in which the new pseudo-family promises liberation from the Oedipal drama of conflict within his biological family:

VOICE 1: But I'm not so sure about the other people in this house.

One is an old man.

The one who is an old man retires early. He is bald.

The other is a woman who wears red dresses.

The other is another man.

[. . .]

At night I hear whispering from the other rooms and do not understand it. I hear steps on the stairs and do not go out to investigate. (135)

At first a stranger, the son gradually assumes a familiarity with the curiously complicated relationships in the Withers family. His insouciant account of a series of potentially sexual encounters with men and women in the house may be either real or fantasized. Whatever the case, his casting of himself as the naive if willing victim of sexual predators recalls the disingenuous attitude of the youthful rakes in Henry Fielding's novels,[3] and seems calculated to shock his mother in order to mark his separation from his own family:

> VOICE 1: I was lying in my bath when the door opened. I thought I had locked it. My name's Riley, he said. How's the bath? Very nice, I said. You've got a wellknit yet slender frame, he said, I thought you only a snip, I never imagined you would be as wellknit and slender as I now see you are. (140)

The son's speeches are cool and facetious. Ventriloquizing the people he meets in a consciously literary manner, he creates a picaresque narrative whose Dickensian exaggerations seem almost to advertise its equivocal relationship with reality:

> Is Lady Withers Jane's mother or sister?

> If either is the case why isn't Jane called Lady Jane Withers? Or perhaps she is. Or perhaps neither is the case? Or perhaps Mrs Withers is actually the Honourable Mrs Withers? But if that is the case what does that make Mr Withers? And which Withers is he anyway? I mean what relation is he to the rest of the Witherses? And who is Riley?

> But if you find me bewildered, anxious, confused, uncertain and afraid, you also find me content. My life possesses shape. (145)

This speech parodies a wide variety of literary stereotypes, archly alluding to the pseudo-scientific idiom of literary detective fiction à la Conan Doyle, the Continental European bildungsroman, the Gothic mystery of a Wilkie Collins novel, the obsession with nuances of class and status typical of the Anglo-Irish comedy of manners, and the Proustian pretensions of the twentieth-century belletrist. The philosophical problem of self and others[4] is jokingly implied yet never didactically explicated. Such comedy of intra- and interfamilial conflict echoes Beckett's assumptions about human personality and theatrical representation, unself-consciously locating its radically skeptical representation of the irrationality and self-contradiction involved in the performance of self within a postmodern drama of consciousness.

The mother's speeches are less fanciful, but no less artificial in their literary style:

> VOICE 2: Sometimes I think I have always been sitting like this. I sometimes think I have always been sitting like this, alone, by an indifferent fire, curtains closed, night, winter.
>
> [. . .]
>
> What I mean is that when, for example, I was washing your hair, with the most delicate shampoo, and rinsing, and then drying your hair so gently, with my soft towel, so that no murmur came from you, of discomfort or unease, and then looked into your eyes and saw you look into mine, knowing that you wanted no-one else, no-one at all, knowing that you were entirely happy in my arms, I knew also, for example, that I was at the same time sitting by an indifferent fire, alone in winter, in eternal night, without you. (140–41)

A Freudian drama of suffering motherhood is compressed into one speech, its unexpected modulations of tense from the present to the past being followed by a kind of continuous present that subsumes both past and present in anticipated retrospect. The mother's fervid imagination construes her son's coy admissions of his sexual flirtations as acts of prostitution:

> The police are looking for you. You may remember that you are still under twenty-one. [. . .] I have stated my belief that you are in the hands of underworld figures who are using you as a male prostitute. [. . .] Women were your downfall, even as a nipper. I haven't forgotten Francoise the French maid or the woman who masqueraded under the title of governess, the infamous Miss Carmichael. You will be found, my boy, and no mercy will be shown to you. (147)

Ironically, Voice 1's need to return to the past ("I'm coming back to you, mother, to hold you in my arms. I am coming home") reveals mother and son to exist in a solipsistic limbo of unrealizable desires. Although the father (Voice 3) only speaks twice, his opposing point of view on events contradicts the mother's claims and he not only confuses the narrative but is himself illogical and self-contradictory. All three voices end up suspended in the no man's land of pure consciousness; they are frozen in time, existing in the purely virtual dimension of the aural. Their total lack of connection is signified by the impossibility of the father's ever being able to communicate with his son: "I have so much to say to you. But I am quite dead. What I have to say to you will never be said" (148).

Victoria Station (first performed as part of a triple bill with A Kind of Alaska and Family Voices) elaborates the metaphor of spatial isolation as emotional alienation in the form of a short black farce. The separate mental worlds of a taxi driver and his controller are indicated visually by their situation in two fragmentary locations—the driver seated in one part of the stage behind the steering wheel of his car, the controller seated behind a microphone in his office in another. Gradually, the desperate loneliness of both men becomes apparent as the controller tries with less and less success to get Driver 274 to pick up a passenger at Victoria Station and drive him to Cuckfield. The controller's increasing exasperation at the driver's refusal to cooperate with him is conceived by him as a disregard for his authority: "I'm talking into this machine, trying to make some sense out of our lives. That's my function. God gave me this job. He asked me to do this job personally. I'm your local monk, 274" (198). The Controller's sarcasm is a joking reference to Pinter's view of the arbitrariness of authority but it also emphasizes the insecurity of its representatives.

The driver claims not to know where Victoria Station[5] is and cannot identify the "dark park" underneath Crystal Palace (200) beside which he says he is parked with a woman on the back seat that he claims to have fallen in love with. Their absurd bickering builds to a pitch of hilarity as the controller becomes progressively more enraged by the driver's disingenuous evasiveness until the surprise reversal when the controller decides to leave his office and join the driver at his car to celebrate his engagement to the female passenger. Although in format no more than a revue sketch, Victoria Station is a richly surreal exploration of loneliness and frustration, the use of disconnected voices in separate spaces being a variation on the experiment with a scenic convention first employed in Family Voices. Here it is clear that the two characters are actually talking to each other, yet each exists for the other only as a disembodied voice, and the controller is compelled to seek a physical connection with the driver in order to verify and empathize with his human reality.

In his foreword to A Kind of Alaska Pinter identifies Oliver Sacks's Awakenings as the inspiration for the one-act play:

In the winter of 1916–17, there spread over Europe, and subsequently over the rest of the world, an extraordinary epidemic illness which presented itself in innumerable forms—as delirium, mania, trances, coma, sleep, insomnia, restlessness, and states of Parkinsonism. It was eventually identified [. . .] and named [. . .] *encephalitis lethargica*, or sleeping sickness. Over the next ten years almost five million people fell victim to the disease [. . .] The worst-affected sank into singular states of "sleep"—conscious of their surroundings but motionless, speechless, and without hope or will. (151)

In 1969 the introduction of the new drug, L-DOPA stimulated the "awakening" of some of these patients. On the surface, the play appears to be a straightforwardly naturalistic dramatization of the case of Sacks's patient Ruth R, confounding the expectations of its first reviewers by its apparent lack of the stylistic hallmarks of Pinter's postmodern dramaturgy. Yet the documentary-style presentation of the forty-five-year-old Deborah's awakening from twenty-nine years of sleep is not strictly naturalistic, but condenses a process that would normally last weeks or even months into a fifty-minute encounter with her sister Pauline and her brother-in-law Hornby, who has attended to her as doctor throughout her illness. The play, however fragmentary, nevertheless evokes a thirty-year history of waste and suffering on the part of all three characters, stimulating new reflections on Pinter's persistent themes of truth, time, and memory. Deborah's conscious mind has frozen at sixteen so she recalls people she knew and events that occurred during her adolescence as recent memories, obliging Hornby and Pauline to try to account for the twenty-nine-year gap in her perception of the world—to explain the meaning of that time passing—in a matter of minutes.

Whereas *Betrayal* takes an audience on a dramaturgical journey from the present through a series of temporal regressions that at last disclose an original event occurring nine years earlier, *A Kind of Alaska* develops the strategy explored tentatively at the end of the first act of *Old Times* and in the second act of *No Man's Land*, when present and past worlds overlap for some moments. Yet Deborah's awakening permits a more immediate confrontation of present and past worlds, as an audience witnesses the simultaneous presence of Deborah's sixteen-year-old mind and her forty-five-year-old body. There is a surreal counterpoint of Pauline and Hornby, each of whom exhibits the integration of mental and physical states that is appropriate to the normal experience of middle age, with Deborah, whose adolescent consciousness is located in a middle-aged female body. On stage Deborah's vivid adolescent past is more colorfully alive than the gray present of her two sad carers, juxtaposing being and consciousness in an alarming opposition. The depredations of time are exposed as powerfully in *A Kind of Alaska* as they are in *Betrayal*. The suffering of Deborah's relatives at first appears to have been worse than her own because they have over twenty-nine years experienced the gradual disillusionment that is inherent in aging. Ironically it is Deborah whose sudden consciousness of aging will ultimately be most traumatic, even though she appears at the end of the play to be imbued with the naive confidence of youth:

> You say I have been asleep. You say I am now awake. You say I have not awoken from the dead. [. . .] You say I am a woman. [. . .] Mummy and Daddy and Estelle are on a world cruise. They've stopped off in Bangkok. It'll be my birthday soon. I think I have the matter in proportion. (190)

Deborah can remember only the ghosts of a lost world. Her sense of having "the matter in proportion" is a complete illusion; the economy of Pinter's writing is such that this is implied by the linguistic contrast between her reporting of the truth told her by Hornby (the repetitions of "You say") and her own first-person assertions of the white lies told her by Pauline to mitigate the shock of discovering that her relatives have been dead for years. She neither possesses the emotional maturity to grasp the full meaning of twenty-nine years of time having passed, nor perhaps is she resilient enough to withstand the traumatic realization that her mother, father, and sister are dead. Not being able to inhabit the existential truth of her condition, Deborah invents an equivocal reality of her own, combining truths, half-truths, and untruths to construct a variant of the *Sleeping Beauty* narrative as explanation for her newly emergent identity. Such a bricolage of autobiographical fragments is consistently identified in Pinter's drama as the dominant strategy by which characters perform their identities.[6]

Deborah's words that begin the play, "Something is happening. / *Silence.* / Do you recognize me?" (153) might jokingly be employed to sum up the experience of the average member of an audience at a Pinter play. Something is always going on but an audience is seldom sure exactly what that is—and the characters are always desperate to have their own sense of self validated. This is precisely the existential condition that *A Kind of Alaska*—and indeed most of Pinter's work from his early novel *The Dwarfs* to *Celebration*—portends. Human beings are always in the middle of "something" without knowing how it began, when it will end, and fearful that, if they are not "recognized," they may not truly exist.[7] During a mere fifty minutes of playing time, *A Kind of Alaska* asks an audience to imagine the waste lands of three interrupted lives, much of the experience of the drama happening in the spaces between the lines, the characteristic hesitations (. . .), pauses and silences halting the flow of the speaking characters to demand a spectator's empathic response to a trauma that transcends the limits of commonsense experience. By daring each member of the audience to fill these gaps with thought and feeling, the play negotiates the boundaries of human consciousness, confronting every witness with the bare facts of Deborah's case without manipulating her or his feelings. Peculiar though Deborah's circumstances are, her unique experience constitutes an apt metaphor for the relationship between the oneiric realm, in which past, present, and imagined events coexist, and the chronological experience of historical time. Possibly in response to the ghostly specters that haunt Beckett's spare plays of the seventies and eighties, *A Kind of Alaska* marks the point at which Pinter reaches toward a form of dramaturgy that elaborates images and performance rhythms capable of invoking penumbral states of consciousness that are normally the province of faith or mystery.

The antinomies of spiritual and material experience staged in the rather different experiments of *No Man's Land* and *A Kind of Alaska*, anticipate the dialectic of grotesquely opposed speech registers and theatrical styles that produces the surreally self-referential collage of *Moonlight* (1993). The play's exaggerated recapitulation of the familiar Pinterian tropes of subjective memory, existential alienation, spatial dislocation, and psychological dysfunction expresses a comic self-consciousness that exults in its ironic reminder that the audience has "known this before."[8] The alternation of playful self-parody and ritualized lyricism produces startling juxtapositions of linguistic style as a substitute for the conventional pleasures of dramatic suspense. Andy is on his deathbed, with his wife Bel by his side; his two sons, Fred and Jake, have cut themselves off from their parents and refuse to answer their mother's telephone calls,[9] while his deceased daughter Bridget wanders around a separate area of stage in moonlight, worrying about having left her parents untended. A married couple, Ralph and Maria, who are family friends, appear in Andy's bedroom and Fred's apartment without any realistic motivation. Each of the four groups of characters is characterized by a particular speech idiom that allows for grotesque contrasts of tone and mood. While the play shifts visually from one place to another, there is no indication of temporal sequence: in this sense *Moonlight* has the quality of a dream in which time is suspended in a continuous present.

Absence and loss are the predominant themes of *Moonlight*, which explores subjects treated a number of times before in Pinter's work, such as death and dying, love and betrayal, the problematic relationship of fathers and sons, and the equivocal nature of friendship. Yet the effect of the play is very different from that of any previous work. The interpellation of situations and conflicts reminiscent of *The Homecoming* with others redolent of *A Kind of Alaska* and *No Man's Land*, situates the dramaturgy of the early play in a dialectical relationship with that of the later two, generating a phantasmagoric effect that seems wholly new. If the lonely and childless Hirst exists in the penumbral space between life and death, with Spooner as the Charon figure ready to ferry him across the river Styx to the underworld, Andy is a foul-mouthed husband and father in his fifties, as scabrous and bad-tempered a patriarch as Max in *The Homecoming*, waiting for death without in any way being prepared to die. Unlike Spooner, Andy's fifty-year old wife, Bel, is unable to empathize with him, and apparently unwilling to comfort him. Their relationship resembles those in Strindberg's late "ghost" dramas, their bitter and petty resentment signifying their refusal to "go gentle into that good night."[10]

Moonlight is set in three separate playing areas and the action divides into twenty short segments although these are not nominated as separate scenes in the script. Action alternates mostly between Andy's and Fred's bedrooms, with a few episodes in a shadowy, less defined space where Bridget appears, Andy on one occasion wanders in search of her, and a flashback to a period before she died takes place. The difference in status between one location and another forms a key to the play's motifs of emotional disconnection and familial dysfunction. Fred and Andy are both confined to bed in their respective bedrooms, in Fred's case because he seems to be suffering from a severe depression or nervous breakdown ("I've got a funny feeling my equilibrium is in tatters" [364]). These locations are paralleled, the only difference being that Andy's is "well-furnished" while Fred's is "shabby." Bridget's location, however, appears as a ghost space, one that was situated somewhere specific in the past, but is now suspended between memory and material reality. Like Bridget herself it has once been fully present in the material world, but is now partly spectral—merely a shadow of its former existence. The enforced separation of Bridget from her family is comparable to the estrangement of the sons from their parents but the feelings involved are complicated; Andy resents his sons and adores Bridget, while Bel is emotionally attached to the boys.

The black comedy of Andy and Bel's irritable arguments about their life together, and Fred and Jake's satirical parody of their father's hypocritical faith in the bureaucratic system that ordered his working life, is framed by the serene and lyrical appearances of their daughter and sister, Bridget. Opening the play "in faint light" with her simple views of her duty to care for her parents, and closing it with her adolescent account of the moment of dying as a solitary trip to a party destination that she never reaches, Bridget's stage presence visually evokes a mystical sense of the continuity of life and death.

> BRIDGET: I can't sleep. There's no moon. It's so dark. [. . .] I don't want to wake my father and mother. They're so tired. They have given so much of their life for me and for my brothers. All their life in fact. [. . .] They need to sleep in peace and wake up rested. I must see that this happens. It is my task. Because I know that when they look at me they see that I am all they have left of their life. (319)

At the start of the play, the audience does not know that Bridget is dead, so her diction appears to be a rather childlike reflection on a young daughter's responsibility for her parents' well-being, resembling the adolescent "thinking-aloud" of Deborah in A Kind of Alaska—her mechanical rationalization of the conventional family values of Judeo-Christian morality formed by a typical middle-class upbringing. With hindsight, the ironic contrast between Bridget's loving care of her parents and the bitter battle that has alienated the sons from their father is rendered terribly poignant by the knowledge that death has enforced a final unwanted estrangement between daughter and parents. As the only character at peace with herself, Bridget in death is signified by what the other characters say about her and through her confinement to the (virtual) space on stage. Her life continues after death through her vivid presence in the memories of each member of the family. The conceit of the drama is to have her behave as if she has simply moved away from the place that was home to inhabit a space her father has not yet reached. The paradoxical effect of her gentle presence in the play ironically implies that Fred and Jake's separation from their parents represents an absence as complete as death, but it also constitutes a telling contrast with Andy's baffled rage at dying and his unsuccessful struggle to come to terms with his life.

No decorum is observed between Bel and Andy on his deathbed; at times it is difficult to know whether the characters are being deliberately self-mocking in their bitter squabbling or whether their self-conscious idiom is merely habitual sarcasm. Instead of the conventional sympathy of a wife for her terminally ill husband, Bel coolly seems to parody the normal concern of a carer for her patient by irrationally eliding the banal questions she would ask into one stream of speech: "Do you feel anything? What do you feel? Do you feel hot? Or cold? Or both? What do you feel? Do you feel cold in your legs? Or hot? What about your fingers? What are they? Are they cold? Or hot? Or neither cold nor hot?" (321). Andy's facetious reply sets the tone for many of their ambivalent exchanges, which teeter on the border between bluntness and sarcasm: "Is this a joke? My God she's taking the piss out of me. My own wife. On my deathbed. She's as bad as that fucking cat" (321). The exchange then takes the form of a ritualized quarrel between long-married partners, their stilted syntax and bombastic diction evoking the specter of years of petty bickering.

The abrupt switch to Fred's bedroom and the brothers' absurdly formal greeting ("Jake: Brother / Fred: Brother") echoes their parents' mocking banter in a less aggressive mode, the parody of adult male pomposity being heightened to the point where it becomes a satire on patriarchal authority of any kind:

JAKE: I've got it.
FRED: You've got it?

JAKE: I've got it.
FRED: Where did you find it?
JAKE: Divine right.
FRED: Christ.
JAKE: Exactly.
FRED: You're joking.
JAKE: No, no, my father weighed it all up carefully the day I was born.
FRED: Oh, your father? Was he the one who was sleeping with your
    mother? (326)

The squash-court volley of dialogue and the deliberate bathos of the old joke at the end is a pastiche of music hall comic cross-talk, parodying the dated idioms of bureaucrats as a routine rehearsal of outmoded social attitudes that involve the repression of genuine feelings. At the end of their first exchange, the sons' accusation that Andy may have gambled away their inheritance offers a possible explanation for the contempt they exhibit toward him:

FRED: The answer is your father was just a little bit short of a few
    krugerrands.
JAKE: He'd run out of pesetas in a pretty spectacular fashion.
FRED: He had, only a few nights before, dropped a packet on the pier
    at Bognor Regis.
JAKE: Fishing for tiddlers.
FRED: His casino life had long been a lost horizon.

[. . .]

JAKE: Yes—it must and will be said—the speech my father gave at
    that trustees meeting [. . .]
was the speech either of a mountebank—a child—a shyster—a fool—
    a villain—
FRED: Or a saint. (330–32)

Their debunking of Andy's patriarchal authority involves a sarcastic recognition of the stereotypical view of the paterfamilias as a kind of saint, reinforcing the play's exposure of the ideology that shaped Bel's and Andy's lives as an outmoded cliché, but it also suggests the sons' inability to grow up and accept the responsibilities of adult life.

An equivalent of a cinematic jump cut is indicated in the direction "Maria to them. Jake stands" (332). As before, no temporal sequence is specified. Maria's speech might be taken to occur immediately after the episode just witnessed ("Do you remember me?" [332]); alternatively, it could be construed as a flashback to a slightly earlier period in the sons' adolescence ("You're both so tall. I remember you when you were little boys" [332]), or it might be merely symbolic—an image produced in memory or dream—a composite representation of the way she habitually communicates with Fred and Jake on the occasions when she meets them. Maria's idiom is redolent of middle-class gentility, mixing nostalgic images of two picture-perfect families with the smug conceit of a proud mother who speaks elliptically of her children's successful careers ("My three are all in terribly good form. Sarah's doing marvelously well and Lucien's thriving at the Consulate and as for Susannah, there's no stopping her" [332]). Her glibly euphemistic speech becomes more disturbing when she talks of Andy and Bel:

> MARIA: But of course in those days—I won't deny it—I had a great affection for your father. And so had your mother—for your father. [. . .] And how he danced. One of the great waltzers. An elegance and grace long gone. [. . .] Your mother was marvelously young and quickening every moment. I—I must say—particularly when I saw your mother being swirled across the floor by your father—felt buds breaking out all over the place. I thought I'd go mad. (332–33)

Maria's recollections of the life of two happy families as a domestic idyll is disrupted by her own partial failure to censor memories of her desire for both Andy and Bel—an inappropriate topic for a conversation with their sons. Her unconscious intimation of such transgressive passions is reinforced by Andy's subsequent assertions that Maria had affairs with both Bel and himself. All four of the separate groups of characters have now been introduced (Maria's husband Ralph has been mentioned but will not appear until the eighth episode, while the ninth episode is a flashback in which Jake, Fred, and Bridget are shown together for the only time in the play).

The fifth segment is a conversation between Bel and Andy that revolves around Andy's bewilderment in the face of death, and Maria's role in their marriage:

> ANDY: I'm dying. Am I dying?
> BEL: If you were dying you'd be dead.
> ANDY: How do you work that one out? (334)

As in most of Pinter's drama, the characters find themselves in the midst of the process of living/dying, without knowing how long life will be or when it will end. Andy could be said to have been dying from the moment he was born. This exchange is elaborated in the twelfth episode of the play when Andy tries to grasp the process and meaning of death, but here it suggests the existential dilemma of having to choose how to live without being able to choose how to die. Although he recalls Bel's relationship with Maria as a lesbian affair, Andy insists he was never jealous:

> BEL: Why should you be jealous? She was your mistress. Throughout the early and lovely days of our marriage.
> ANDY: She must have reminded me of you.
>
> *Pause.*
>
> The past is a mist.
>
> *Pause.*
>
> Once . . . I remember this . . . once . . . a woman walked towards me across a darkening room.
>
> *Pause.*
>
> BEL: That was me. (336)

Andy's sarcastic quip that he was attracted to Maria because she reminded him of Bel can also suggest an archetypal pattern of male fantasy. The psychic economy of such typology reduces all women to a sexualized archetype of the feminine, so that mistress and wife ultimately become indistinguishable in Andy's memory.

In the succeeding episode, Bridget contrasts her sheltered and liberating experience of "walking slowly in a dense jungle" where "no one in the world can find me" (337) with the memory of a no man's land that might have come directly from *No Man's Land:* "I crossed so many fierce landscapes to get here. Thorns, stones, stinging nettles, barbed wire, skeletons of men and women in ditches. There was no hiding there. There was no yielding. There was no solace, no shelter" (337). Bridget evokes the liminal space between life and death that haunts Hirst's imagination, but the image might also be interpreted as a memory of her brief life, between the peace before birth and the peace of death. The lyrical tone and sensuous imagery of Bridget's speech creates a mood that is utterly incongruous with Jake and Fred's mockery of their father's civil service career, facetiously enacted at intervals during the remainder of the play. Their elaborate make-believe game is played as a burlesque of the typical British radio revue of the fifties,[11] much of its absurdity deriving from the farcical antics of bureaucrats with stereotypically blimpish British names like Macpherson, Kellaway, Saunders, Jim Sims, Manning, Rawlings, Horsfall, Bellamy, Bigsby, and Buckminster, which are incongruously juxtaposed with joke-names like Belcher, Pratt, and Hawkeye, and foreign names like Gonzalez, Rausch, and Lieutenant-Colonel Silvio d'Orangerie.

Fred and Jake's game of mistaken identities is a comic emblem of each son's failure to achieve an adult identity, while their refusal to assume the normal responsibilities of sons toward their dying father is signified when Bel attempts to make contact by telephone, by their pretending as a cruel and immature practical joke that she has reached a Chinese laundry. Their arrested adolescence is presented as a consequence of the dysfunctional relationship with their father. These episodes are interspersed with others in Andy's bedroom, including a scene with Ralph and Maria, Andy's attempt to "find" Bridget and the flashback scene of the three siblings together. Male insecurity is also represented in the parallel ways in which Andy and Ralph view each other as friends. Ralph's speech to the sons, which constitutes the eighth episode, echoes Maria's (fourth episode) in its depiction of Ralph's relationship with Andy and Bel, but it also reveals an undercurrent of masculine competitiveness.

Ralph at first conceives himself as the outdoor man (sailor and amateur referee) in opposition to Andy, who he claims "was a thinker" (342). But he admits that "after years at sea I decided to give the Arts a chance generally" (343). Ralph asserts, somewhat incongruously in the light of the philistine mentality thus far exhibited by Andy and Bel, "It was your mother and father woke me up to poetry and art. They changed my life" (343). Unconsciously perhaps, Ralph is blaming Andy and Bel for making him effeminate, for he admits that although he drank "the occasional pint [. . .] he] preferred a fruity white wine but you couldn't actually say that in those days" (343). In the ninth episode, Andy remembers Ralph as a completely ineffectual amateur referee, although he cannot recall his name: "Charming bloke. They treated him like shit. A subject of scorn [. . .] They shouted at him, they screamed at him, they called him every kind of prick" (349). The memory of Ralph's "impotent whistle" suggests that Andy has made a Freudian connection between Ralph's lack of assertiveness as a referee and his virility. Ralph's opinion of Andy as a lover of poetry and art is called into question by the gross insensitivity that leads Andy to reduce the emotional complexity of the ménage à trois to the crudest sexual level:

> ANDY: . . . [W]here is Maria? Why isn't she here? I can't die without her.
> BEL: Of course you can. And you will.
> ANDY: But think of our past. We were all so close. Think of the months I betrayed you with her. How can she forget? Think of the wonder of it. I betrayed you with your own girlfriend, she betrayed you with your husband and she betrayed her own husband—and me—with you! She broke every record in sight! She was a genius and a great fuck. (351)

The speech sounds like a coarsely comic parody of the situation in *Betrayal*, in marked contrast with Andy's wish to see Bridget and the grandchildren she was too young to provide:

> Is she bringing my grandchildren to see me? Is she? To catch their last look of me, to receive my blessing? [. . .] And what is the weather like? Is it uncertain with showers or sunny with fogpatches? Or unceasing moonlight with no cloud? Or pitch black for ever and ever? . . . There must be a loophole. The only trouble is, I can't find it. If only I could find it I would crawl through it and meet myself coming back. Like screaming with fright at the sight of a stranger only to find that you're looking into a mirror [. . .]
>
> *Pause.*
>
> But what if I cross this horizon before my grandchildren get here? They won't know where I am. (357–58)

In Andy's thoughts, questions of personal identity are linked with his position as patriarch, grandchildren representing some degree of immortality. In struggling to make sense of a life that has been fractured by the loss of his daughter and separation from his sons, he visualizes death merely as existence in an alternative dimension of space-time, a mysterious continuation in a place beyond the horizon that confers a new identity on its inhabitants. His confused attempts to conceive of a life beyond death ironically parallel Bridget's vivid and childlike descriptions of the places through which she has journeyed since "leaving" her family, Andy's vagueness contrasting with her metaphorical intimations of a transcendent realm of experience that can be conceived in visual images as absence from the spatiotemporal here-and-now.

When in the thirteenth section of the action Fred's telephone rings six times in half-light, followed by a click and a silence, the parents' experience of their sons' absence is poignantly evoked as a death comparable with that of Bridget. The theatrical image is more powerful than speech. The paradoxical experience of Bridget's material absence/presence in memory is succinctly conjured by the funny and sad fourteenth episode in which Andy stumbles about in the dark in Bridget's (ghost) area of the stage, swearing profusely as he struggles to find a drink while she is visible behind in "growing moonlight." Bel's entrance to the moonlight and her moments of silent communion with Andy convey the couple's love for Bridget and their sadness at losing her in the form of two brief tableaux whose simplicity belies the powerful depths of their emotional impact: "Andy and Bel look at each other. They turn away from each other. They stand still, listening" (360).

In the sixteenth segment, Bel's memory of finding a new identity in her relationship with Maria ("Sometimes it happens, doesn't it? You're speaking to someone and you suddenly find that you're another person" [373]) is a declaration of liberation from the confines of her relationship with Andy that elaborates the theme of identity permeating the play, while Andy's somewhat fanciful claim to have witnessed the moment to which Bel alludes in a restaurant could almost be a parody of Deeley's equivocal narrative about how he encountered Anna and Kate at the Wayfarers' Arms in *Old Times:*

> ANDY: I was spying on you both from a corner table, behind a vase of flowers and *The Brothers Karamazov.*
> [. . .]
> I was there. I heard every word.
> BEL: Not my thoughts.
> ANDY: I heard your thoughts. I could hear your thoughts.
>
> [. . .]
>
> She's the one we should both have married.

BEL: Oh no, I don't think so. I think I should have married your friend
     Ralph. (374–75)

Not only do Andy's absurd claims suggest that he, like Deeley, is
either fantasizing or lying, the echo of pulp detective fiction renders
inauthentic the feelings that may have been involved. The Strindber-
gian malice of a sexual competition conducted at Andy's deathbed is
incongruously followed by the routine chatter of Maria and Ralph in
the next episode, the banal news of their bourgeois life in a country
cottage a habitual way of avoiding knowledge of the unpleasant reality of Andy's condition until it is referred to directly by Bel ("He's on
the way out"), at which point they deny the seriousness of the situation staring them in the face ("He looks in the pink" [380]) before
beating a hasty retreat.

The desolation of an unhappily married wife obliged to wait beside her husband's bed until he dies is movingly expressed when, on
finally answering the telephone to Bel in the seventeenth episode,
Jake pretends she has reached a Chinese laundry. The cruel trick by
which both sons refuse to acknowledge her in spite of her repetition
of "Your father is very ill" (381) prompts Bel to join in the absurd
game by asking twice, "Do you do dry cleaning?" (382)—a desperate
attempt to make some sort of contact with them. In the eighteenth
episode, Andy and Bel express genuine bewilderment in the face of
death, coming closer to an honest realization of its mystery ("I don't
know. I don't know how it feels. How does it feel?" [383]); Andy reveals uncharacteristic tenderness in his wish to spare Bridget unnecessary fear. Jake and Fred then resume the acting out of their civil service parody, acknowledging the reality of their father's imminent
death in their account of the imaginary d'Orangerie's memorial service. Fred's brief eulogy for d'Orangerie ironically highlights their
failure to grieve for their own father: "I loved him. I loved him like a
father" (386).

Although it constitutes the central focus of the action, Andy's
death is never shown in *Moonlight*; during the final episode, Bridget's
recollection of being on her own, waiting for the moon to go down
before the beginning of a party, represents dying in simple but almost
mystical imagery:

BRIDGET: [T]hey told me the party wouldn't begin until the moon had gone down.

Pause.

When I got to the house it was bathed in moonlight. The house, the glade, the lane, were all bathed in moonlight. But the inside of the house was dark and all the windows were dark. There was no sound.

Pause.

I stood there in the moonlight and waited for the moon to go down.
  (387)

In language of austere beauty, the absence of Bridget's family renders her isolation in moonlight a metaphor for her death. The darkness of the house is a poignant image of her final exclusion from the party, which represents the life that is continuing without her. Poignantly, the play ends not with a conclusive image of Andy's dead body in bed but with the ghostly figure of Bridget, evoking an apparently endless moment of waiting.

No other play by Pinter runs through such a gamut of moods and styles. *Moonlight* is a late masterpiece, recapitulating motifs from all phases of Pinter's work to create a coherent drama that is innovative in its eschatological meditation on what constitutes a satisfying life—romantic love, desire, family relationships, the value of work, and the inevitability of loss. *Moonlight* is the fullest articulation of the Pinterian ghost drama in which past and present—the worlds of the living and the dead—co-exist phenomenally in a ceremonious invocation of the continuous present/s of experience/memory.

CHAPTER 9

The New World Order:
One for the Road, Mountain
Language, Party Time

After Pinter entered the public arena in the mid-1980s to express his views about the support of Western democracies for oppressive political regimes that make regular use of torture and violence, he became the target of much derision in the popular British press.[1] Nevertheless he continued to use his high profile to draw attention to the moral bankruptcy of successive British and American governments, most recently excoriating Tony Blair and George W. Bush for misleading their countrymen into supporting a war against Iraq with the alleged aim of destroying weapons of mass destruction that subsequently turned out not to exist. While ridiculed in some quarters, Pinter's stance subsequently proved to be the correct one; his plays about political interrogation and torture in prisons now appear prophetic in their envisioning of the systematic violence known to have been practiced at Guantánamo Bay, Abu Ghraib. and similar political prisons where human rights have been routinely violated in the name of democracy. In an interview first published in *The Observer* (5 October 1980) he said,

> While we are talking now, for example, people are locked up in prisons all over the place, being tortured in one way or another. I'm quite raddled with these kind of images, with the sense that these things are ever present. I have plenty of violence within me, and from a child I've lived in a world in which there has been more and more violence of one sort or another. (Smith, 72)

As early as 1977, his comments on the premiere of *The Hothouse* clarified the anti-authoritarian political stance that motivated his writing of that play as well as *The Birthday Party* and *The Dumb Waiter*, but his first attempt to deal directly with the systemic violence against political prisoners was *One for the Road* (1985). This play initiated a series of overtly political one-act dramas that caused many critics to assume that the playwright had abandoned the philosophical complexity and multi-layered ambiguity of his previous work to become a writer of didactic protest plays. Such a view is not only a crass oversimplification of Pinter's "political" plays but also ignores their new exploration of the language of power and its psychosexual pathology.

One for the Road explores the psychology of the interrogation rather than the effects of torture itself. It is the totalitarian assumption of the power of the state that renders Nicolas's insouciant attitude so horrifying. Set in an office located in a secret penal institution, the play never specifies in what country the institution is situated, nor whether its government is a democracy or a dictatorship; indeed the precise historical details are irrelevant to the play's unremitting focus on the banal fact of human cruelty. The scene is simple—a room with a desk and some chairs. The appearance of the bruised prisoner Viktor, who has clearly been tortured, belies Nicolas's assertion that they are both civilized men. Nicolas quietly intimidates Viktor, not by abusing him physically, but by a verbal intimation of the unlimited power conferred on him by the institution:

> NICOLAS: I wave my big finger in front of your eyes. Like this. And now I do the same with my little finger. I can use both . . . at the same time. Do you think I'm mad? My mother did. [. . .] But would you take the same view if it were my boot—or my penis? Why am I so obsessed with eyes? [. . .] Not my eyes. Other people's eyes. The eyes of people who are brought to me here. They're so vulnerable. The soul shines through them. (223–24)[2]

Throughout the play Nicolas reminds the prisoners that he is having a drink—"one for the road"—thereby drawing attention ironically to the humiliating fact that he can do what he wants in their presence, while they can only do what he tells them.[3] The most horrifying way in which Nicolas tortures Viktor is through the apparently off-the-cuff insinuations that his wife Gila and seven-year-old son Nicky might come to harm, beginning in the first scene with his observation that she is a "good-looking woman" (224) and continuing at intervals throughout the action.

Pinter's early preoccupation with authority reappears in a wholly different context with Nicolas's ironic assertion of godlike authority ("I run the place. God speaks through me" [225]), before he demonstrates his point by ordering Viktor to stand up and sit down. His unnecessary gesture of thanking Viktor for obeying orders proves that the velvet glove he wears has no need to conceal its iron fist. The politeness is a form of humiliation that reinforces the abject status of the victim by the pretense that he has freedom to choose. The feigned politeness of the "civilized" man continues to be exploited as a strategy with which to humiliate Viktor, as Nicolas rationalizes the thuggish behavior of his henchmen:

> NICOLAS: I hear you have a lovely house. Lots of books. Someone told me some of my boys kicked it around a bit. Pissed on the rugs, that sort of thing. I wish they wouldn"t do that. I do really. But you know what it's like—they have such responsibilities [. . .] and so, sometimes, they piss on a few rugs. You understand. You're not a fool.
>
> *Pause.*
>
> Is your son all right? (228)

By appealing to Viktor as a gentleman and man of the world he tacitly asks him to condone the abuse that has been meted out to his family and himself, the ultimate strategy in a process whereby the dissident is conditioned to accept that the violation of his rights is for his own good. The sinister implications of the feigned concern about Viktor's son are calculated to remind him of his utter powerlessness at the mercy of Nicolas and his establishment. Nicolas knows that Viktor must be extremely anxious about the fate of his son since he is presumably responsible for arranging their separate incarcerations, yet he persists with the question in order to suggest that Nicky is actually in danger.

Nicolas now plays a game with Viktor, tormenting him with the thought that he may be killed without directly saying that he will be. In doing so, he teasingly alludes to the psychological motivation of professional interrogators like himself, possibly revealing more of his own fantasies than he intends:

> NICOLAS: I'm prepared to be frank as a true friend should. I love death. What about you?
>
> *Pause.*
>
> What about you? Do you love death? Not necessarily your own. Others? The death of others. [. . .] do you love the death of others as much as I do?
>
> [. . . . .]
>
> Death. Death. Death. Death. As has been noted by the most respected authorities, it is beautiful. The purest, most harmonious thing there is. Sexual intercourse is nothing compared to it. (229)

Although the pleasure Nicolas derives from possessing the power of life or death over his prisoners reveals the psychosexual desire that is the motor of such an institution—its heart of darkness—he does not intend these words merely to express his sadistic impulses, but to taunt Viktor with the absolute power he wields over him, appealing to his supposed fellow-feelings in order to make him collude in his own torture.[4] He then terrorizes Viktor more crudely with respect to his wife, implying that she is bleeding as a resulting of having been sexually assaulted:

> NICOLAS: Does she . . . fuck? Or does she . . . ? Does she . . . like . . . you know . . . what?
>
> [. . .]
>
> Your wife and I had a very nice chat but I couldn't help noticing that she didn't look her best. She's probably . . . menstruating. Women do that.
>
> [. . .]
>
> Tell me . . . truly . . . are you beginning to love me?
>
> *Pause.*
>
> I think your wife is. Beginning. She is beginning to fall in love with me. (230–31)

In response to this perverse game of intimidation, Viktor asks Nicolas to kill him, which Nicolas claims is a sign that he is hungry or thirsty, counseling him against despair and ending the scene with the astonishing comment, "Your soul shines out of your eyes" (233).

The second scene shows Nicolas subjecting Viktor's son to a subtle yet insidious form of psychological cruelty, which involves an absurd parody of conventional interrogation strategies for adults:

NICOLAS: Do you like your mummy and daddy?

Pause.

Do you like your mummy and daddy?
NICKY: Yes.
NICOLAS: Why?

Pause.

Why?

Pause.

Do you find that a hard question to answer?

Pause.

NICKY: Where's mummy?
NICOLAS: You don't like your mummy and daddy?
NICKY: Yes, I do.
NICOLAS: Why? (235–36)

In the third scene, after subjecting Viktor's wife Gila to the same type of interrogation as her son, asking her unanswerable questions such as *why* she met her husband, Nicolas call her a "fuckpig" and attacks her verbally for insulting "the memory of [. . . her] father [who] . . . fought for his country" (140), before asking her repeatedly how many times his men have raped her, thereby attempting to make it her responsibility to account for the atrocities committed against her.

The final moments of her intimidation by Nicolas as the scene ends seem entirely gratuitous, his exultation in his power over her shown by his nonchalant objectification of her as a woman, while his veiled suggestion that her son will be killed is calculated to cause her intolerable anguish:

You're a lovely woman. Well, you were.

He leans back, drinks, sighs.

Your son is . . . seven. He's a little prick. You made him so. You have
  taught him to be so.

[. . .]

Oh well . . . in one way I suppose it's academic

Pause.

You're of no interest to me. I might even let you out of here, in due
course. But I should think you might entertain us all a little more before you go. (244)

The intimation that Gila will be interned a bit longer so that she can
be further used to pleasure his associates completes her debasement
to the status of a sexual object. The final scene reveals Nicolas's upper-class understatement as a habitual mode of euphemism that permits the oppressor to normalize the systematic torture and degradation of political prisoners by referring to it as a necessary function of
government.

The irony of Nicolas's question, "How have you been? Surviv-
ing?" can be seen in context as a horrifying joke: Viktor has had his
tongue cut out and has barely survived his period of incarceration.
His final humiliation comes when Nicolas again adopts the fiction
that they are equals enjoying the good news of Viktor's imminent re-
lease:

What about a drink? One for the road. What do you say to a drink?
[. . .] our business [. . .] is, I remind you, to keep the world clean for
God. Get me? Drink up. Drink up. Are you refusing to drink with
me?

Viktor drinks. His head falls back.

Cheers.

Nicolas drinks.

You can go.

Pause.

You can leave. (246)

Nicolas's alternation between subtly threatening and ostensibly
friendly postures suggests a degree of insecurity, hinting that he ac-

tually desires the prisoner to approve the behavior of his torturer. His character provides an appalling illustration of the psychological implications of the truism, "power corrupts." He has become addicted to the sadistic pleasure of wielding unlimited power, and even seems to believe the horrible cliché that his brutality is "keeping the world clean for God" (246). The most morally repugnant moment comes at the very end of the play when in response to Viktor's struggle to ask about his son, Nicolas coolly replies, "Your son? Oh don't worry about him. He was a little prick" (247).

The dramatic economy of the reference to Nicky in the past tense is devastating. Without risking a voyeuristic response by showing an audience any act of violence on stage, the play evokes the bleakest landscape of human suffering and evil, anticipating the horrors so graphically illustrated on television during the wars in the former Yugoslavia and in Iraq over the last twenty years. Through its brilliant representation of the interrogator's language of euphemism, irony, and equivocation, *One for the Road* exposes the dishonesty endemic in any intelligence agency that justifies the use of torture in the service of state security. By concentrating exclusively on the relationship between the head of the organization and a family of prisoners, the play depicts the mentality that allows unspeakable cruelty to persist, and shows that brutality and torture are unacceptable, no matter what value system they are used to defend. The focus on a few temporal fragments that obliquely infer an "offstage" narrative of deprivation and torture is typical of Pinter's minimalist "art of taking away" (Kael, 218). More unsettling than a conventional representation of violent interrogation, these elliptical scenes stimulate each member of the audience to imagine a dizzying set of putative scenarios; conventional devices of suspense are avoided by the arrangement of action as a sequence of conversational duets that repeatedly infer the literal horror of the victims' experience while pretending to mask it through the use of euphemistic clichés. Such a technique of representation foregrounds the sophisticated misuse of language by modern societies as a systematic method of justifying atrocities committed in the name of state security.

The violation of human rights also comprises the central theme of *Mountain Language* (1988), an austere twenty-minute play that explores the implications of the systematic denial of the right to speak one's own language in four shocking, yet darkly humorous scenes. Inspired by Pinter's investigation of the plight of the Kurds on a trip to Turkey with Arthur Miller in 1985, the play does not attempt to articulate an argument concerning the particular historical circumstances of political oppression in the contemporary world, but to confront audiences with the mechanisms of repression typically employed to enforce the individual's conformity to state authority. Pinter's early interest in the arbitrariness of authority and in the dual function of language to reveal and conceal individual identity motivates a new concern with the power to exploit language as a means of political control. Whereas *One for the Road* portrays the misuse of language in the process of neutralizing political dissidents, *Mountain Language* goes further in exploring the subjection of a population through the systematic policing of their language. By depriving the mountain people of their right to speak their own local language, the state undermines the integrity of these individuals, denying them their humanity and reducing them to the level of animals, unable to express their thoughts and feelings.

Mountain Language depicts the corporeal reality of state power in the context of the corruption and manipulation of language as a system of control, but again, without ever portraying an act of violence on stage. When the play opens an elderly woman is nursing a wounded hand that has been bit by a Doberman Pinscher belonging to one of the soldiers, so an audience is shown the effect of violence on an individual, rather than being excited by a representation of the act itself. From the opening scene, the audience observes the use of language to discipline and control the mountain people. The Sergeant bullies the women by repeatedly demanding their names, while the young woman resists by claiming, "We've given our names" (251). The officer insults the young woman in a more sophisticated manner by asking who bit her and then demanding to know the name of the dog that did it:

> OFFICER: Every dog has a *name*! They answer to their name. They are given a name by their parents and that is their name. That is their *name*! Before they bite, they *state* their name. It's a formal procedure. They state their name and then they bite. (253–54)

The insane obsession with bureaucratic correctness that pertains even to dogs illustrates the inhumanity of a system that exists to maintain its authority rather than to protect its citizens (the dog is permitted to bite as long as it follows correct procedure); it is obliquely suggested that the status of prisoners and their families is below that of dogs. The Sergeant bluntly advertises the power of the state to define good and evil for its citizens through the manipulation of language: "Your husbands, your sons, your fathers, these men you have been waiting to see, are shithouses. They are enemies of the State. They are shithouses" (255). The officer's approach is more subtle, yet every bit as ruthless in suppressing the citizens' freedom: "Your language is dead. It is forbidden. It is not permitted to speak your mountain language in this place. You cannot speak your language to your men. [. . .] Your language no longer exists. Any questions?" (255–56).

The only woman named in the play is Sarah Johnson, a sign of her individual resistance to the state authority. By distinguishing herself from the mountain people ("I do not speak the mountain language" [256]) she lays herself open to sexist abuse by the Sergeant ("What language do you speak? What language do you speak with your arse?" [256])—a dehumanized object reduced to her biological functions. In the next scene in the visitor's room, Pinter breaks the naturalistic convention of conversation by combining this with a voice-over technique whereby the prisoner and his mother "hear" in their heads the things the other wishes to say in the forbidden mountain language. The mastery of a minimalist aesthetic is complete; on the surface the scene is little more than a tableau, the bullying guard illustrating the phallic power of patriarchy by jabbing her with his truncheon in order to stop her from speaking the mountain language, while the elderly woman and her son communicate through the empathic process of looking into each other's eyes and imagining what the other wishes to say. The guard criminalizes the woman's inability to understand his language, as though he was making her responsible for repressing the use of her own language, and he uses the crudest linguistic tactic to dehumanize the son and his family: "I've got a wife and three kids. And you're all a pile of shit" (260). The silences indicated in the script are telling, as the scene manifests a subtextual drama of unspoken thoughts and feelings that overwhelms the spare dialogue. The prisoner's assertion of his own humanity ("I've got a wife and three kids" [260]) in response to the Guard's bullying is perceived as an act of resistance that prompts the Guard to telephone the Sergeant and inform him, "I think I've got a joker in here" (260), a hint that the prisoner will be brutally punished for his insolence.

The voice-overs, heard in half-light with the human figures frozen, are profoundly moving in their evocation of a language of loving humanity that transcends the ugly brutality of the prison system:

ELDERLY WOMAN'S VOICE: The baby is waiting for you.

[. . . . .]

When you come home there'll be such a welcome for you. Everyone is waiting for you. They're all waiting for you. They're all waiting to see you. (261)

The spell of this loving "exchange" of thoughts is broken by the Sergeant's abrupt entrance with the brusque question "What joker" as the lights fade up suddenly before the scene ends in a blackout.

The third scene entitled "Voice in the Darkness" begins literally with the Sergeant's voice in darkness:

Who's that fucking woman? What's that fucking woman doing here? Who let that fucking woman through that fucking door?
SECOND GUARD'S VOICE: She's his wife.

Lights up.

A corridor. (262)

With the utmost economy, the scene is established as a surreal tableau in which Sarah Johnson discovers the hooded figure of her husband, presumably being escorted from an interrogation room to his cell. The impact of the repeated expletive "fucking" is both a realistic representation of the demeaning and violent idiom of prison speech and a surreal foreshadowing of the ending of the scene where Sarah shows her comprehension of the currency of sexual favors that operates in this world. The Sergeant's sarcastic gallantry in addressing a woman he identifies as more educated than himself hints at the possibility of barter: "Hello, Miss. Sorry. A bit of a breakdown in administration. They've sent you through the wrong door. [. . .] Anyway, what can I do for you, dear lady, as they used to say in the movies?" (262–63).

The voice-over convention of the previous scene is repeated as the audience witnesses Sarah Johnson staring at her husband in half-light, the gentle reminiscences of their shared affection in stark contrast to the brutal image of his confinement. When the lights come up again, the hooded figure collapses and the guard drags him off. In a bizarre version of the incident where the dog is treated as a person, the computer is spoken of as a live person—an instance of anthropomorphosis that is the logical inverse of a system that reduces people to material objects: "The computer's got a double hernia." When recommended to contact Joseph Dokes if she wants any information about the prison, Sarah demonstrates her understanding of the way power operates here by saying, "Can I fuck him? If I fuck him will everything be all right?" (264). Her gesture of defiance is indicated in the way she linguistically assumes the active role. The sergeant's cynicism is implied in his reply, "Sure. No problem," while Sarah's "Thank you" sarcastically reveals her ability to play the game of subservient whore to the authorities in power. The exchange is grimly humorous yet also profoundly unsettling in its revelation of the way even the most intelligent resistance gives way to the complete control of bodies and minds that defines a totalitarian regime.

In the final scene in the visitors room, the elderly woman's son has blood on his face and is trembling—the visible effects of the torture that has occurred offstage. The scene concisely illustrates the inhumanity of the police system by revealing the arbitrariness of the rules that determine the mental and physical abuse suffered by prisoners and their families:

> GUARD: Oh, I forgot to tell you. They've changed the rules. She can speak. She can speak in her own language. Until further notice.
> PRISONER: She can speak?
> GUARD: Yes. Until further notice. New rules. (265)

The arbitrariness is implied by casual repetition by the guard of "until further notice," indicating that the mountain people are entirely subject to the whim of their rulers; the fact that he forgot to inform them being a subtle reminder that the jailer has completely arbitrary power over every aspect of the oppressed individual's life. But the real evil of this system is evoked in the mother's terrified incomprehension of her son's invitation to her to speak in her own language.

She does not reply, either because she is scared to risk being tricked into doing the wrong thing, or because she has been so terrorized that she no longer has the will to communicate with her son. Her failure to respond to her son's appeals ("Do you hear me?" [266]) seems to upset him so much that his trembling grows until he falls from the chair gasping and shaking as the sergeant enters and concludes the play: "Look at this. You go out of your way to give them a helping hand and they fuck it up" (267).

The repetition of the word "fuck" is strangely powerful at this point, not only reinforcing the utter dehumanization of the prisoner and his mother, but echoing the strategic use of the word in scene 3, where fucking becomes a matter of choice for the individual who can either cooperate with the obscene system or become its helpless victim. The sergeant's words are a grotesque example of how individuals are made responsible for the violence suffered by them at the hands of the totalitarian system, the moral that "they asked for it" signifying the victim's ultimate degradation.

Party Time

In *Party Time* Pinter continues to anatomize the systems whereby postmodern societies mask the brutal reality of state power. Here he extends the technique of *One for the Road* in which a series of conversations comprise a fragmented narrative whose gaps and silences indicate a subtextual story of military force and police violence. The implied contrast between the conspicuous consumption witnessed at the onstage party and the material deprivation of the prisoner Jimmy—an "offstage" presence only seen as a ghostly figure at the end of the play—offers a devastating illustration of the power of the modern state to neutralize opposition by means of exclusion. The beginning of the action establishes Gavin as the suave host of a party, engaged in conversation with the insecure and somewhat obsequious Terry, who is extolling the virtues of an exclusive new club. Social pleasantries are disrupted by the entrance of Terry's wife Dusty, whose urgent question, "Did you hear what's happened to Jimmy?" (284), introduces an apparently inappropriate note of personal anxiety that causes the other guests to freeze for a moment, disturbing the complacent poise of the social celebration. Terry's momentarily angry response is a further socially inappropriate expression of genuine emotion: "Nobody's discussing this. Nobody's discussing this, you follow? If you're not a good girl, I'll spank you" (284). The unease introduced by Dusty's question is compounded a few moments later by Dame Melissa's more urbane but nonetheless perplexing entrance speech:

> What on earth's going on out there? It's like the Black Death . . . The town is dead, there's nobody on the streets, there's not a soul in sight apart from some . . . soldiers. My driver had to stop at a . . . you know, what d'you call it? A roadblock. We had to say who we were. It really was a trifle . . . (286)

In its opening minutes the play not only maps the emblematic divide between the insiders and the excluded, the scene (a luxurious apartment) and the unseen (the contiguous offstage world of the street outside), but in parallel exposes the Establishment's rituals of social self-approbation. The true identities of individual characters are never explicitly revealed. For the whole duration of the play the audience is therefore challenged to decipher clues about the precise nature of the network of power relationships that lies below the surface of the characters' behavior.

There are eighteen segments of action/conversation. The plot unfolds simply as a series of constantly reforming conversation groups in which guests jockey to establish their positions within the supposed hierarchy of the group (emblematized by the idea of joining "the club"). The snippets of gossip and chatter are juxtaposed as fragmented narratives that repeatedly provoke unanswered questions about who the speakers are and what their relationship is with the unexplained "round-up" that is apparently occurring in the streets outside. As representatives of the power of the Establishment, the behavior of Dame Melissa and Gavin is in complete harmony with their social environment. By contrast, Liz and Terry are desperately eager to adopt the trappings of this lifestyle and therefore each attempts to play the role of appreciative guest. In this context "becoming a member of the club" involves keeping one's body trim and sexually attractive. This discourse of the body is overtly elaborated in Liz's and Charlotte's gossip over sexual adventuring in the fifth section of the play. Their language provides a surreal echo of the previous speech of Terry ("You keep hearing all these things spread by pricks about pricks" [288]), amplifying the objectification of the body through a fetishizing of male body parts:

LIZ: So beautiful. The mouth, really. And of course the eyes.
CHARLOTTE: Yes
LIZ: Not to mention his hands [. . . . .
. . . .]
LIZ: But that bitch had her legs all over him
[. . . . .]
CHARLOTTE: That's why you're in such pain
LIZ: Yes, because that bigtitted tart—
CHARLOTTE: Raped the man you loved. (290)

In an absurdly comic inversion of the traditional sexual conquest of a passive woman by a lustful man, Liz and Charlotte speak of Liz's female rival as a rapist, appropriating conventions of masculine sex-talk in order to assert the force of Liz's own desires. Such a conflation of pornographic fantasies and sentimental love reflects the psychological clichés of women's magazines of the eighties and nineties, ironically emblematizing the pervasive sexualization of culture for commercial profit. The conversation clearly introduces a psychosexual dimension into the discourse of power and privilege that the stage image embodies.

The behavior of the characters seems to suggest that Gavin and Melissa are at the apex of a hierarchy determined by social status, with Fred, Douglas, Charlotte, and Liz below them, and Pamela, Emily, Suki, Sam, Harlow, and Smith[5] on the lowest rung of the ladder. Terry and Dusty's comparative lack of urbanity and Terry's working-class London dialect indicate that they are part of a class of ambitious "servants" given privileged access to the social rituals of the ruling class in order to do its dirty work. The precise nature of the hierarchy is never directly revealed, and is complicated by the coexistence of a shadowy nexus of power relationships dominated by Gavin, in which men have unquestioned power over women and all the men other than Jimmy are Gavin's assistants and henchmen. In one respect *Party Time* represents the way in which the monetarist government policies of the eighties constituted a realignment of privilege and power, effecting the rapprochement between new money and the old ruling elite (aristocracy and the Oxbridge-educated upper middle class).

Douglas and Fred's conversations elliptically allude to the reasons for the military activity that seems to be taking place in the street. They attempt to justify it in the threatening language of military or police strategy—without any concern for justice or human rights:

> DOUGLAS: We want peace and we're going to get it. But we want that peace to be cast iron . . .
> Tight as a drum. That's the kind of peace we want. And that's the kind of peace we're going to get. A cast iron peace. *(He clenches his fist)* Like this.
> FRED: You know, I really admire people like you.
> DOUGLAS: So do I. (292–93)

On the surface, their mutual admiration comically evokes the homoerotic frisson of young sportsmen, but the smug self-righteousness of these middle-aged men is horrifying in its narcissistic intimation of the attractiveness of brute force as a proto-fascist means of maintaining social harmony.

The conversation rather disturbingly implicates Fred and Charlotte in some kind of previous sexual liaison, compressing unemotional references to what must have been the political execution of her husband in a cool line of cocktail party chatter wholly unsuited to the discussion of such a grave matter.

> CHARLOTTE: Oh my husband. Oh yes. That's right. He died.
> FRED: Was it a long illness?
> CHARLOTTE: Short.
> FRED: Ah.
>
> *Pause.*
>
> Quick then
> CHARLOTTE: Quick, yes. Short and quick.
> [. . . . .]
> FRED: [. . .] A quick death must be better than a slow one. It stands to reason—
> CHARLOTTE: No it doesn't.
>
> *Pause.*

CHARLOTTE: Anyway, I'll bet it can be quick and slow at the same time. Oh by the way, he wasn't ill.

Pause.

FRED: You're still very beautiful. (305–7)

Their behavior here emblematizes the postmodern collapse of the ethical order of society into a sexualized regime of consumption in which people become potential playthings, objects of desire rather than moral agents. The masculine desire for power that exults in its ability to torture and kill Charlotte's husband is the same impulse that derives pleasure from the contemplation of possessing her sexually:

CHARLOTTE: God, your looks! No, seriously. You're still so hand-some! How do you do it? What's your diet? What's your regime? What is your regime, by the way? What do you do to keep yourself so . . . I don't know . . . so trim, so fit?
FRED: I lead a clean life. (307)

References to sport playfully thematize the corporeal presence and visual display of bodies in the mise-en-scène.

As in *The Birthday Party*, the artist (musician) is considered by the Establishment as the social nonconformist whose threat to authority must be ruthlessly repressed. As they quaff champagne, Smith and Harlow's crude platitudes are reminiscent of the school bully's pleasure at hurting the sensitive child:

SAM: I mean—I met a man at a party the other day. I couldn't believe it. He was talking the most absolute, bloody crap. His ideas about the world and that kind of thing. He was a complete and utter and total arsehole. A musician or something.
SMITH: Stoddard.
SAM: That's it. Now you see, these kind of people, they're an infection.
SMITH: Don't worry about Stoddard. We've seen him off.
HARLOW: We've had him for breakfast.[6]

Harlow's last line is a commonplace euphemism for violence that grimly exploits the motif of consumption, and Sam's use of the word "infection" invokes images of bodily health variously reiterated throughout *Party Time* as metonymic signs of the body politic.

The repeated attempts of the characters at the party to join or construct groups and subgroups reveal their need to gain or demonstrate their access to society's locus of power as represented by the club Terry introduces at the opening of the play. The party ends with Melissa and Gavin being applauded for their self-congratulatory speeches in celebration of the selfish and narcissistic ethos institutionalized by the club. Melissa's references to the replacement of the tennis and swimming clubs of her youth by the new club emblematizes the old Establishment's reconstitution of itself during the eighties in a less traditionally class-based form. Her membership of the new club demonstrates a conjunction of the authority of the traditionally aristocratic Establishment with the consumerist Darwinism of the New Right, her casual dismissal of her old friends ("they weren't my friends, anyway" [311]) revealed as a ruthlessly self-serving betrayal of old loyalties.[7]

As a coda to the main action of the play, Jimmy, dressed in immaculately white clothes, appears in the outer doorway; his appearance identifies his body in direct visual opposition to the sleek bodies of the partygoers—conspicuous consumers whose fashionable black evening dress fetishizes the power and glamour of their "designer" bodies. His significant absence from the plenitude emblematized by the party defamiliarizes the games of social competition and conformity represented by the unceasing attempts of the party guests to avoid social ostracism. Excluded from the comfortable world of the power elite—outside the door to Gavin's elegant apartment—are those like Jimmy. Although the performance stresses Jimmy's vulnerability, there is no literal representation of the physical torture he must have endured. His oppression is implied by his words, suggesting that he has been deprived of light, that he lives in a world of sounds, and that his identity has been negated by his isolation from human society:

> I had a name. It was Jimmy. People called me Jimmy. That was my name [. . .] Sometimes, a door bangs. I hear voices, then it stops. Everything stops. It all stops. It closes down. It shuts. It all shuts. It shuts down. It shuts. I see nothing at anytime any more. I sit sucking the dark. It's what I have. The dark is in my mouth and I suck it. It's the only thing I have. It's mine. It's my own. I suck it. (313–14)

Jimmy's total deprivation is the inverse of the comforts of material plenitude that the party represents. The political theme of the drama is thus articulated through the contrast between the plenitude of here and the void of an unlocated and terrifying elsewhere. Exclusion is identified as the definitive modern form of oppression. The battle taking place "in the street" involves the protection of such locations of conspicuous consumption from the have-nots, those excluded by accident of birth or by political choice from the material power of plenty.

The last piece of dramatic writing Pinter completed was the seven-minute sketch *Press Conference*, premiered at his invitation by the Department of Drama, Goldsmiths College, in 2001 before he performed in it himself on the set of the National Theatre production of *No Man's Land* in February 2002 as part of a 40-minute program of his sketches. Pinter's suavely sinister portrayal of a government minister at a press briefing was understood by some critics as a comment on African dictators, but his speech to the House of Commons less than a year later makes it obvious he had in mind a leader closer to home.

> One of the more nauseating images of the year 2002 is that of our Prime Minister [Tony Blair] kneeling in the church on Christmas Day praying for peace on earth and good will towards all men while simultaneously preparing to assist in the murder of thousands of totally innocent people in Iraq [. . .] Power, as has often been remarked, is the great aphrodisiac, and so, it would seem, is the death of others [. . .] The planned war can only bring about [. . .] widespread death, mutilation and disease, an estimated one million refugees and escalation of violence throughout the world, but it will still masquerade as a "moral crusade," a "just war," a war waged by "freedom loving democracies," to bring "democracy" to Iraq. The stink of the hypocrisy is suffocating. (House of Commons Speech, 21 January 2003)

Although his political views were repeatedly caricatured by the British press as eccentric and extreme, he proved to be utterly correct about the war in Iraq, and gained the respect and admiration of millions of Britons when on 15 February he addressed the demonstration and march—estimated at between one and two million people—to protest against the war. His late poem *Death* reminds those who, like Blair and Bush, authorize wars, of the vast gulf between death as a statistic and as a personal confrontation with a person who is no longer living:

Death (Births and Deaths Registration Act 1953)

Where was the body found?
Who found the dead body?
Was the dead body dead when found?
How was the dead body found?
Who was the dead body?
Who was the father or daughter or brother
Or uncle or sister or mother or son
Of the dead and abandoned body?

Was the body dead when abandoned?
Was the body abandoned?
By whom had it been abandoned?
Was the dead body naked or dressed for a journey?
What made you declare the dead body dead?
Did you declare the dead body dead?
How well did you know the dead body?
How did you know the body was dead?
Did you wash the dead body
Did you close both its eyes
Did you bury the body
Did you leave it abandoned
Did you kiss the dead body

CHAPTER 10

A Postmodern Aesthetics of Power:
Ashes to Ashes, Celebration

For Pinter, it was a paradox that while he as a citizen believed it was imperative to assume personal responsibility for the dictates of his political conscience, drama itself was not a didactic form of political agitprop. Although he made speeches and wrote articles to excoriate both corrupt dictators and Western leaders—he believed Western democracies to be morally as culpable of abusing human rights in the establishment and maintenance of a "new world order" as overtly totalitarian regimes—he insisted that his plays were poetic visions of how things are that arose from his unconscious mind. He maintained that he never wrote plays as arguments but as deeply felt images; those that illuminated the hidden abuses of power in the contemporary world certainly represented his personal experience of the world but were not written to order as a comment on it.

In *Ashes to Ashes* Pinter returns to the form of conversational duologue first developed in *Night* and subsequently elaborated with variations in the opening section of *Old Times:* a man is attempting to assert some kind of dominance over his wife as they reminisce about the past. Whereas in *Night* a comic drama emerges from the discrepancy between his and her memories of their first meeting, in both *Old Times* and *Ashes to Ashes,* the man struggles to prevent the woman from resisting his desire to interpret her memories in a way that gratifies him. There is a minimum of physical action and the conversation follows the associative logic of the unconscious; it is possible to identify twenty-two moments when one topic of conversation elicits another before giving way to it, yet occasionally the new subject appears to have no rational connection with that which preceded it.

The dramatic rhythm of the play is established at the outset by Devlin's voyeuristic insistence on pursuing his enquiry into Rebecca's sadomasochistic memory or fantasy of an earlier lover:

> REBECCA: Well . . . for example . . . he would stand over me and clench his fist. And then he'd put his other hand on my neck and grip it and bring my head towards him. His fist... grazed my mouth and he'd say, "Kiss my fist."
>
> [. . . . .]
>
> *Pause.*
>
> And then I would speak.
>
> DEVLIN: What did you say? You said what? What did you say?
>
> *Pause.*
>
> I said, "Put your hand round my throat." I murmured it through his hand, as I was kissing it . . . (395–96)[1]

After revealing more details of this intimate sexual encounter, Rebecca is silent before Devlin attempts to change the subject by asking her if she feels she is being hypnotized, a strange form of displacement, because it appears as if he himself is mesmerized by her account. Devlin tries to rationalize his own fixation on her liaison:

> DEVLIN: You understand why I'm asking you these questions. Don't you? Put yourself in my place. I'm compelled to ask you questions. There are so many things I don't know. I know nothing . . . about any of this. Nothing. I'm in the dark. I need light. Or do you think my questions are illegitimate? (399)

Devlin assumes the archetypically domineering posture of masculine rationality, casting Rebecca as the traditionally emotional female. The repetition of words like "questions" and the somewhat melodramatic rhetoric of being in the dark needing light betrays a degree of paranoia on his part, while the odd choice of the word "illegitimate" in this context seems portentous. As in both *Night* and *Old Times*, the man's insistence on the reasonable nature of his inquiry together with the woman's constant evasiveness establishes a pattern of interrogation that transforms an intimate conversation into a bullying cross-examination.

Devlin's demand that Rebecca "define" her past lover is expressed in language whose pretended attitude of scientific objectivity betrays the irrational jealousy that is his true motivation:

> DEVLIN: Physically, I mean, what did he actually look like. [. . .] Can't you give him a shape for me, a concrete shape? I want a concrete image of him, you see . . . an image I can carry about with me. I mean all you can talk of are his hands, one hand over your face, the other on the back of your neck, then the first one on your throat. There must be more to him than hands. What about eyes? Did he have any eyes?
>
> REBECCA: What colour? (400)

At this point images of body parts are positioned in an almost surrealistic syntactical jumble. The naming of parts in three short lines of a speech—hands, hands, face, neck, throat, hands, eyes, eyes—constitutes an effect of defamiliarization that transforms them into material objects divorced from a human context. Rebecca's response ("What colour?") is a non sequitur, suggesting that she is not concentrating on his questions but is lost in her own reverie, so that Devlin's mention of eyes only acts as a prompt to her involuntary memory.

Rebecca's reply cues the next change of topic, a further association being provoked by Devlin addressing her as darling: "How odd to be called darling. No one has ever called me darling. Apart from my lover" (400). In this speech Rebecca rejects any implication that Devlin might see himself in the same relationship to her as her "lover," causing him to use the word "illegitimate" again: "Do you think my use of the word is illegitimate?" (401). Rebecca then rejects any claim Devlin makes to being her darling, which introduces an extraordinary exchange:

> REBECCA: I'm nobody's darling
> DEVLIN: That's a song
> REBECCA: What?
> DEVLIN: "I'm nobody's baby now"
> REBECCA: It's "You're nobody's baby now." But anyway, I didn't use the word baby. (401–2)

The exchange harks back to the device in *Old Times* when Deeley and Anna engage in a competition to remember lyrics of old songs, but this moment in *Ashes to Ashes* anticipates a harrowing image of a baby that dominates the concluding section of the play.

After revealing that her lover was some sort of guide in a tourist agency, Rebecca switches from answering Devlin's question about the man's physical appearance to recall a "kind of factory" he took her to, where all the workers doffed their caps to him:

> They had great faith in him. They respected his ... purity, his ... conviction. They would follow him over a cliff and into the sea, if he asked them, he said. And sing in a chorus, as long as he led them. They were in fact very musical, he said. (405)

The images of order and authority are somewhat unsettling, even more so when Rebecca recalls how she looked for a bathroom but could not find one.[2] The sudden shock created by her memory that her lover "used to go to the local railway station and walk down the platform and tear all the babies from the arms of their screaming mothers" (406–7) is a further example of the surrealist technique of juxtaposing verbal images that are utterly incongruous. In this case the violent image of babies being torn from their mothers' arms is alarmingly suggestive of a Holocaust narrative, with Rebecca's lover in the position of a ruthless Nazi officer.

After a silence the surrealist technique is continued as Rebecca says she is "terribly upset" about "that police siren we heard a couple of minutes ago" (407), explaining that "as the siren faded away in my ears I knew it was becoming louder and louder for someone else" (408). Rebecca claims that she feels "terribly insecure" because she hates "losing it. I hate somebody else possessing it. I want it to be mine, all the time" (408). This bizarre image is an emblem of the key theme elaborated in *Ashes to Ashes*—the relationship between the primary experience of those who suffer and the ambivalent identification of those who did not actually share it.[3] As the conversation continues in a cyclical pattern, Rebecca keeps reliving her voyeuristic experience of moments redolent of a Holocaust narrative, while Devlin compulsively strives to possess a full image of Rebecca's fascist lover, finally attempting to re-enact their sadomasochistic encounter as she guiltily recalls giving up a baby to be murdered by the man. From the conversation about the police siren to the end of the play, every one of Rebecca's visions/memories involves some notion of guilt or responsibility for unnamed crimes or sins. She assumes some kind of moral responsibility for a pen she had left on the coffee table falling onto the carpet, referring to it, somewhat uncannily, as "innocent." In denying her right to express a point of view on the matter, Devlin anthropomorphizes the pen: "You can't know it was innocent [. . .] Because you don't know where it had been. [. . .] You know nothing of its history [. . .] of its parents' history" (410).

Devlin's insistent denial of her authority to discuss the kind of atrocity she has described, his words echoing his earlier question of whether it was "legitimate" for him to call Rebecca "darling," prompts her to reply: "I have no authority. Nothing has ever happened to me. Nothing has ever happened to any of my friends. I have never suffered. Nor have my friends" (413). Although as a middle-class English woman Rebecca has no firsthand experience of the kind of atrocities that occurred during the Holocaust, she is haunted—as indeed are many people born after the war—by nightmare images of inhumanity that produce a kind of "survivor guilt" in those who feel compelled to imagine its horrors. Devlin cannot imagine how such an evil man could love Rebecca ("He suffocated you and strangled you"), but she remains under his spell ("No, no. He felt compassion for me. He adored me" [414]). Rebecca continues to recall images derived from accounts of the Holocaust. One in particular involves a dreamlike image of a group of people she saw from the window of a house in Dorset, walking through the woods and into the sea dressed in winter coats: "It was such a lovely day. It was so still and the sun was shining. And I saw all those people walk into the sea" (416). The startling contrast between a Dorset summer and the freezing cold typical of documentary images of extermination camps is another variant on the surrealist juxtapositions of contradictory images within a single frame.

Ignoring Devlin's questions about when she lived in Dorset, Rebecca almost whimsically recalls hearing about the condition of mental elephantiasis:

> . . . when you spill an ounce of gravy, for example, it immediately expands and becomes a vast sea of gravy [. . .] which surrounds you on

all sides and you suffocate in a voluminous sea of gravy. It's terrible. But it's all your own fault. You brought it on yourself. [. . .] Because it was you who spilt the gravy in the first place, it was you who handed over the bundle. (417)

Rebecca's reference to mental elephantiasis provides a metaphor for the unconscious connections among the apparently random phantasmagoria of images, in her own intuitive way explicating the function of her own moral imagination as it relates her own failure to prevent atrocities from being committed to the helplessness of the historical victims of genocide. Like the gravy adduced in her example, her guilt is suffocating her, to the extent that she herself feels responsible for the atrocities. Her love for the "guide" renders her complicit by association, and the audience later learns that "the bundle" is a baby she was carrying for its mother in her dream/vision before handing it over to a man at the station, an action that establishes her symbolic responsibility for failing to prevent its murder. Most disturbing in *Ashes to Ashes* is the fact that Rebecca is sexually stimulated by the sadism of the man who in her dreams/fantasies is responsible for genocide. In a series of astonishing metaphors, the play evokes the guilt and responsibility of those who accept the reality of people's inhumanity to others without doing anything to prevent it. In this respect, Pinter universalizes the notion of "survivor guilt," challenging every member of an audience to place themselves in a personal relationship with Rebecca's horrific vision of an individual's collusion with fascism.

When Devlin addresses her as "sweetheart," Rebecca's memory of the man who was her lover calling her by the same term of endearment "in [. . . a] dream or as I opened my eyes" (418), symbolically connects Devlin with the fascist. As though sick with mental elephantiasis, Rebecca cannot resist the compulsion to return to thoughts of her lover: "The man I knew was the man for me from the moment we met, my dear, my most precious companion, I watched him walk down the platform and tear all the babies from the arms of their screaming mothers" (419). Devlin's attempt to draw her away from such morbid fantasy to the cozy reality of her domestic world by asking her about her sister Kim and her children, elicits a rueful story about how Kim's ex-husband has asked her to take him back, although "she says she'll never share a bed with him again. Never. Ever" (422). Rebecca's recollections at this point all seem to revolve around men who have hurt or betrayed women. The film that she sees after meeting her sister is a comedy about a woman and her male partner, which she could not laugh at, and—in an image reminiscent of Deeley's visit to the cinema in *Old Times*—she recalls sitting behind a man who "never moved, he was rigid, like a body with rigor mortis, he never laughed once, he just sat like a corpse" (424).

Although the man is never identified, he completes the list of male figures who have oppressed or hurt women in some way. In order to reassure or placate Rebecca, Devlin now makes reference to the peace and beauty of her domestic surroundings, his reference to the "wonderful garden" she has "created [. . .] all by yourself" (424), a reference to the garden of the country house that can be seen through the "large window" (393) of the room in which *Ashes to Ashes* is set. There is a third echo of *Old Times* when Rebecca and Devlin each sing alternate lines of the song from which the later play takes its title:

REBECCA: (*singing softly*) "Ashes to ashes"—
DEVLIN: "And dust to dust"—
REBECCA: "If the women don't get you"—
DEVLIN: "The liquor must." (425)

On being admonished by Devlin for having previously omitted to tell him about her lover, Rebecca adopts her typical strategy of evasion by introducing her recollection of watching an old man and a little boy walking through the middle of town at night ("Oh by the way there's something I meant to tell you" [426]) before launching into an account of how she followed them to the trains mentioned earlier:

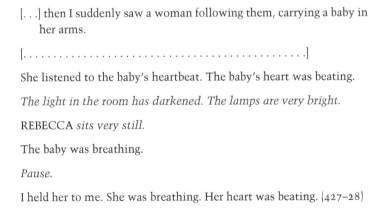

[. . .] then I suddenly saw a woman following them, carrying a baby in her arms.

[. . . . .]

She listened to the baby's heartbeat. The baby's heart was beating.

The light in the room has darkened. The lamps are very bright.

REBECCA *sits very still.*

The baby was breathing.

Pause.

I held her to me. She was breathing. Her heart was beating. (427–28)

Without any explanation, Rebecca introjects herself into the mother's situation, suggesting such complete identification with the woman's plight that she cannot separate her own identity from that of this other. Devlin immediately adopts a parallel strategy of attempting to put himself in the position of her lover, but her refusal to play along denies him the possibility of assuming the role of fascist male:

> He clenches his fist and holds it in front of her face. He puts his left hand behind her neck and grips it. He brings her head towards his fist. His fist touches her mouth.
>
> Kiss my fist.
>
> She does not move.
>
> He opens his hand and places the palm of his hand on her mouth.
>
> She does not move. (428)

Devlin tries again without success to assert himself as her sadistic lover, but her continued rejection of his attempts is a sign that she has resisted the earlier need to surrender sexually to the spell of fascist masculinity as she now takes responsibility for her own inability to save the baby's life.

For the first time in the play, a recorded echo is employed to heighten the impact of certain words and phrases. This is an elaboration of the voice-over technique utilized in *Mountain Language* to suggest the thoughts of the prisoners and their loved ones. Here the echo serves not only to emphasize the intensity of Rebecca's feelings, but also to create an incantatory effect that transforms the individual act of remembering into a ritual recital provoking associations with universal resonances:

REBECCA: I took my baby and wrapped it in my shawl
ECHO: my shawl
REBECCA: And I made it into a bundle
ECHO: A BUNDLE

[. . . . . . .]

REBECCA: But the baby cried out
ECHO: cried out
REBECCA: and the man called me back

ECHO: called me back
REBECCA: And he said what do you have there
ECHO: have there
REBECCA: He stretched out his hand for the bundle
ECHO: for the bundle
REBECCA: And I gave him the bundle
ECHO: the bundle (429–31)

Rebecca's imagined act of surrendering the baby becomes a key to her personal sense of responsibility for the fate of modern history's innocent victims. Her guilt is confirmed in her narration of an incident that occurred after she had been transported by train to "this place" where she met a woman she knew:

REBECCA: And she said what happened to your baby
ECHO: your baby
REBECCA: Where is your baby
ECHO: your baby
REBECCA: And I said what baby
ECHO: what baby
REBECCA: I don't have a baby
ECHO: a baby
REBECCA: I don't know of any baby
ECHO: of any baby

Pause.
REBECCA: I don't know of any baby
Long silence.
Blackout. (432–33)

In the intensity of her recall of the imagined narrative, Rebecca uncannily creates a dream vision that she begins to own as though it were a memory of her personal experience. The nature of her identification with mothers who did experience such atrocities as having their babies torn from their hands is so intense that she situates herself in an archetypal Holocaust narrative, assuming both the mother's guilt at giving up her baby and her own at having lived a life protected from such horrors. When she finally states that she does not "know of any baby" she is not merely admitting that she has no first-hand experience of the incidents recalled but is accepting moral responsibility for her "onlooker" position in history arrived at via a complex process of imaginative identification with the suffering of others.

Ashes to Ashes shows Pinter at the height of his powers as a playwright. Its minimalist precision in the elaboration of dramaturgical structure is in inverse proportion to its complex and resonantly poetic verbal images. The play tackles a central ethical question—possibly *the* central ethical question—of the twentieth century: how is it possible to retain a belief in the value of being human in the face of the kind of evil manifested during the Holocaust and the attempted genocides of the past seventy years? Rebecca takes responsibility for the implications of her romantic infatuation with a ruthless perpetrator of cruel atrocities at the end of the play by refusing to enter into the sexual ritual of abject surrender to the absolute power of the fascist male; Devlin however remains in thrall to the sadomasochistic masculine fantasy of life-and-death power over a loved one. In some respects a recapitulation of the themes of authority and power initially addressed in *The Birthday Party* and *The Hothouse, Ashes to Ashes* combines echoes of the psychosexual battles for dominance between male and female characters in *The Lover, Night,* and *Old Times,* with a deeper exploration of the theme of the ambivalent aura of brute masculinity that is explored in *One for the Road, Mountain Language,* and *Party Time.* The archetypal images of the Holocaust and the startling conjunctions of sexual pleasure and fascist brutality, personal selfishness and collective historical responsibility are entirely new, returning Pinter's theater to one of its originary impulses—his adolescent haunting by images of the Gestapo. The play is surprisingly allusive in demanding the active participation of the audience to relate one image to another, and profoundly disturbing in its invocation of a cultural unconscious determined by memories of the Holocaust.

A first response to *Celebration* (2000) might suggest that the play has little in common with the more overtly political dramas that preceded it. Its darkly comic representation of the duplicity, violence, and banal sexualization that characterizes the culture produced by the global system of consumer capitalism revealed Pinter at the age of seventy to be as finely attuned to the changing language and values of English society as always. The stage picture of a fashionable restaurant displaying a banquette at which two middle-aged couples are seated on one side and at the other, a table with a younger couple, the investment banker Russell and his wife Suki, represents the aspirational culture of conspicuous consumption at the start of the new millennium. In this respect, there are obvious parallels with *Party Time*, the contrast between what Lambert and Matt actually do as "strategy consultants" and the faux-aristocratic ambience of the restaurant lending intimations of menace to the vulgarity of the couples' behavior that echo much of Pinter's earlier drama.[4]

The restaurant is a kind of temple to the gross materialism of contemporary consumer culture:

> SUKI: Everyone is so happy in your restaurant. I mean women *and* men.
> You make people so happy.
> RICHARD: Well, we do like to feel that it's a happy restaurant.
> RUSSELL: It is a happy restaurant. For example, look at me. Look at me. I'm basically a disordered personality, some people would describe me as a psychopath . . . But when I'm sitting in this restaurant I suddenly find I have no psychopathic tendencies at all. I don't feel like killing everyone in sight. (38–39)[5]

The true function of the ambience is to mask the contradictions within the status quo, appeasing its diners by offering them sensory pleasures and the comfort of exclusive privilege as gratification designed to dull their naked fear and aggression. Beneath the stylish surface of the restaurant, the world these characters actually inhabit operates according to the principle of repression by brute force. Lambert and Matt are "Taking charge. Keeping the peace. Enforcing the peace. Enforcing peace" (61).

The aim of satisfying the customers degrades the waiters to the level of prostitutes, food and sex apparently being equally available in exchange for money. The aspiration toward high cultural value is continually undermined by the characters' gross materialism, represented in dialogue as a lack of sophistication. The two couples celebrating a wedding anniversary appear unable to tell whether they have attended the ballet, the opera, or the theater. Cordon Bleu dishes are referred to as the duck, the chicken, or the steak while "Osso"[6] becomes arsehole in a world in which restaurants are merely "caffs." The play exposes the way postmodern culture not only fragments but flattens hierarchies of value so that the difference between one pleasure and another is merely a matter of price.

A more poignant discourse of aesthetic and moral value, however, remains partially obscured by the rampant materialism of the physical scene. The young waiter's recurring interjections of a seeming nostalgia for traditional or intrinsic values obliquely challenges the commodified nature of the consumer environment. His initial interruption of Russell and Suki on the pretext of having overheard them talk about T. S. Eliot comically introduces his grandfather as an acquaintance of major English literary figures of the twentieth century—W. H. Auden, C. Day Lewis, Louis Macniece, Stephen Spender, and others, as well as the American writers Ezra Pound, Ernest Hemingway, William Faulkner, and Carson McCullers. Asserting that his grandfather "stood four square in the centre of the intellectual and literary life of the tens, twenties and thirties" (32), he makes the palpably absurd claim that "He was James Joyce's godmother" (32). The young waiter makes two further interjections, alternately informing the first group of celebrating couples of his grandfather's improbable connections with the great names of Hollywood's heyday and later telling the whole company of his grandfather's acquaintance with political and literary figures, including Churchill, Mussolini, Brecht, Kafka, the Inkspots, and the Three Stooges—a surrealistic concatenation of famous names from modern history, literature, and popular culture that reduces their value to items on a restaurant menu.

Although the young waiter's attempt to interpellate himself into the cultural history of the twentieth century is never explained, it forms a wonderfully witty reminder of the cultural value system that a postmodern environment such as the restaurant has eradicated. As the youngest person in the play, the young waiter's intellectual confusion is understandable, but what is remarkable is the naive desire to assert his literary-cultural credentials in the face of the barbarity of global capitalism.[7] The ending of *Celebration* with the young waiter's inability to complete his final interjection forms a poignant coda to the play, offering an emblem of Pinter's own lifelong dramaturgical exploration of the equivocal nature of human experience:

> WAITER: My grandfather introduced me to the mystery of life and I'm still in the middle of it. I can't find the door to get out. My grandfather got out of it. He got right out of it. He left it behind and he didn't look back.
>
> He got that absolutely right.

And I'd like to make one further interjection.

He stands still.

Slow fade. (72)

After twenty-five minutes of scabrous social comedy *Celebration* ends on a hauntingly introspective note, the waiter's silence in the face of his own inability to resolve "the mystery of life" (72) challenging the audience to probe the void beneath the noisy jocularity of the characters' vulgar behavior. This suspension of noisy humor forms a coda to the play that aptly demonstrates Pinter's view that "The comic, in a way, is the best of what we are . . . but on the whole, the laughter goes out of any play I've written before it's finished" (Smith, 95). The darkness pervading common experience is illuminated in *Don't Look,* one of the last poems Pinter wrote; it paradoxically evokes the horror of the destructive impulse toward profit that he believed was threatening to destroy contemporary civilization:

> Don't look.
> The world's about to break.
>
> Don't look.
> The world's about to chuck out all its light
> and stuff us in the chokepit of its dark,
> That black and fat suffocated place
> Where we will kill or die or dance or weep
> Or scream or whine or squeak like mice
> To renegotiate our starting price.

In the last decade of his life Pinter devoted more of his time and energy to fighting against what he believed to be the misuse of power by Western democracies (in particular, the United States and Britain) than to writing plays, although he did publish a number of new poems. Although much imitated, his work still appears unique: his plays retain both their comic and their enigmatic qualities, and their power to disturb. Although Pinter's drama possesses a unique style, the plays are never mere exercises in style; their blend of realism and abstraction always deployed as a means of disclosing the equivocal nature of human experience and exposing the compulsive—and at times ruthless—exercise of power in diverse societies and cultures.

In October 2005 the Swedish Academy announced that Pinter had been awarded the Nobel Prize in Literature, judging his unique contribution to dramatic art to be that it revealed "the precipice under everyday prattle and forced entry into oppression's closed rooms." Because his throat cancer prevented him from attending the Nobel Prize ceremony in Sweden, Pinter chose to deliver his laureate lecture via satellite link on 7 December 2005. Speaking from a wheelchair, and appearing very weak, he demonstrated his lifelong aversion to authority by using this media opportunity to deliver a powerful attack on the United States and Britain for initiating the Iraq war, and to demand that Tony Blair and George W Bush be prosecuted for war crimes.

Only a year before he died, Pinter bravely played the sixty-nine-year-old Krapp to great acclaim in *Krapp's Last Tape*—a monodrama by his literary and theatrical hero, Samuel Beckett. Like that of Beckett, Pinter's theater has changed the landscape of English-language and European drama. Four decades of important English-language playwrights including Edward Bond,[8] David Mamet, Sam Shepard,[9] Caryl Churchill,[10] Sarah Kane, and Martin Crimp have been profoundly influenced by his approach to drama, and his plays continue to be read and performed around the world as modern classics.

Chronology

Life

1930   Harold Pinter born in Hackney, East London
1948   Risked imprisonment as a conscientious objector to compulsory military service
1948   Studied at RADA but left in 1949 after two terms
1950   Began to publish poems under the name of Harold Pinta
1950   Studied for a year at the Central School of Speech and Drama
1951   Toured Ireland as an actor with actor-manager Anew McMaster
1952   Started acting in English regional repertory theatre
1953   Acted for a year with Donald Wolfit
1954   Started acting under the name of David Baron
1956   Married the actress Vivien Merchant
1958   Birth of his son, Daniel
1963   Wrote the screenplay for *The Pumpkin Eater*, the first of twenty-seven screenplays for television and film
1966   Awarded the CBE
1971   Directed Simon Gray's *Butley*, the first of fifty plays he has directed
1975   Separated from Vivien Merchant to live with the historian, Lady Antonia Fraser
1980   Divorced Vivien Merchant and married Antonia Fraser
1985   Visit to Turkey with Arthur Miller marks the beginning of his career as a political activist
2001   Diagnosed with esophageal cancer
2002   Awarded the Companion of Honour
2005   Awarded the Nobel Prize for Literature
2007   Performed Beckett's *Krapp's Last Tape*
2008   Died of liver cancer in London

Plays

1957   *The Room* (first performed 1958)
1957   *The Birthday Party*
1957   *The Dumb Waiter* (first performed 1960)
1958   *A Slight Ache* (radio broadcast 1959)
1958   *The Hothouse* (first performed 1977??)
1959   *A Night Out* (television broadcast 1960)

Notes

Introduction

1. Epistemology is the branch of philosophy that treats of knowledge and thinking, investigating the foundations of knowledge and the principles that determine thought.

2. *The Proust Screenplay* was published to general acclaim; it was later adapted by Pinter and Di Trevis as *Remembrance of Things Past* and staged at the National Theatre in 2000.

3. John Russell Taylor's influential book *Anger and After* grouped Pinter with the "angry young men" who were in the vanguard of the Royal Court "revolution," although in some respects Pinter's stagecraft had less in common with the new theater of Osborne and Wesker than with that of the previous generation exemplified by the work of Terence Rattigan and Noël Coward.

4. In the fifties and early sixties, it was a critical commonplace that Pinter was a brilliant mimic of working-class London dialects, a view that ignores the subtle and complex effects of defamiliarization that characterize his simultaneously poetic and theatrical deployment of stage dialogue.

5. The label "kitchen-sink drama" was applied indiscriminately to a diverse group of pseudo-naturalistic plays by a new generation of anti-establishment playwrights whose gritty, realistic representations of working-class life included Arnold Wesker's *The Kitchen* (1957), *Chicken Soup with Barley* (1958), *Roots* (1958), Shelagh Delaney's *A Taste of Honey* (1958), Brendan Behan's *The Hostage* (1958), and John Arden's *Live Like Pigs* (1959). These plays were somewhat misleadingly thought to follow the example of John Osborne's iconic *Look Back in Anger* (1956) in giving voice to the resentment and frustration of the postwar generation at the spiritual poverty of fifties British society.

6. Beckett, although born in Ireland, is often regarded as a Continental European writer, because he spent his working life in Paris and wrote in French as well as English.

7. In her essay "The World of Harold Pinter," Ruby Cohn succinctly analyzed the anti-authoritarian theme of Pinter's first four plays: "Pinter's anger [. . .] is directed vitriolically, against the System. But his System cannot be reduced to a welfare state [. . .] John Wain approaches closest to Pinter's intention when he states that 'the artist's intention is to humanize the society he is living in, to assert the importance of humanity in the teeth of whatever is currently trying to annihilate that importance' *(Declaration)*. Pinter's as-

sertion, however, takes a negative form; it is by his bitter dramas of *dehu-manization* that he implies 'the importance of humanity.' The religion and society which have traditionally structured human morality, are, in Pinter's plays, the immoral agents that destroy the individual. [. . .] Situating him between Beckett and the Angries is only a first approximation of his achievement."

8. T. S. Eliot claims to have adopted in *The Waste Land* notions of mythology concerning patterns of ritualistic action and narrative structures from Jessie Weston's interpretation of the myth of the Holy Grail in *From Ritual to Romance* that refer to the myth of the year-king as initially adumbrated by J.G. Frazer in *The Golden Bough*.

9. The exception is *Silence* (1969), a stream-of-consciousness drama that is staged in an abstract setting; *Family Voices* (1981) also takes place in an unlocalized space, but this was conceived and originally produced as a radio play.

10. Phatic communication is speech that does not convey information but functions to produce social connection—what is commonly referred to as "small talk."

11. Chekhov's use of the device was first recognized in the employment of the term "subtext" by the actor-director Stanislavski, who produced Chekhov's four dramatic masterpieces at the Moscow Art Theatre between 1898 and 1904.

12. See chapter 3.

13. "I made a fatal mistake in the early part of my career when, to my eternal regret, I wrote the word 'pause'. All I was talking about was a natural break, when people don't quite know what to do next. [. . .] But this damn word 'pause' and those silences have achieved such significance that they have overwhelmed the bloody plays." "Breaking the Silence," *London Daily News*, 19 June 1987, 19.

14. This production transferred from the Gate Theatre in Dublin to the Lincoln Centre, New York, in 2001.

15. The reading of *The Dumb Waiter* with his friend and fellow actor and playwright Ronald Harwood, was filmed and broadcast by Arena, BBC2, 2002.

16. For a full discussion of the transformation of conventional genre categories in Pinter's drama, see Bernard Dukore, *Where Laughter Stops*.

17. See John Lahr, "Pinter and Chekhov: The Bond of Naturalism."

18. With the exception of Tom Stoppard, none of the other British or European dramatists regarded as avant-garde from 1955 to the present day would ever be likely to receive open-ended productions of their work in the commercial theater. Even the work of such a widely read playwright as Samuel Beckett is not normally considered suitable for presentation by commercial producers, and is usually presented by not-for-profit organizations in repertory or limited engagements.

19. See David Thompson, *The Players' Playwright.*

20. Katherine Burkman, *The Dramatic World of Harold Pinter*; Martin Esslin, *The Peopled Wound.*

21. In the interest of brevity, I have limited myself to a study of plays written for the theater or those written initially for radio and television that have been transposed for the stage and are regularly performed there. I have not included any analysis of Pinter's many excellent film screenplays.

22. Phenomenology is a twentieth-century philosophical approach that aims to explain the meaning of phenomena by accurately describing the way in which they are experienced or apprehended by consciousness, rather than through attempting to analyze things through the causal logic of traditional philosophy and science.

23. See Susan Hollis Merritt, *Pinter in Play,* for an exhaustive analysis of the many different critical approaches adumbrated by Pinter scholars.

24. A phenomenological approach to the analysis of drama in performance was first proposed by Bert O. States in *Great Reckonings in Little Rooms: On the Phenomenology of Theater.* States countered the excessive emphasis on hermeneutic meaning concomitant on semiology's exclusive approach to signification with a contrary approach to how the experiential dimension of meaning unfolds within the space and time of dramatic performance. A phenomenological approach to modern drama with specific reference to the plays of Beckett and Pinter, among others, was systematically pursued by Stanton B. Garner Jr. in *Bodied Spaces: Phenomenology and Performance in Contemporary Drama.*

Chapter 1

1. Auriol Smith, one of the original cast members, remembered how the cast dealt with the difficulty of understanding the play: "We accepted . . . [the play's] oddity and the fact we weren't going to understand everything going on. But it gave us such rich dialogue to speak. . . . It was like going into someone's house for a day and picking up the strange vibrations going on. You don't have to know every detail of the relationships to pick up on the atmosphere."

2. Page references to *The Room* indicate Harold Pinter, *Plays One.*

3. In the first decade of his career Pinter became famous for the perfect accuracy of his rendering of London speech registers; this mimicking of the minute details of demotic idiom was interpreted as a metaphoric representation of the alleged breakdown of communication in contemporary life.

4. Such a plot motif anticipates *The Birthday Party,* in which the central character Stanley, who has been "lying low" at a boarding house in a coastal town in England, is sought out by two apparent strangers who force him to conform to societal norms by escorting him away from his haven in

order to "take him to Monty," who as psychiatrist or doctor somewhat sinisterly represents the arbitrary power of state authority.

5. It may not be merely a coincidence that Pinter was acting in a production of Rattigan's pair of linked one-act plays, *Separate Tables*, at the Pavilion Theatre in Torquay while writing *The Room* for his friend Henry Woolf. One of the plays concerns the revelation of the "secret" that a character claiming to be a former army major is in reality a pathetic and lonely sham who spends his afternoons trying to pick up women in cinemas by touching them up in the dark. Rattigan's handling of the one-act play form was masterly—very much in the "well-made" tradition of English drama that persisted from the late nineteenth century to the 1950s.

6. "Art is by nature an origin: a distinctive way in which truth comes into being, that is, becomes historical." Martin Heidegger, "The Origin of the Work of Art," 27.

Chapter 2

1. A rave review in the Sunday *Times* by its influential drama critic Harold Hobson appeared only after the production had closed and could not be reprieved. Hobson's prophetic words are often cited:

> One of the actors in Harold Pinter[']s *The Birthday Party* at the Lyric, Hammersmith, announces in the programme that he read History at Oxford, and took his degree with Fourth Class Honours. Now I am well aware that Mr Pinter[']s play received extremely bad notices last Tuesday morning. At the moment I write these it is uncertain even whether the play will still be in the bill by the time they appear, though it is probable it will soon be seen elsewhere. Deliberately, I am willing to risk whatever reputation I have as a judge of plays by saying that *The Birthday Party* is not a Fourth, not even a Second, but a First; and that Pinter, on the evidence of his work, possesses the most original, disturbing and arresting talent in theatrical London. . . . Mr Pinter and *The Birthday Party*, despite their experiences last week, will be heard of again. Make a note of their names. (Harold Hobson, *The Sunday Times*, 25 May 1958)

2. All page references to *The Birthday Party* and *The Hothouse* indicate *Harold Pinter: Plays One.*

3. The technical term for such conversation without informational content is phatic communication.

4. Defamiliarization is the artistic technique of representing the everyday world as if it were strange or unfamiliar in order to provoke the reader or viewer to perceive it in a new way.

5. Cf. Behan's *The Hostage*, Arnold Wesker's *Chicken Soup with Barley*, Bernard Kops, *The Hamlet of Stepney Green* (1959); by contrast, Osborne's

Look Back in Anger and *The Entertainer* (1957) express the unthinking racism, sexism, and homophobia of an imperialistic British culture.

6. Music hall is an English equivalent of American vaudeville; while there were differences in its style and context of presentation, many of the "turns" on a musical hall bill were directly comparable to individual vaudeville acts.

7. The Albigensenists were thirteenth-century heretics.

8. The conception of otherness as treason or disease appears to be an imaginative transformation of the Cold War discourse that linked communists (social rebels) with homosexuals (diseased people) as potential traitors who might be spying for the Soviets.

9. Ruby Cohn, "The World of Harold Pinter."

10. In act 3 the audience learns that this was an accident.

11. The paradigmatic instance of this theme in Western drama is Sophocles' *Oedipus the King*.

12. This is what the existentialist philosopher Jean-Paul Sartre calls *bad faith*.

13. "All Petey says is one of the most important lines I've ever written . . . I've lived that line all my damn life" (quoted in Gussow, 71).

14. Rosette Lamont has interpreted the play as an allegory of the way in which the Nazis masked the real function of concentration camps as institutions of genocide in the guise of social and mental "rehabilitation" centers. See Burkman and Kundert-Gibbs, 37–48.

Chapter 3

1. Comedy of menace is also a verbal pun on comedy of manners.

2. The combination of Pinter's personal admiration for Beckett's writing and his inclusion of a tramp as the play's central character inevitably led to comparisons with *Waiting for Godot*, but in most respects these represented facile and misleading attempts to classify his drama as absurdist. As much as he had from an early age admired Beckett's novels, Pinter consistently exploited—and subverted—the conventions of well-made West End theater in a manner that would have seemed entirely alien to his Irish literary hero: "If Beckett's influence shows in my work, that's all right with me. You don't write in a vacuum; you're bound to absorb and digest other writing; and I admire Beckett's work so much that some of its texture might appear in my own. . . . However, I do think that I have succeeded in expressing something of myself" (Smith, 45).

3. All page numbers refer to *Harold Pinter: Plays Two*.

4. The significance of stage props in modern drama is discussed in detail in Andrew Sofer's *The Stage Life of Props*; for a phenomenological approach

to the way the actor's body, her or his costume, and props create a kinetic/visual/spatial gestalt in the performance of Pinter's drama, see Stanton Garner, *Bodied Spaces.*

5. *A Room of One's Own* is an extended essay by the novelist Virginia Woolf, first published in 1929.

6. It was the British theater critic, Irving Wardle, who in 1958 described Pinter as "the poet of the London Underground."

7. These suburbs are in west London, the area in which Mick's house is located.

8. Austin Quigley's groundbreaking volume *The Pinter Problem* explains the dramaturgical strategy represented by Pinter's complex and subtle use of demotic idiom on stage by way of Wittgenstein's later philosophy, as it has been developed in the tradition of Anglo-American linguistic pragmatism by J. L. Austin and others. Wittgenstein's often-quoted observation, "The meaning of a word is its use," signaled a paradigm shift in twentieth-century linguistic philosophy: earlier attempts to explain how language means what it does by analyzing the meaning of propositional statements according to the rules of artificial languages such as logic, were abandoned in favor of the pragmatic analysis and demystification of the way natural language communicates in particular contexts. Wittgenstein identified the "language games" that people elaborate through custom and practice as keys to the understanding of the contextual meaning of words under specific conditions of utterance. Quigley illuminates the power battles among Pinter's characters by analyzing the rhetorical strategies each deploys in seeking to advance her or his status and power within the particular situations the characters find themselves in.

9. This structural pattern was first noted and analyzed by Quigley.

10. Pinter himself stated in a conversation with Richard Findlater published as "Writing for Myself" in *Twentieth Century* CLXIX (Feb. 1961): 175: "*The Caretaker* wouldn't have been put on, and certainly wouldn't have run, before 1957. The old categories of comedy and tragedy and farce are irrelevant" (xi).

Chapter 4

1. Luigi Pirandello is famous as a writer (*Six Characters in Search of an Author, The Rules of the Game, Right You Are If You Think So*) who constructed his plays as philosophical discourses that reflect on the foundation of the ineluctable conflict between characters' views of a situation that is logically one but appears in each individual's subjective experience of it to be wholly different and to contradict the way it is experienced by every other.

2. The play's complex conception of sexual identity chimes perfectly with the current notion in queer studies of gender and sexuality as performative.

3. Page references to *The Collection* and *The Lover* indicate *Harold Pinter: Plays Two.*

4. In *Pinter's Female Portraits*, Elizabeth Sakellaridou is more skeptical in reading the writer's treatment of his female characters as symptomatic of the patriarchal construction of woman as mother-or-whore pervasive in Western culture (and many others). In my view, he begins as early as *The Collection* to be critically self-aware in identifying as masculine insecurity the projection onto women of such a misogynistic archetype.

5. Page references to *The Homecoming* indicate *Harold Pinter: Plays Three.*

6. In his *Leviathan* (1651), Thomas Hobbes adumbrated his view of human life as a perpetual "war of all against all."

7. The first director of the play, Peter Hall, interpreted Teddy as the "villain" of the play. See Peter Hall interview in Smith, 136.

8. Freud first employed the term *phantasy* to indicate the psychological process of conscious or unconscious daydreaming, the latter functioning as a meditation between desire and reality. Both meanings are now commonly denoted as *fantasy.*

9. "Homosociality" is a sociological term to describe same-sex bonding that is not of a sexual or romantic nature, traditionally manifest, for example in single-sex schools, clubs, sororities, fraternities, football teams, feminist groups, the armed services, etc.

10. See Pinter's letter to Mosley regarding "objectivity," in Billington, 187.

11. "Pinter must stylize more than any writer in England apart from Ivy Compton-Burnett, which is why Peter Hall is right to direct the play so anti-naturalistically. His people are entirely creatures of manoeuvre, hence the peculiar freezing mood of their moments of randiness. The sexual instinct in Pinter isn't at all emotional or even physical; it is practically territorial." Penelope Gilliat, *The Observer*, 6 June 1965, in *File on Pinter*, 32–33.

12. Between the writing of *The Caretaker* (1960) and *The Homecoming* (1965), Pinter had successfully completed screenplays for *The Servant* (1963), *The Pumpkin Eater* (1964), and a film version of *The Caretaker* (1963), and written the television plays *Night School* (1961), *The Collection*, and *Tea Party* (1965).

Chapter 5

1. Page references to *Landscape, Silence, Night,* and *Old Times* indicate *Harold Pinter: Plays Three.*

2. See Elizabeth Sakellaridou, *Pinter's Female Portraits.*

3. Meg in *The Birthday* Party and Ruth in *The Homecoming* provide the most obvious examples.

4. The names are a teasing allusion to Shakespeare's *Macbeth*, in which

Vivien Merchant was appearing as Lady Macbeth while Pinter was writing the play.

5. *Odd Man Out* (1946) is an iconic British thriller directed by Carol Reed and starring James Mason as Johnny MacQueen, an Irish revolutionary desperately trying to escape from being hunted down after a raid on a Belfast factory one night. Robert Newton plays Lukey, a mad and alcoholic painter.

6. Deeley's statement is not logical, as there is no evidence that Christy exists in the present time of the drama.

7. Pinter had played Garcin in a production of Sartre's *Huis Clos* (*In Camera*) on television in 1965; apart from the very small role of the waiter, Sartre's play also concerns the triangular relationship of two women—one of whom is a lesbian in love with the other—and a man who is attracted to the heterosexual woman.

Chapter 6

1. Chalk Farm is an area in northwest London at the southern border of Hampstead.

2. This is a term first used by the phenomenological philosopher Edmund Husserl (1859–1938).

3. In response to its premiere production in 1975, a number of reviewers commented adversely on the self-reflexive nature of *No Man's Land*.

4. Page references to *No Man's Land* indicate *Harold Pinter: Plays Three*.

5. "I have known this before. Morning. A locked door. A house of silence and strangers" (363).

6. Early in his career, critics habitually but misleadingly praised his virtuoso use of London idioms for the purposes of characterization as a kind of naturalistic mimicry of speech he had heard and recorded.

Chapter 7

The subtitle of Chapter 7 is taken from Pauline Kael, "Pinter's art is the art of taking away." Pauline Kael, 197.

1. *The Dwarfs* contains a great deal of autobiographical material, but it was conceived and written as a novel, being adapted into a radio play some years later, and only after that transferred to the stage—not entirely successfully.

2. There can be little doubt that some aspects of the play unconsciously reflect the experience of his very happy relationship with Lady Antonia Fraser but, although they were both legally married to other people at the time *Betrayal* was first produced at the National Theatre in 1978, there is no similarity between the plot of *Betrayal* and the events of their lives. Pinter had been estranged from his wife Vivien Merchant for some years before

meeting the woman who in 1980 was to become his second wife; he and Lady Antonia Fraser began to live together in 1975, and no deception was involved in their affair.

3. Page references to *Betrayal* indicate *Harold Pinter: Plays Four*.

Chapter 8

1. All page references in this chapter indicate *Harold Pinter: Plays Four*.

2. A bildungsroman is a coming-of-age novel about a young person's moral and spiritual growth to maturity. Famous examples are Goethe's *Wilhelm Meister's Apprenticeship* and *The Sorrows of Young Werther*.

3. The most famous of these fictional heroes are Tom Jones and Joseph Andrews.

4. I can only know other people through their behavior (i.e., as they represent themselves to me); they can only know me as I represent myself to them. Since direct access to the consciousness of others is not available, it is logically impossible to distinguish self from persona.

5. Victoria Station is one of the locations in London best known to taxi drivers.

6. By way of example, see, in particular, the various autobiographical stories told by Lenny and Max in *The Homecoming*.

7. This idea is famously implied in Beckett's *Waiting for Godot*, when Vladimir asks the Boy in act 1 to tell Mr Godot, "Tell him [. . .] tell him you saw us. *(Pause)* You did see us, didn't you?" (Beckett, 52), and in act 2, "that you saw me [. . .] You're sure you saw me, you won't come and tell me tomorrow that you never saw me!" (Beckett, 92).

8. *No Man's Land*, in *Harold Pinter: Plays Three*, 340 and 372.

9. Despite Pinter's denial that the alienation of Andy from his sons in *Moonlight* is autobiographical, it is difficult to avoid the conclusion that his representation of this situation in some way reflects his own sadness at the agreement he made with his only child, Daniel, in 1993 that it was better for them not to meet.

10. Do not go gentle into that good night,
Old age should burn and rage at close of day;
Rage, rage against the dying of the light.
                    Dylan Thomas, 1951

11. The most famous English radio show of this type was the *Goon Show*, which with its surreal collection of funny voices made Spike Milligan, Peter Sellers, and Harry Secombe household names in Britain. Other comic radio shows such as *Round the Horne* that also popularized this type of comic surrealism and were progenitors of the globally popular *Monty Python* shows on television and film.

Chapter 9

1. Among other things, he has been labeled a "Bollinger Bolshevik."
2. Page references indicate *Harold Pinter: Plays Four*.
3. At the conclusion of the play, when Viktor is released after having been humiliated and tortured, his tongue cut out, and his son killed, Nicolas forces him to have a drink with him.
4. In *The Times Literary Supplement*, 9 August 1985, Peter Kemp commented: "*One for the Road* doesn't so much disturb you by authentic insights into the world of a torturer as leave you slightly uneasy at having watched a piece of elegant juggling with vileness." In my view, this is precisely what the play intends to do, Nicolas's witty conversations about death and sex with victims who he pretends are equals deliberately provoking feelings of alarm and disgust in members of an audience.
5. Pamela, Emily, Suki, Sam, Harlow, and Smith do not appear in the printed text of the stage play but are introduced in the slightly amplified version, written and directed for television by Pinter himself and broadcast on London Weekend Television in November 1992. The television version adds a few exchanges that express some of the themes of the play in more explicit terms.
6. This exchange does not appear in the stage play, but the dialogue is quoted from the London Weekend Television production.
7. Gavin's final speech refers euphemistically to the "round-up" that security forces have carried out during the evening as a resumption of "normal service" (312), political repression being justified as though it were merely a question of restoring a disrupted rail service.

Chapter 10

1. Page references to *Ashes to Ashes* indicate *Harold Pinter: Plays Four*.
2. This detail is derived from Gitta Sereny's book, *Albert Speer: His Battle with Truth*, which Pinter had read a few weeks before commencing the writing of *Ashes to Ashes*.
3. In the 1960s, survivor guilt was first recognized as a syndrome associated with survivors of extremely traumatic events that had caused the death of family members, friends, or colleagues. Now classified as one type of posttraumatic stress disorder, it has been recognized by psychologists that various forms of such guilt can be experienced by children of survivors or groups of people with connections to the event or to those responsible for it.
4. Russell's job as investment banker can in retrospect be viewed as a startlingly appropriate emblem for the power of the contemporary ideology of consumer capitalism.

5. Page references to *Celebration* and *The Room* indicate Harold Pinter, *Celebration* and *The Room*.

6. It refers to Osso Bucco on the menu.

7. During rehearsals for the first production of *Celebration* at the Almeida Theatre in London, Pinter revealed that the waiter's interjections were drawn from his own memory of an incident in which as a young waiter he had "overheard a conversation on a table about T.S. Eliot, which he dared to interrupt. He was sacked the same day" (Raine, 28).

8. Bond's *The Pope's Wedding* has always been regarded by critics as "Pinteresque" and the language of Bond's masterpiece, *Saved*, reveals his indebtedness to Pinter's heightened use of working-class speech.

9. Shepard's *Buried Child* has structural and thematic similarities with *The Homecoming* and is often regarded as an American "version" of Pinter's play.

10. Churchill's *Far Away* seems clearly indebted to Pinter's plays of the 1990s.

Bibliography

Baker, William, and Stephen Ely Tabachnik. 1973. *Harold Pinter.* London: Oliver & Boyd.

Bakewell, Joan. 1969. Interview with Harold Pinter. *The Listener,* 6 November.

Batty, Mark. 2005. *About Pinter: The Playwright and the Work.* London: Faber and Faber.

Beckett, Samuel. 1965. *Waiting for Godot.* London: Faber and Faber.

Begley, Varun. 2005. *Harold Pinter and the Twilight of Modernism.* Toronto: University of Toronto Press.

Billington, Michael. 1996. *The Life and Works of Harold Pinter.* London: Faber & Faber.

Brown, John Russell. 1972. *Theatre Language: A Study of Arden, Osborne, Pinter and Wesker.* London: Allen Lane, the Penguin Press.

Burkman, Katherine. 1971. *The Dramatic World of Harold Pinter: Its Basis in Ritual.* Columbus: Ohio State University Press.

Burkman, Katherine, and John Kundert-Gibbs, eds. 1993. *Pinter at Sixty.* Bloomington: Indiana University Press.

Cave, Richard Allen. 1987. *New British Drama in Performance on the London Stage 1970–1985.* Gerrards Cross: Colin Smythe.

Cohn, Ruby. 1972 [1962]. "The World of Harold Pinter." In *Pinter: A Collection of Critical Essays,* ed. Arthur Ganz. Englewood Cliffs: Prentice-Hall, 78–92.

Diamond, Elin. 1985. *Pinter's Comic Play.* New York: Associated University Presses.

Dukore, Bernard F. 1976. *Where Laughter Stops: Pinter's Tragicomedy.* Columbia: University of Missouri Press.

Dukore, Bernard F. 1982. *Harold Pinter.* New York: Grove Press.

Esslin, Martin. 1961. *The Theatre of the Absurd.* New York: Doubleday Anchor.

Esslin, Martin. 1970. *The Peopled Wound.* New York: Doubleday Anchor.

Gabbard, Lucinda Paquet. 1976. *The Dream Structure of Pinter Plays: A Psychoanalytic Approach.* Rutherford, NJ: Fairleigh Dickenson University Press.

Gale, Stephen H. 1977. *Butter's Going Up: A Critical Analysis of Harold Pinter's Work.* Durham, NC: Duke University Press.

Gale, Steven H. 2003. *Sharp Cut: Harold Pinter's Screenplays and the Artistic Process.* Lexington: University Press of Kentucky.

Garner, Stanton B., Jr. 1994. *Bodied Spaces: Phenomenology and Perfor-mance in Contemporary Drama*. Ithaca, NY: Cornell University Press.

Gordon, Lois. 1969. *Stratagems to Uncover Nakedness: The Dramas of Harold Pinter*. Columbia: University of Missouri Press.

Gordon, Lois. 1990. *Harold Pinter: A Casebook*. New York: Garland.

Grimes, Charles. 2005. *Harold Pinter's Politics: A Silence beyond Echo*. Rutherford, NJ: Fairleigh Dickinson University Press.

Gussow, Mel. 1994. *Conversations with Pinter*. London: Nick Hern Books.

Heidegger, Martin. 1971. "The Origin of the Work of Art." In *Poetry, Lan-guage, Thought*, trans. Alfred Hofstadter. New York: Harper and Row.

Kael, Pauline. 1975. *When the Lights Go Down*. New York: Holt, Rinehart and Winston.

Lahr, John. 1972 [1968]. "Pinter and Chekhov: The Bond of Naturalism." In *Pinter: A Collection of Critical Essays*, ed. Arthur Ganz. Englewood Cliffs: Prentice-Hall, 60–71.

Merritt, Susan Hollis. 1990. *Pinter in Play*. Durham, NC: Duke University Press.

Page, Malcolm, ed. 1993. *File on Pinter*. London: Methuen.

Pinter, Harold. 1996. *Plays Two*. London: Faber and Faber.

Pinter, Harold. 1996. *Plays One*. London: Faber and Faber.

Pinter, Harold. 1997. *Plays Three*. London: Faber and Faber.

Pinter, Harold. 1998. *Plays Four*. London: Faber and Faber

Pinter, Harold. 2000. *Celebration & The Room*. London: Faber and Faber.

Prentice, Penelope. 2000. *The Pinter Ethic: The Erotic Aesthetic*. New York: Garland.

Quigley, Austin. 1975. *The Pinter Problem*. Princeton, NJ: Princeton, Uni-versity Press.

Raby, Peter, ed. 2001. *The Cambridge Companion to Pinter*. Cambridge: Cambridge University Press.

Raine, Nina. 2009. "Pinter in Rehearsal." *Areté* 28 (Spring–Summer): 23–43.

Renton, Linda. 2002. *Pinter and the Object of Desire: An Approach through the Screenplays*. Oxford: Legenda, European Humanities Research Cen-tre.

Sakellaridou, Elizabeth. 1988. *Pinter's Female Portraits*. Basingstoke: Macmillan.

Sereny, Gitta. 1995. *Albert Speer: His Battle with Truth*. New York: Alfred Knopf.

Silverstein, Marc. 1993. *Harold Pinter and the Language of Cultural Power*. Lewisburg, PA: Bucknell University Press.

Smith, Ian. 2005. *Pinter in the Theatre*. London: Nick Hern Books.

Sofer, Andrew. 2003. *The Stage Life of Props*. Ann Arbor: University of Michigan Press.

States, Bert O. 1992. *Great Reckonings in Little Rooms: On the Phenome-nology of Theater*. Berkeley: University of California Press.

Taylor, John Russell. 1972. *Anger and After*. London: Allen Lane, the Penguin Press.

Thompson, David T. 1985. *Pinter: The Player's Playwright*. Basingstoke: Macmillan.

Trussler, Simon. 1973. *The Plays of Harold Pinter: An Assessment*. London: Victor Gollancz.

Worth, Katharine. 1972. *Revolutions in Modern English Drama*. London: Bell & Sons.

Index

Printed and bound by CPI Group (UK) Ltd, Croydon, CR0 4YY

09/06/2025

14685638-0002